Alfred Hitchcock s
Psycho

A CASEBOOK

ALFRED HITCHCOCK'S
Psycho

◆ ◆ ◆

A CASEBOOK

Edited by
Robert Kolker

OXFORD
UNIVERSITY PRESS

2004

OXFORD

UNIVERSITY PRESS

Oxford   New York
Auckland   Bangkok   Buenos Aires   Cape Town   Chennai
Dar es Salaam   Delhi   Hong Kong   Istanbul   Karachi   Kolkata
Kuala Lumpur   Madrid   Melbourne   Mexico City   Mumbai   Nairobi
São Paulo   Shanghai   Taipei   Tokyo   Toronto

Copyright © 2004 by Oxford University Press, Inc.

Published by Oxford University Press, Inc.
198 Madison Avenue, New York, New York 10016

www.oup.com

Library of Congress Cataloging-in-Publication Data
Alfred Hitchcock's psycho: a casebook / edited by Robert Kolker.
p. cm.—(Casebooks in criticism)
Includes bibliographical references.
ISBN 0-19-516919-0; 0-19-516920-4 (pbk.)
1. Psycho (Motion picture) I. Kolker, Robert Phillip. II. Series.
PN1997.P79 P78 2004
791.43'72—dc22   2003016992

1 3 5 7 9 8 6 4 2
Printed in the United States of America
on acid-free paper

Acknowledgments

◆ ◆ ◆

Many thanks to Steven Schneider and Jay Telotte for making the bibliography better than it would have been without them. Linda Williams was helpful in supplying material for her essay. At Oxford University Press, Elissa Morris supported the project with humor and a strong sense of what a book should look like. Jeremy Lewis was tireless in helping me hack through the thickets of permissions and the myriad of details of putting the book together. William Smith demonstrated a saint's patience. Stacey Hamilton and Robin Miura were of great assistance with the complicated job of copy editing. My special thanks to Katherine Calhoun, head of the Information Delivery Department of the Georgia Institute of Technology Library, whose assistance was nothing short of amazing.

Credits

✦ ✦ ✦

Contents

❖ ❖ ❖

Alfred Hitchcock's
Psycho

A CASEBOOK

1

"Good Evening . . ."

Alfred Hitchcock Talks to François Truffaut about "Pure Cinema," Playing His Audience Like an Organ, and Psycho

◆　◆　◆

◆　◆　◆

Once a week for ten years, beginning in 1955, Hitchcock introduced his popular television show with a formal "good evening, ladies and gentlemen" spoken in an exaggerated British accent, sounding something like a movie version of an English butler. He was sarcastic and ironic; he mocked his sponsors and himself. He had, in short, a good time at everyone's expense, his own included. The publicity and public exposure his appearances provided was invaluable. Despite the fact that Hitchcock coveted a quiet, creative life, he wanted everyone to know who was responsible for the films he created, as evidenced by the fact that he quite literally wrote himself into his films by means of brief, silent cameos in almost all of them. These, and the television series, guaranteed an almost personal engagement with his audience.

Hitchcock wanted another kind of engagement, however. As Robert Kapsis has pointed out, he wanted critical, even scholarly, recognition of his work. This began in the late fifties in France, a country that always took filmmaking seriously. The first book-length study of his work was written in 1957 by two French critics who would soon become important directors in their own right: Eric Rohmer and Claude Chabrol. In 1962, one of the most famous of the "new wave" of French directors working in the late fifties and throughout the sixties, François Truffaut (who made, among many other films, *The Four Hundred Blows, Shoot the Piano Player*, and *Fahrenheit 451*), began a career-long interview with Hitchcock. The result was many days of conversation, conducted with the assistance of a translator, that finally appeared in a book called, simply enough, *Hitchcock/Truffaut*. In it, Hitchcock continued what he did in most other interviews. He talked about the structure of his films, his love of the form of film itself, and all the things that could be accomplished with it. He talked about his profound awareness of the audience and how they could be manipulated to respond the way he wanted them to. He never talked about the narrative depth of his work, about its emotional and psychological complexities (the closest he gets is the reference in the interview to his own desire for orderliness in his life). Otherwise, he always left interpretation to others.

FRANÇOIS TRUFFAUT. Mr. Hitchcock, this morning you mentioned that you had had a bad night and indicated that you were probably disturbed by all of the memories that our talks have been stirring up these past several days. In the course of our conversations we've gone into the dreamlike quality of many of your films, among them *Notorious, Vertigo*, and *Psycho*. I'd like to ask whether you dream a lot.

ALFRED HITCHCOCK. Not too much . . . sometimes . . . and my dreams are very reasonable.

   In one of my dreams I was standing on Sunset Boulevard, where the trees are, and I was waiting for a Yellow Cab to take me to lunch. But no Yellow Cab came by; all the automobiles that drove by me were of 1916 vintage. And I said to myself, "It's no good standing here waiting for a Yellow Cab because this is a 1916 dream!" So I walked to lunch instead.

F.T. Did you really dream this, or is it a joke?

A.H. No, it's not a gag; I really had a dream like that!

F.T. It's almost a period dream! But would you say that dreams have a bearing on your work?

A.H. Daydreams, probably.

F.T. It may be an expression of the unconscious, and that takes us back once more to fairy tales. By depicting the isolated man who's surrounded by all sorts of hostile elements, and perhaps without even meaning to, you enter the realm of the dream world, which is also a world of solitude and of danger.

A.H. That's probably me, within myself.

F.T. It must be, because the logic of your pictures, which is sometimes decried by the critics, is rather like the logic of dreams. *Strangers on a Train* and *North by Northwest,* for instance, are made up of a series of strange forms that follow the pattern of a nightmare.

A.H. This may be due to the fact that I'm never satisfied with the ordinary. I'm ill at ease with it.

F.T. That's very evident. A Hitchcock picture that didn't involve death or the abnormal is practically inconceivable. I believe you film emotions you feel very deeply—fear, for instance.

A.H. Absolutely, I'm full of fears, and I do my best to avoid difficulties and any kind of complications. I like everything around me to be clear as crystal and completely calm. I don't want clouds overhead. I get a feeling of inner peace from a well-organized desk. When I take a bath, I put everything neatly back in place. You wouldn't even know I'd been in the bathroom. My passion for orderliness goes hand in hand with a strong revulsion toward complications.

F.T. That accounts for the way you protect yourself. Any eventual problem of direction resolved beforehand by your minute predesigned sketches that lessen the risks and prevent trouble later on. Jacques Becker used to say, "Alfred Hitchcock is undoubtedly the director who gets the least surprises when he looks at the rushes."

A.H. That's right. I've always dreamed of the day I wouldn't have to see the rushes at all! And since we're back to dreams, I'd like to digress a moment to tell you a little story. There was a movie writer who always seemed have his best ideas in the middle of the night and when he woke up in the morning, he never remembered them. So one day the man had brilliant idea. He said to himself, "I'll put paper and pencil beside my bed, and when I get the idea, I'll write it down." So he went to bed and, sure enough, in the middle of the night he awoke with a terrific idea. He wrote it down and went back to sleep. When he awoke the next morning, he'd forgotten the whole thing, but all of a sudden, as he was shaving, he thought to himself, "Oh God, I had a terrific idea again last night, and now I've forgotten it. But wait, I had my paper and pencil; that's right, I wrote it down!" So he rushed into the bedroom and picked up the note and read what he'd written: "Boy meets girl!"

F.T. That is funny.

A.H. There's some truth to the story, you see, because you have what seems to be a really great idea in the middle of the night, but when you think it over in the cold light of dawn, it's pretty awful!

F.T. I see we're not getting anywhere with this discussion on the impact of dreams on your work. At any rate, you don't seem to be too interested in this angle.

A.H. One thing for sure: I never have any erotic dreams!

F.T. And yet love and even eroticism play important roles in your work. We haven't talked about that yet. After *Notorious* you were regarded not only as the master of suspense, but also as an expert on physical love on the screen.

A.H. I suppose there is a physical aspect to the love scenes of *Notorious*. You're probably thinking of the kissing scene between Ingrid Bergman and Cary Grant.

F.T. As I remember it, the publicity blurbs described it as "the longest kiss in screen history."

A.H. As a matter of fact, the actors hated doing it. They felt terribly uncomfortable at the way in which they had to cling to each other. I said, "I don't care how you feel; the only thing that matters is the way it's going to look on the screen."

F.T. I imagine the reader will want to know why these two professionals were so ill at ease during this scene. To be specific, there was a close-up on their two faces together as they moved across the whole set. The problem for them was how to walk across, glued to each other in that way, while the only thing that concerned you was to show their two faces together on the screen.

A.H. Exactly. I conceived that scene in terms of the participants' desire not to interrupt the romantic moment. It was essential not to break up the mood, the dramatic atmosphere. Had they broken apart, all of the emotion would have been dissipated. And, of course, they had to be in action; they had to go over to the phone that was ringing and keep on embracing throughout the whole call and then they had to get over to the door. I felt it was indispensable that they should not separate, and I also felt that the public, represented by the camera, was the third party to this embrace. The public was being given the great privilege of embracing Cary Grant and Ingrid Bergman together. It was a kind of temporary *ménage à trois*.

The idea not to break up that romantic moment was inspired by the memory of something I witnessed in France several years earlier.

I was on the train going from Boulogne to Paris, and we were moving slowly through the small town of Etaples. It was on a Sunday afternoon. As we were passing a large, red brick factory, I saw a young couple against the wall. The boy was urinating against the wall and the girl never let go of his arm. She'd look down at what he was doing, then look at the scenery around them, then back again at the boy. I felt this was true love at work.

F.T. Ideally, two lovers should never separate.

A.H. Quite. It was the memory of that incident that gave me an exact idea of the effect I was after with the kissing scene in *Notorious*.

F.T. Your mention of the actors' irritation when they don't understand what the director is aiming at raises an interesting point. Many directors, I think, will shoot a scene within the context of the whole setting rather than solely in the context of that frame, which ultimately is what appears on the screen. I often think of that, especially when I look at your pictures, which makes me realize that great cinema, pure cinema, can stem from an establishing shot that may seem completely absurd to the cast as well as to the crew.

A.H. Absolutely. For instance . . .

F.T. The long kissing scene in *Notorious* is one illustration; another is the embrace between Cary Grant and Eva Marie Saint in the train coach in *North by Northwest*. Their bodies glide along the panel, making two complete turns as they kiss each other. On the screen it's absolutely perfect, yet it must have seemed completely illogical during the shooting.

A.H. Yes, they rotate against the wall. There, again, we applied the same rule of not separating the couple. There's just so much one can do with a love scene. Something I wish could work out is a love scene with two people on each side of the room. It's impossible, I suppose, because the only way to suggest love would be to have them exposing themselves to each other, with the man opening his fly and the girl lifting her skirt, and the dialogue in counterpoint. Something like: "What are going to have for supper tonight?" But I suppose that would come under the heading of out-and-out exhibitionism. Anyway, we used that counterpoint dialogue in *Notorious*, where they talk about a chicken dinner and who is going to wash the dishes, while they're kissing.

F.T. Can we go back a little? I think that I interrupted you just as you were about to say something about the realism of the frame and the mood on the set.

A.H. Well, I agree with you that many directors are conscious of the over-all atmosphere on the set, whereas they should be concerned only with what's going to come up on the screen. As you know, I never look into the view finder, but the cameraman knows very well that I don't want to have any air or space around the actors and that he must follow the sketches exactly as they are designed for each scene. There's no need to be concerned over the space in front of the camera if you bear in mind that for the final image we can take a pair of scissors to eliminate the unnecessary space.

Another aspect of the same problem is that space should not be wasted, because it can be used for dramatic effect. For instance, in *The Birds*, when the birds attack the barricaded house and Melanie is cringing back on the sofa, I kept the camera back and used the space to show the nothingness from which she's shrinking. When I went back to her, I varied that by placing the camera high to convey the impression of the fear that's rising in her. After that, there was another movement, high up and around her. But the space at the beginning was of key importance to the scene. If I'd started, at the outset, right next to the girl, we'd have the feeling that she was recoiling in front of some danger that she could see but the public could not. And I wanted to establish just the contrary, to show that there was nothing off-screen. Therefore, all of that space had a specific meaning.

Some directors will place their actors in the decor and then they'll set the camera at a distance, which depends simply on whether the actor happens to be seated, standing, or lying down. That, to me, seems to be pretty woolly thinking. It's never precise and it certainly doesn't express anything.

F.T. In other words, to inject realism into a given film frame, a director must allow for a certain amount of unreality in the space immediately surrounding that frame. For instance, the close-up of a kiss between two supposedly standing figures might be obtained by having the two actors kneeling on a kitchen table.

A.H. That's one way of doing it. And we might even raise that table some nine inches to have it come into the frame. Do you want to show a man standing behind a table? Well, the closer you get to him, the higher you must raise the table if you want to keep it inside the image. Anyhow, many directors overlook these things, and they hold their camera too far away to keep that table inside the image. They think that everything on the screen will look just the way it looks on the set. It's ridiculous!

You've raised a very important point here, a point that's fundamental. The placing of the images on the screen, in terms of what you're expressing, should never be dealt with in a factual manner. Never! You can get anything you want through the proper use of cinematic techniques, which enable you to work out any image you need. There's no justification for a short cut and no reason to settle for a compromise between the image you wanted and the image you get. One of the reasons most films aren't sufficiently rigorous is that so few people in the industry know anything about imagery.

F.T. The term "imagery" is particularly appropriate, because what we're saying is that it isn't necessary to photograph something violent in order to convey the feeling of violence, but rather to film that which gives the impression of violence.

This is demonstrated in one of the opening scenes of *North by Northwest*, in which the villains in a drawing room begin to manhandle Cary Grant. If you examine that scene in slow motion, on the small screen of the cutting room, you will see that the villains aren't doing anything at all to Cary Grant. But when projected on theater screens, that succession of quick frames and the little bobbing movements of the camera create an impression of brutality and violence.

A.H. There's a much better illustration in *Rear Window* when the man comes into the room to throw James Stewart out of the window. At first I had filmed the whole thing completely realistically. It was a weak scene; it wasn't impressive. So I did a close-up of a waving hand, a close-up of Stewart's face and another one of his legs; then I intercut all of this in proper rhythm, and the final effect was just right.

Now let's take a real-life analogy. If you stand close to a train as it's speeding through a station, you feel it; it almost knocks you down. But if you look at the same train from a distance of some two miles, you don't feel anything at all.

In the same way, if you're going to show two men fighting with each other, you're not going to get very much by simply photographing that fight. More often than not, the photographic reality is not realistic. The only way to do it is to get into the fight and make the public feel it. In that way you achieve true realism.

F.T. One method of unrealistic shooting to get a realistic effect is to set the decor behind the actors into motion.

A.H. That's one way to do it, but it isn't a rule. It would entirely depend upon the movements of the actors. As for myself, I'm quite satisfied to let the pieces of film create the motion. For instance, in *Sabotage*, when the little boy is in the bus and he's got the bomb at his side, I cut to that bomb from a different angle every time I showed it. I did that to give the bomb a vitality of its own, to animate it. If I'd shown it constantly from the same angle, the public would have become used to the package: "Oh well, it's only a package, after all." But what I was saying was: "Be careful! Watch out!"

F.T. To get back to that train you mentioned a while back, in *North by Northwest,* there's a scene in which the action takes place inside the train, but you show the whole of the train from the outside. To do that you didn't set your camera on the outside, in the fields, but you attached it to the train so that it was entirely dependent on it.

A.H. Planting the camera in the countryside to shoot a passing train would merely give us the viewpoint of a cow watching a train go by. I tried to keep the public inside the train, *with* the train. Whenever it went into a curve, we took a long shot from one of the train windows. The way we did that was to put three cameras on the rear platform of the *Twentieth Century Limited*, and we went over the exact journey of the film at the same time of the day. One of our cameras was used for the long shots of the train in the curves, while the two others were used for background footage.

F.T. In your technique everything is subordinated to the dramatic impact; the camera, in fact, accompanies the characters almost like an escort.

A.H. While we're on the subject of the camera flow and of cutting from one shot to another, I'd like to mention what I regard as a fundamental rule: When a character who has been seated stands up to walk around a room, I will never change the angle or move the camera back. I always start the movement on the close-up, the same size close-up I used while he was seated.

In most pictures, when two people are seen talking together, you have a close-up on one of them, then a close-up on the other, then you move back and forth again, and suddenly the camera jumps back for a long shot, to show one of the characters rising to walk around. It's wrong to handle it that way.

F.T. Yes, because that technique *precedes* the action instead of *accompanying* it. It allows the public to guess that one of the characters is about to stand up, or whatever. In other words, the camera should never anticipate what's about to follow.

A.H. Exactly, because that dissipates the emotion, and I'm convinced that's wrong. If a character moves around and you want to retain the emotion on his face, the only way to do that is to travel the close-up.

F.T. Before talking about *Psycho* I would like to ask whether you have any theory in respect to the opening scene of your pictures. Some of them start out with an act of violence; others simply indicate the locale.

A.H. It all depends on what the purpose is. The opening of *The Birds* is an attempt to suggest the normal, complacent, everyday life in San Francisco. Sometimes I simply use a title to indicate that we're in Phoenix or in San Francisco. It's too easy, I know, but it's economical. I'm torn between the need for economy and the wish to present a locale, even when it's a familiar one, with more subtlety. After all, it's no problem at all to present Paris with the Eiffel Tower in the background, or London with Big Ben on the horizon.

F.T. In pictures that don't open up with violence, you almost invariably apply the same rule of exposition: From the farthest to the nearest. You show the city, then a building in the city, a room in that building. That's the way *Psycho* begins.

A.H. In the opening of *Psycho* I wanted to say that we were in Phoenix, and we even spelled out the day and the time, but I only did that to lead up to a very important fact: that it was two-forty-three in the afternoon and this is the only time the poor girl has to go to bed with her lover. It suggests that she's spent her whole lunch hour with him.

F.T. It's a nice touch because it establishes at once that this is an illicit affair.

A.H. It also allows the viewer to become a Peeping Tom.

F.T. Jean Douchet, a French film critic, made a witty comment on that scene. He wrote that since John Gavin is stripped to his waist, but Janet Leigh wears a brassiere, the scene is only satisfying to one half of the audience.

A.H. In truth, Janet Leigh should not have been wearing a brassiere. I can see nothing immoral about that scene, and I get no special kick out of it. But the scene would have been more interesting if the girl's bare breasts had been rubbing against the man's chest.

F.T. I noticed that throughout the whole picture you tried to throw out red herrings to the viewers, and it occurred to me that the reason for that erotic opening was to mislead them again. The sex angle was raised so that later on the audience would think that Anthony Perkins is merely a voyeur. If I'm not mistaken, out of your fifty works, this is the only film showing a woman in a brassiere.

A.H. Well, one of the reasons for which I wanted to do the scene in that way was that the audiences are changing. It seems to me that the straightforward kissing scene would be looked down at by the younger viewers; they'd feel it was silly. I know that they themselves behave as John Gavin and Janet Leigh did. I think that nowadays you have to show them the way they themselves behave most of the time. Besides, I also wanted to give a visual impression of despair and solitude in that scene.

F.T. Yes, it occurred to me that *Psycho* was oriented toward a new
      generation of filmgoers. There were many things in that
      picture that you'd never done in your earlier films.

A.H. Absolutely. In fact, that's also true in a technical sense for
      The Birds.

F.T. I've read the novel from which *Psycho* was taken, and one of
      the things that bothered me is that it cheats. For instance,
      there are passages like this: "Norman sat down beside his
      mother and they began a conversation." Now, since she
      doesn't exist, that's obviously misleading, whereas the film
      narration is rigorously worked out to eliminate these dis-
      crepancies. What was it that attracted you to the novel?

A.H. I think that the thing that appealed to me and made me
      decide to do the picture was the suddenness of the murder
      in the shower, coming, as it were, out of the blue. That was
      about all.

F.T. The killing is pretty much like a rape. I believe the novel
      was based on a newspaper story.

A.H. It was the story of a man who kept his mother's body in
      his house, somewhere in Wisconsin.

F.T. In *Psycho* there's a whole arsenal of terror, which you gen-
      erally avoid: the ghostly house . . .

A.H. The mysterious atmosphere is, to some extent, quite acci-
      dental. For instance, the actual locale of the events is in
      northern California, where that type of house is very com-
      mon. They're either called "California Gothic," or, when
      they're particularly awful, they're called "California ginger-
      bread." I did not set out to reconstruct an old-fashioned
      Universal horror-picture atmosphere. I simply wanted to be
      accurate, and there is no question but that both the house
      and the motel are authentic reproductions of the real thing.
      I chose that house and motel because I realized that if I had
      taken an ordinary low bungalow the effect wouldn't have
      been the same. I felt that type of architecture would help
      the atmosphere of the yarn.

F.T. I must say that the architectural contrast between the vertical house and the horizontal motel is quite pleasing to the eye.

A.H. Definitely, that's our composition: a vertical block and a horizontal block.

F.T. In that whole picture there isn't a single character with whom a viewer might identify.

A.H. It wasn't necessary. Even so, the audience was probably sorry for the poor girl at the time of her death. In fact, the first part of the story was a red herring. That was deliberate, you see, to detract the viewer's attention in order to heighten the murder. We purposely made that beginning on the long side, with the bit about the theft and her escape, in order to get the audience absorbed with the question of whether she would or would not be caught. Even that business about the forty thousand dollars was milked to the very end so that the public might wonder what's going to happen to the money.

You know that the public always likes to be one jump ahead of the story; they like to feel they know what's coming next. So you deliberately play upon this fact to control their thoughts. The more we go into the details of the girl's journey, the more the audience becomes absorbed in her flight. That's why so much is made of the motorcycle cop and the change of cars. When Anthony Perkins tells the girl of his life in the motel, and they exchange views, you still play upon the girl's problem. It seems as if she's decided to go back to Phoenix and give the money back, and it's possible that the public anticipates by thinking, "Ah, this young man is influencing her to change her mind." You turn the viewer in one direction and then in another; you keep him as far as possible from what's actually going to happen.

In the average production, Janet Leigh would have been given the other role. She would have played the sister who's investigating. It's rather unusual to kill the star in the first third of the film. I purposely killed the star so as to make the killing even more unexpected. As a matter of fact, that's why I insisted that the audiences be kept out of the theaters once the picture had started, because the late-comers would have been waiting to see Janet Leigh after she has disappeared from the screen action.

Psycho has a very interesting construction and that game with the audience was fascinating. I was directing the viewers. You might say I was playing them, like an organ.

F.T. I admired that picture enormously, but I felt a letdown during the two scenes with the sheriff.

A.H. The sheriff's intervention comes under the heading of what we have discussed many times before: "Why don't they go to the police?" I've always replied, "They don't go to the police because it's dull." Here is a perfect example of what happens when they go to the police.

F.T. Still, the action picks up again almost immediately after that. One intriguing aspect is the way the picture makes the viewer constantly switch loyalties. At the beginning he hopes that Janet Leigh won't be caught. The murder is very shocking, but as soon as Perkins wipes away the traces of the killing, we begin to side with him, to hope that he won't be found out. Later on, when we learn from the sheriff that Perkins' mother has been dead for eight years, we again change sides and are against Perkins, but this time, it's sheer curiosity. The viewer' emotions are not exactly wholesome.

A.H. This brings us back to the emotions of Peeping Tom audiences. We had some of that in *Dial M for Murder*.

F.T. That's right. When Milland was late in phoning his wife and the killer looked as if he might walk out of the apartment without killing Grace Kelly. The audience reaction there was to hope he'd hang on for another few minutes.

A.H. It's a general rule. Earlier, we talked about the fact that when a burglar goes into a room, all the time he's going through the drawers, the public is generally anxious for him. When Perkins is looking at the car sinking in the pond, even though he's burying a body, when the car stops sinking for a moment, the public is thinking, "I hope it goes all the way down!" It's a natural instinct.

F.T. But in most of your films the audience reaction is more innocent because they are concerned for a man who is wrongly suspected of a crime. Whereas in *Psycho* one begins by being scared for a girl who's a thief, and later on one is scared for a killer, and, finally, when one learns that this killer has a secret, one hopes he will be caught just in order to get the full story!

A.H. I doubt whether the identification is that close.

F.T. It isn't necessarily identification, but the viewer becomes attached to Perkins because of the care with which he wipes away all the traces of his crime. It's tantamount to admiring someone for a job well done.

I understand that in addition to the main titles, Saul Bass also did some sketches for the picture.

A.H. He did only one scene, but I didn't use his montage. He was supposed to do the titles, but since he was interested in the picture, I let him lay out the sequence of the detective going up the stairs, just before he is stabbed. One day during the shooting I came down with a temperature, and since I couldn't come to the studio, I told the cameraman and my assistant that they could use Saul Bass's drawings. Only the part showing him going up the stairs, before the killing. There was a shot of his hand on the rail, and of feet seen in profile, going up through the bars of the balustrade. When I looked at the rushes of the scene, I found it was no good, and that was an interesting revelation for me, because as that sequence was cut, it wasn't an innocent person but a sinister man who was going up those stairs. Those cuts would have been perfectly all right if they were showing a killer, but they were in conflict with the whole spirit of the scene.

Bear in mind that we had gone to a lot of trouble to prepare the audience for this scene: we had established a mystery woman in the house; we had established the fact that this mystery woman had come down and slashed a woman to pieces under her shower. All the elements that would convey suspense to the detective's journey upstairs had gone before and we therefore needed a simple statement. We needed to show a staircase and a man going up that staircase in a very simple way.

F.T. I suppose that the original rushes of that scene helped you to determine just the right expression. In French we would say that "he arrived like a flower," which implies, of course, that he was ready to be plucked.

A.H. It wasn't exactly impassivity; it was more like complacency. Anyway, I used a single shot of Arbogast coming up the stairs, and when he got to the top step, I deliberately placed the camera very high for two reasons. The first was so that I could shoot down on top of the mother, because if I'd shown her back, it might have looked as if I was deliberately concealing her face, and the audience would have been leery. I used that high angle in order not to give the impression that I was trying to avoid showing her.

But the main reason for raising the camera so high was to get the contrast between the long shot and the close-up of the big head as the knife came down at him. It was like music, you see, the high shot with the violins, and suddenly the big head with the brass instruments clashing. In the high shot the mother dashes out, and I cut into the movement of the knife sweeping down. Then I went over to the close-up on Arbogast. We put a plastic tube on his face with hemoglobin, and as the knife came up to it, we pulled a string releasing the blood on his face down the line we had traced in advance. Then he fell back on the stairway.

F.T. I was rather intrigued by that fall backward. He doesn't actually fall. His feet aren't shown, but the feeling one gets is that he's going down the stairs backward, brushing each step with the tip of his foot, like a dancer.

A.H. That's the impression we were after. Do you know how we got that?

F.T. I realize you wanted to stretch out the action, but I don't know how you did it.

A.H. We did it by process. First I did a separate dolly shot down the stairway, without the man. Then we sat him in a special chair in which he was in a fixed position in front of the transparency screen showing the stairs. Then we shot the chair, and Arbogast simply threw his arms up, waving them as if he'd lost his balance.

F.T. It's extremely effective. Later on in the picture you use another very high shot to show Perkins taking his mother to the cellar.

A.H. I raised the camera when Perkins was going upstairs. He goes into the room and we don't see him, but we hear him say, "Mother, I've got to take you down to the cellar. They're snooping around." And then you see him take her down to the cellar. I didn't want to cut, when he carries her down, to a high shot because the audience would have been suspicious as to why the camera has suddenly jumped away. So I had a hanging camera follow Perkins up the stairs, and when he went into the room I continued going up without a cut. As the camera got up on top of the door, the camera turned and looked back down the stairs again. Meanwhile, I had an argument take place between the son and his mother to distract the audience and take their minds off what the camera was doing. In this way the camera was above Perkins again as he carried his mother down, and the public hadn't noticed a thing. It was rather exciting to use the camera to deceive the audience.

F.T. The stabbing of Janet Leigh was very well done also.

A.H. It took us seven days to shoot that scene, and there were seventy camera setups for forty-five seconds of footage. We had a torso specially made up for that scene, with the blood that was supposed to spurt away from the knife, but I didn't use it. I used a live girl instead, a naked model who stood in for Janet Leigh. We only showed Miss Leigh's hands, shoulders, and head. All the rest was the stand-in. Naturally, the knife never touched the body; it was all done in the montage. I shot some of it in slow motion so as to cover the breasts. The slow shots were not accelerated later on because they were inserted in the montage so as to give an impression of normal speed.

F.T. It's an exceptionally violent scene.

A.H. This is the most violent scene of the picture. As the film unfolds, there is less violence because the harrowing memory of this initial killing carries over to the suspenseful passages that come later.

F.T. Yet, even better than the killing, in the sense of its harmony, is the scene in which Perkins handles the mop and broom to clean away any traces of the crime. The whole construction of the picture suggests a sort of scale of the abnormal. First there is a scene of adultery, then a theft, then one crime followed by another, and, finally, psychopathy. Each passage puts us on a higher note of the scale. Isn't that so?

A.H. I suppose so, but you know that to me Janet Leigh is playing the role of a perfectly ordinary bourgeoise.

F.T. But she does lead us in the direction of the abnormal, toward Perkins and his stuffed birds.

A.H. I was quite intrigued with them: they were like symbols. Obviously Perkins is interested in taxidermy since he'd filled his own mother with sawdust. But the owl, for instance, has another connotation. Owls belong to the night world; they are watchers, and this appeals to Perkins's masochism. He knows the birds, and he knows that they're watching him all the time. He can see his own guilt reflected in their knowing eyes.

F.T. Would you say that *Psycho* is an experimental film?

A.H. Possibly. My main satisfaction is that the film had an effect on the audiences, and I consider that very important. I don't care about the subject matter; I don't care about the acting; but I do care about the pieces of film and the photography and the sound track and all of the technical ingredients that made the audience scream. I feel it's tremendously satisfying for us to be able to use the cinematic art to achieve something of a mass emotion. And with *Psycho* we most definitely achieved this. It wasn't a message that stirred the audiences, nor was it a great performance or their enjoyment of the novel. They were aroused by pure film.

F.T. Yes, that's true.

A.H. That's why I take pride in the fact that *Psycho*, more than any of my other pictures, is a film that belongs to film-makers, to you and me. I can't get a real appreciation of the picture in the terms we're using now. People will say, "It was a terrible film to make. The subject was horrible, the people were small, there were no characters in it." I know all of this, but I also know that the construction of the story and the way in which it was told caused audiences all over the world to react and become emotional.

F.T. Yes, emotional and even physical.

A.H. Emotional. I don't care whether it looked like a small or a large picture. I didn't start off to make an important movie. I thought I could have fun with this subject and this situation. The picture cost eight hundred thousand dollars. It was an experiment in this sense: Could I make a feature film under the same conditions as a television show? I used a complete television unit to shoot it very quickly. The only place where I digressed was when I slowed down the murder scene, the cleaning-up scene, and the other scenes that indicated anything that required time. All of the rest was handled in the same way that they do it in television.

F.T. I know that you produced *Psycho* yourself. How did you make out with it?

A.H. *Psycho* cost us no more than eight hundred thousand dollars to make. It has grossed some fifteen million dollars to date.

F.T. That's fantastic! Would you say this was your greatest hit to date?

A.H. Yes. And that's what I'd like you to do—a picture that would gross millions of dollars throughout the world! It's an area of film-making in which it's more important for you to be pleased with the technique than with the content. It's the kind of picture in which the camera takes over. Of course, since critics are more concerned with the scenario, it won't necessarily get you the best notices, but you have to design your film just as Shakespeare did his plays—for an audience.

F.T. That reminds me that *Psycho* is particularly universal because it's a half-silent movie; there are at least two reels with no dialogue at all. And that also simplified all the problems of subtitling and dubbing.

A.H. Do you know that in Thailand they use no subtitles or dubbing? They shut off the sound and a man stands somewhere near the screen and interprets all the roles, using different voices.

2

Introduction

ROBERT KOLKER

◆ ◆ ◆

"I . . . know that the construction of the story and the way in
which it was told caused audiences all over the world to react
and become emotional." There are few American filmmakers who
would openly announce that they were more interested in form
than content. (Let us note that Hitchcock was British and made
many films in England before the.American producer, David O.
Selznick, brought him over to his new home in the late 1930s,
where he became, in very short order, an American filmmaker.)
In Hollywood, the emphasis is on "story" and characters. Cinematic form is meant to be a clear window, through which the
viewer looks at that story unfolding, as if by magic. Hitchcock
did not believe in magic, and he understood that "content" or
story is not something that floats around waiting for a novelist,
poet, or filmmaker to catch and pour it into the waiting form of
his or her art.

Quite the opposite, like most artists, Hitchcock was deeply
aware that form creates content, and form is specific to each kind
of artistic expression. The artist, like the Thai interpreter Hitch-

cock mentions at the end of the interview, uses different voices, expressing him or herself in the specific languages of the medium. But unlike that interpreter, the artist is not simply a vessel through which the material passes. A good filmmaker, like any other artist, uses form, pushes and tests it, speaks through his or her characters and how they interact, speaks through the very spaces of the story that is created out of the visual stuff of cinema and gives it life.

This is what makes *Psycho* such an important film. It was an experiment in form that was a commercial success. It was built to generate an emotional charge that cannot be ignored no matter how often it is seen. Few films before it had such a shocking effect on their audience. And few other films—perhaps those of Stanley Kubrick and Orson Welles (whose 1958 film, *Touch of Evil* was an enormous influence on *Psycho*)—keep revealing more and more on subsequent viewings. The reason for this is exactly the intricate way Hitchcock molds, defines and structures the visual narrative that tells the story of his film.

The very conditions under which the film was made, with Hitchcock attempting to duplicate the shooting methods of his television show (down to using his television cameraman, John Russell, to film it) indicated, first of all, an economy of form—as well as cost—but also indicates the initial desire to make *Psycho* different from what was usually seen at the movies in the late fifties. The final product does not look like television; but it does not quite look like any film made before it. It is stark and compact, and each shot is packed with information, much of which is unavailable on a single viewing.

Part of that compactness is a result of another experiment, an abstract design that underpins almost every composition, and which is foreshadowed in Saul Bass's credit sequence. Saul Bass was an important industrial designer, as well as a designer of film credit sequences, and a film director in his own right. Martin Scorsese—a director greatly influenced by all things Hitchcockian—had Saul Bass create the credit sequences for some of his own films, including the *Psycho*-like credits for *GoodFellas*. Bass's design for *Psycho*, which I will examine closely in the last essay in this book, acts like a grid that ties together all the images in the film. This persistent visual design allows for a kind of subliminal cohesion for the viewer as well as a very conscious, very economical cohesion for the director. It is, in fact, the closest that Hitchcock, or perhaps any American director other than Kubrick, has come to abstract expressionist art.

This visual economy is present in many other ways: in the framing of the shots, the choice of gray and black tones of the images and the precise camera movements, each signifying a point of view at, or from, a character—even if, as in the tracking shot from Marion Crane's dead eye to the money lying on the motel table, they are dead ends. There is yet another economy at work, this one in the way Hitchcock folds his narrative into a tightly packed joke. When you watch *Psycho* a second, third, or fourth time, you begin to see how everything in the film's story is revealed in almost every scene of its narrative. A close examination of, for example, the sequence in which Marion and Norman have sandwiches in the parlor—just before Marion is murdered—reveals both in dialogue and in visual composition everything about Norman and his mother. This is part of the "joke" that many of the critics represented in this volume, as well as Hitchcock himself, keep referring to. That sequence, too, will be fully analyzed later in my essay on the visual structure of the film.

The structure and narrative form of *Psycho* may indeed be a joke played on the audience, but, in the end, what makes the film so enduring is the dark, closed, bleak, and joyless world that its structure creates. Few previous films, perhaps only some films noir of the late forties, depicted a world where life is so nasty, brutish, and short. No previous film had ended with such an unanswered, grinning question mark as *Psycho* does. This is another part of the joke and the horror. There is no rational answer to the questions the film raises, certainly not those offered by the smug psychiatrist in the cop house—that place of order that can impose order on nothing. No, *Psycho* ends with the grinning face of Norman, his mother's grinning skull superimposed, and a thick chain pulling the car carrying Marion's corpse out of the swamp. The world of the film is closed with this shot, which, like the slashing of the knife that kills Marion—a movement itself fore-shadowed in the windshield wipers of Marion's car as she drives to her death—breaks the horizontal and vertical lines that buttress the rest of the film. We are left without a pattern, a narrative anchor, an answer; left only to face our own fears of madness and the unknown.

We are left, as well, with memories and anxieties of the past. Hitchcock made films during the forties that had the Second World War as a background or subject. *Lifeboat* (1944) and *Notorious* (1946) are among the best known. What is little known—though it is referred to in Robin Wood's essay—is that in 1945 Hitchcock briefly collaborated with a colleague on a British documentary on the concentration camps. The film was never shown until the PBS series *Frontline* broadcast it in 1985 under the title *Memory of the Camps*. Hitchcock did not have a great deal to do with the film, but I think whatever his experience with it, along with the cultural memory of Nazis' killing of six million people (*Psycho* was begun in 1959, less than fifteen years after the war), along with the political and social repressions of the fifties themselves, resonate in this film about psychotic repression, the unpredictability of enormous violence, and the inability to rationalize it.

The essays and book excerpts that follow touch on many of these issues, from the film's inception and initial reception through serious, critical analysis of its construction, meanings, and the reasons audiences react to it the way they do. The essays also represent the progress of film criticism itself. I have tried to include a variety of critical approaches that have developed over the span of film studies, from formal analysis through the methodologies of gender and psychoanalytical criticism, theories of the gaze, and that rarest of all things, analysis of the film's music. Rather than summarize the pieces here, I have provided a brief introduction before each essay, explaining the historical context, the methodology, and any special vocabulary employed. I have written an essay of my own that closely analyzes *Psycho*'s visual form and its influence on other filmmakers, in effect summarizing the essays that come before by seeing, through stills, how Hitchcock structured his film.

There is a richness of thought and passion in these essays that match that of the film, which is, strangely enough, very passionate, if not compassionate, in its director's devotion to the forms of his art and his fears about the world.

Note

A history of the making of *Memory of the Camps* can be found on the PBS Web site, http://www.pbs.org/wgbh/pages/frontline/camp/

3

The Inception

❖ ❖ ❖

❖ ❖ ❖

Making of" books (or those DVD supplements on the "making of" a movie) are a bit treacherous. We are given the point of view of many people who work to create a film, but none of them—except usually the producer and sometimes the director—know what the final film will be. We learn some facts and get many anecdotes. However, the following excerpt from *Alfred Hitchcock and the Making of* Psycho gives excellent background information about the deal making that lead to the film and the writing process that, for Hitchcock, along with the storyboarding of the images, was one of the most important parts of filming. The remarks by screenwriter Joseph Stefano in the following excerpt are important in revealing what Hitchcock did and did not want from his writer. Note Stefano's comment that Hitchcock was most interested in visual ideas and that he wanted any sentimentality cut from the script. Think about the naïveté of Stefano's remark that Hitchcock was not aware of the utter darkness of the film he was making.

STEPHEN REBELLO ◆ From *Alfred Hitchcock and the Making of Psycho*

The Deal: Hitchcock Outmaneuvers

Developing passion for a movie property can be like falling madly for someone who leaves one's friends cold. Hitchcock had been battling indifference, or outright bewilderment, toward his projects from the start. Producer David O. Selznick, who railed constantly against the director's "damned jigsaw cutting," seemed to have imported Hitchcock from England without comprehending that the sort of talent who can create *The 39 Steps* or *The Lady Vanishes* does not tend to flourish on a leash. Cary Grant complained throughout the shooting of *North by Northwest* that he could make neither heads nor tails of the script. A Paramount executive admitted: "I never saw what Hitchcock did in *Rear Window* until I saw the finished movie." Lack of vision is one thing. Across-the-board contempt for a proposed Hitchcock movie was something new.

Hitchcock refused to kowtow to Paramount. After all, studio executives came and went like this year's starlet. Hitchcock had become a legend for being right more often than wrong. The director and his production staff quietly began exploring how to minimize the investment downside of *Psycho*. Hitchcock hit on the solution: plan his new production as scrupulously as he would any big-budget feature film, but shoot it quickly and inexpensively, almost like an expanded episode of his TV series, *Alfred Hitchcock Presents*.

That popular anthology series, which debuted on CBS on October 2, 1955, had been a master plot of Hitchcock's MCA agent and confidant, Lew R. Wasserman. A former burlesque-house usher and sweets peddler, Wasserman had been promoted by Jules Stein to vice president of MCA [Universal's then parent company] after two years. Wasserman had risen to becoming one of the shrewdest, most powerful and respected power brokers in the trade. In 1946, Stein appointed the tall, spindly Wasserman head of MCA, and his style and comportment became the house style. It pleased Hitchcock that Wasserman negotiated charmingly and relentlessly in a dark suit, white shirt, and slim tie. MCA agents became known as "the black-suited Mafia."

In 1951, despite a storm of controversy over a bylaw of the Screen Actors Guild that prohibited agents from producing films without a Guild waiver, MCA created its first television show, *Stars over Hollywood*, through its newly formed Revue Productions. Granted a waiver by then president of SAG, Ronald Reagan, MCA premiered *GE Theater* in 1953; Wasserman hired Reagan to host that series. Soon, MCA and Revue enjoyed an ongoing arrangement with NBC, for which they produced such popular TV series as *Wagon Train*, *Wells Fargo*, and *M Squad*.

Lew Wasserman had been waiting for an opportunity to capitalize on the offbeat charisma given off by Hitchcock's manner of a macabre cherub. The director had recently agreed to lend his name to *Alfred Hitchcock Mystery Magazine*, an enterprise funded by a rich Floridian, in which Hitchcock played no role in story selection or editing. Even the first-person story lead-ins were penned by attorney-novelist Harold Q. Masur. But the Hitchcock name was sufficient to send circulation skyward. Movie audiences, too, awaited the walk-on appearance the director made in each of his films. Wasserman understood Hitchcock's seemingly contradictory dynamic of the exhibitionist and the recluse. "About his appearance," observed an associate of the director, "Hitch was very contradictory. He seemed sometimes to delude himself into thinking that because he *directed* Cary Grant that he *looked* like him."

Lew Wasserman also avidly hoped to give MCA a greater toehold in the production side of film and television. In the late fifties, top Hollywood talent generally steered clear of the "overexposure" that TV appearances seemed to threaten. But in 1959, when Wasserman orchestrated the sale of Universal-International Studios and absorbed the Revue production facilities for MCA for $11,250,000, Hitchcock took notice. "We ought to put Hitch on the air," Hitchcock biographer John Russell Taylor quoted Wasserman as saying. The conglomerate mogul contended that a top box-office draw like Hitchcock would lend class to the weekly half-hour suspense-mystery series he envisioned for Revue. Bristol-Meyers readily agreed to bankroll the show, provided Hitchcock act as host as well as director of "several" episodes per season. Certain that Hitchcock would balk at any activity that he perceived as a diversion from feature-film making, Wasserman pitched the proposition masterfully. All rights to each of the episodes, budgeted at $129,000 each, would revert to the director after the first broadcast. Hitchcock consented.

The director installed himself as president and chief executive officer of Shamley Productions, named after a summer place he and Alma, his wife, had bought in a village south of London in 1928. Housed in a modest bungalow, Shamley Productions was entirely separate from the Hitchcock Production Company, the corporation under which Hitchcock did his film work. To make certain he kept his schedule clear for movies, Hitchcock brought on Joan Harrison, who had risen from his secretary in 1935 to script collaborator (*Rebecca, Foreign Correspondent, Suspicion*) to independent producer (*Phantom Lady, They Won't Believe Me*). Sharp, worldly, handsome, experienced, and genre-wise—Harrison was the wife of mystery writer Eric Ambler—she was a matchless choice.

Hitchcock limited his role in the series to reading droll segue monologues scripted by playwright James Allardice and to directing the scripts selected and developed for him by Harrison. A crack cadre of technicians made certain the boss needed to lavish no more than three days—one for rehearsals, two for shooting—on such episodes as "Revenge," "Breakdown," and "Back for Christmas."

In forming a creative team for his TV endeavors, Hitchcock duplicated the situation that he enjoyed on his feature-film work. Movie cameraman Leonard South explained: "[Hitchcock] was ill at ease around people. That's basically why he had the same camera crew for fifteen pictures. After we finished *Vertigo* at Paramount, Hitch told us he was going to be inactive for a while because he had to have gallbladder surgery. So George Tomasini [editor], Bob Boyle and Henry Bumstead [art directors], Bob Burks [chief cinematographer], and I were signed to a two-picture deal with the producers William Perlberg and George Seaton. In the middle of our making for them *But Not for Me*, with Gable and Carroll Baker, Hitch decided to make something out of nothing: *Psycho*." [Actually, after *Vertigo*, Hitchcock and his regular crew made *North by Northwest* for MGM.]

Among members of his TV team were cinematographer John L. Russell, assistant director Hilton A. Green, set designer George Milo, and script supervisor Marshal Schlom. Schlom, son of one of the prolific RKO B-movie producers, Herman Schlom, observed: "Mr. Hitchcock was the biggest thing around, especially on TV. To the studio, he was a hands-off client who got anything he wanted. The crews for the other Revue TV shows, *The Jane Wyman Show*, *The Millionaire*, kept changing, but he said, 'I want my own little family.' While we were doing the hour and half-hour shows, we kept hearing rumblings that he was toying with the idea of doing something different. One day, word came that he was about to make a feature and those of us that were close to him were going to do it with him."

With a trusted, competent talent pool at the ready, Hitchcock devised the idea of shooting *Psycho*—his "smallest" project since *The Wrong Man*—utilizing his television collaborators. The director reconvened the heads of production at Paramount to present this new cost-conscious option. He suggested that he thoroughly prepare the project at Paramount, then import his TV crew to shoot the picture on the studio lot, where he would also complete the editing and postproduction. The executives made it clear: Paramount would not finance *Psycho*. Further, they told Hitchcock that every studio soundstage was either occupied or booked, even though everyone on the lot knew that production was in a slump.

Hitchcock was ready for them. He agreed to finance *Psycho* personally and to shoot at Universal-International if Paramount agreed to distribute the picture. As the sole producer, Hitchcock would defer his director's fee of $250,000 in exchange for 60 percent ownership of the negative. Such an offer Paramount could not—and did not—refuse.

In his book *Dark Victory: Ronald Reagan, MCA, and the Mob*, Dan E. Moldea weaves a politically nefarious, byzantine plot regarding the financing of *Psycho*. In interviews conducted by the FBI for an investigation of ties between MCA and Paramount, a source told Antitrust Division attorney Leonard Posner, "[*Psycho*] was produced on the Universal lot by MCA. . . . Financing for the picture came from the company that is going to distribute the picture—Paramount. . . . In other words, MCA represented Hitchcock and told Paramount that if it wanted to finance and release the Hitchcock picture, it would have to be produced on the Universal lot so that MCA could get its cut from the below-the-line facilities. This arrangement was made in spite of the fact that Paramount had a lot that was half empty at the time. Obviously, Paramount would have preferred to have had the picture made on its own lot, so that it could have gotten some of its money back toward overhead."

If Hitchcock savored his coup, few in his inner circle shared his glee. Producer Herbert Coleman, perhaps the director's closest on-line associate, had served as second-unit director on all Hitchcock productions since *Rear Window*. Coleman had been with Paramount for over thirty years, having risen from the script department to assistant director to William Wyler on such films as *Roman Holiday*. Throughout the summer of 1959, the seasoned, exacting Coleman helped Hitchcock steer *Psycho* through the straits of preproduction. Having worked several times on abandoned Hitchcock projects in the past several years, Coleman apparently hoped this might be another of them. As *Psycho* looked more and more like a "go" project toward the fall, Coleman withdrew. He intended to establish an identity within the movie community outside of Hitchcock. He also had objections to the direction the dark project was taking. Similarly, Shamley production head Joan Harrison reportedly refused profit points in *Psycho* in lieu of a raise. "This time, you're going too far," Harrison reputedly advised Hitchcock about his new project. Not even his closest colleagues envisioned just how far Hitchcock planned to go.

The Screenplays: Writing Is Rewriting

The deeper Hitchcock waded into preproduction on his forty-seventh picture the more obvious it became that to make it would cut him adrift from his moorings: longtime associates plus production values, picture-postcard locations, major stars, and expensive screenwriters of the reputation of Samuel Taylor (*Vertigo*) or Ernest Lehman (*North by Northwest*). By necessity, *Psycho* would mark Hitchcock's break with his moviemaking past and put the industry on notice that a sixty-year-old directorial workhorse could shock and innovate with the best of the young bloods. For an insulated and entrenched creature such as Hitchcock, one might liken that prospect to the dizzying attraction-repulsion that acrophobic Scottie Ferguson (James Stewart) experienced when he looked down from the heights in *Vertigo*.

Hitchcock kept secret the specifics of his new project from all but his closest remaining associates and began to search for a suitable screenwriter. "This is going to need someone with a sense of humor," the director insisted. According to Hitchcock, "When you mention murder, most writers begin to think in low-key terms. But the events leading up to the act itself might be very light and amusing. Many murderers are very attractive persons; they have to be in order to attract their victims." Among writers whom Hitchcock considered to adapt *Psycho* was novelist Robert Bloch, who was eking out a living in the Midwest. According to Bloch, a client of another agency, MCA agents advised Hitchcock that the writer was "unavailable." The "black-suited Mafia" played upon Hitchcock's loyalty (and frugality) by suggesting that he hire from their wide client list.

In the end, Joan Harrison and MCA prevailed upon the director to hire thirty-eight-year-old client James P. Cavanagh, which Hitchcock did on June 8, 1959. Cavanagh had impressed Harrison with his flair for macabre comedy in teleplay credits for Shamley, including "The Hidden Thing" (broadcast May 20, 1956), "The Creeper" (broadcast June 17, 1956), and "Fog Closes In," all *Alfred Hitchcock Presents* episodes, and the last an Emmy winner. *Psycho* would mark Cavanagh's motion picture screenplay debut.

To bolster the case for Cavanagh, Harrison reminded her boss that he had directed the writer's teleplay, "One More Mile to Go," based on a story by F. J. Smith, in January 1957. Broadcast on April 7, 1957, the show virtually suggests a dry run for *Psycho*. In it, David Wayne plays a henpecked husband who—when his wife dies accidentally—stuffs her corpse into a sack in his car trunk, then heads for a lake to dispose of the body. En route, a menacing motorcycle cop hounds him, and a burned-out taillight leads to disclosure of his cargo.

A *Hollywood Reporter* squib on June 10 announced that Hitchcock had signed Cavanagh, who was en route from Paris to begin work on his next film. The same article leaked the title of the project as *Psyche*, which led some observers to wonder whether Hitchcock might be turning to Greek tragedy in search of unusual suspense material. The director teased: "It's the story of a young man whose mother is a homicidal maniac." While on a publicity tour to promote *North by Northwest* and awaiting a first draft of the Cavanagh script in late July, Hitchcock dropped the first hints about his new project to the general public in a June 22 *New York Times* piece by A. H. Weiler. Although he suppressed the title of the Bloch novel ("It would undo any effects I will try to put into the picture"), Hitchcock showed uncharacteristic candor when he promised a film "in the *Diabolique* genre."

"It takes place near Sacramento, California, at a dark and gloomy motel," elaborated the director. "Some very ordinary people meet other ordinary people and horror and death ensue in a manner that can't be unraveled unless you have the book as a guide." Making virtue of necessity, he underscored how modest a budget he planned for the project. Observed Hitchcock: "Nothing about it to distract from the telling of the tale, just like in the old days." In other words, just like in the years in England before Hitchcock came to expect the posh production values that only a Selznick or a Paramount could provide him.

An undated, first-draft screenplay by James Cavanagh, stamped "Revue Studios," not only provides a glimpse of a *Psycho* that might have been but also illustrates the early stages of the development of Hitchcock's visual scheme. As in [Robert Bloch's] novel, the action begins with Mary Crane's absconding with cash from her banker boss, Mr. Lowery, to free her to marry her lover, Sam. By the twelfth page of the script—or, approximately, twelve minutes into the film—the fugitive Mary has traded in her car and, in a rainstorm, taken shelter at the brooding Bates Motel. As she unpacks, Mary overhears Norman Bates and his invalid mother bickering viciously, then joins Bates for an awkward late supper. Much of Cavanagh's script has a sketched-in, tentative feel with little of the density of detail common to Hitchcock scripts. Yet the supper bill of fare is oddly specific: "sausage, cheese, pickles, and rye."

During the supper conversation, the empathy that develops between Mary and Norman deepens when Bates reveals that the bank is about to foreclose on the motel. Both Mary and Norman are trapped by lack of money. Their sympathy toward each other builds and peaks when Norman makes an embarrassing pass, that Mary only *just* rebuffs. "You don't like me, do you?" he asks. "As a matter of fact, I do," she replies. "But I wouldn't like you to think your mother was right about me." As Mary begs off and returns to her cabin, it is apparent that she intends to return the stolen cash. As she begins to undress, Cavanagh employs tedious description to misdirect the audience as to Norman's action and whereabouts. With frequent cuts to a ticking clock, Cavanagh details Norman checking in on mother ("a sleeping figure lying in bed") and, later, drinking himself into oblivion after reading the foreclosure letter.

At this stage of the screenwriting process, Hitchcock and Cavanagh took so indecisive a tone as to suggest that one or both of them were questioning whether the ideal venue for *Psycho* would be theaters or TV. One almost hears them hedging their

bets: "How much should we moralize on the actions of Mary?";
"How much or little can we 'show' of Mother Bates without
tipping off the audience?"; "How graphically can we depict the
murders?" As described by Cavanagh, the shower scene is quite
cinematic, complete with the slashings of an "old-fashioned
straight razor" that slits Mary's throat. And this: "For a brief
moment, we see the mad figure of old Mrs. Bates and hear her
high, shrill, hysterical laughter."

After the killing, Norman wakes from "a drunken stupor,"
discovers Mary's cabin door ajar, then finds a bloody dress and
razor in Mother's room. In the finale of the first act, Bates sinks
Mary's car in the nearby swamp. Unlike the earlier sections of
the script, the latter scene reads like a virtual blueprint for filming—down to the moment when "The car stops sinking. Norman's terror mounts."

Unfortunately, Cavanagh himself sinks in the second and third
acts of the script. Scene after scene fritters away the action to
detail an unconvincing romance between the dead girl's lover,
Sam, and her sister, Lila. Rather than propel us headlong toward
the Bates horror house, Sam and Lila discuss whether Mary was
"good" or "bad" as if they were team captains in a high school
debate. The pot boils anew when "Mrs. Bates comes walking
down the stairs" toward private detective Arbogast: "Now that
she is this close, even in the dim light, the grotesque makeup,
the disordered hair and mad eyes makes [sic] him take a step back
almost in fear."

In the matter of Mother, the Cavanagh script cheats. In a scene
in which two policemen confer outside the room in which the
corpse of Arbogast lies (unlike in the film, the motel and house
are connected), Bates and Mother "converse" in frantic whispers,
"his head buried against her breast." In other matters, the script
fumbles. When Arbogast fails to return, Sam and Lila carry on
the investigation. As they approach the office of the motel—
despite their fear/certainty that Norman is lurking just out of
sight and that he is behind the disappearances of Mary and the
detective—they kiss passionately.

Finally, in Mary's cabin, Sam and Lila turn up a clue in a bloodstained earring; in the film, a scrap of paper with "figuring" on it serves the same function. Then, Sam confronts Norman, who bashes Sam with a liquor bottle and drags the body into a closet. From there, the thrills unfold much as they do in the novel and in the finished film, except that the local sheriff, not a psychiatrist, explains Bates's psychological kinks for the audience.

Hitchcock spent a weekend at home with a script that straddled episodic television and feature films. But long before he reached the climactic revelation of Mrs. Bates as "a dummy with staring glass eyes and the blank face of a huge doll," Hitchcock undoubtedly knew the script did not play. In fact, the script falls so short of the mark, one might question the motivations of Joan Harrison. After all, she was neither a fan of the project nor did she lack for experience in matching a writer with a project. Yet Harrison had taken special pains to recommend to one of *the* most exacting directors in the business *this* inexperienced, inexpensive writer. Did she hope that the collaboration might persuade Hitchcock to get *Psycho* out of his system by doing it for TV? Or to drop it altogether?

Despite the letdown Hitchcock surely experienced, many typical details that had presumably evolved during story conferences with Cavanagh were to find their way into the competed film: the elaborate details of the heroine's harrowing car trip; the poignant, impactful supper conversation between Bates and Mary; the obsessive cleanup by Bates after the shower murder; and the swamp's gobbling Mary's car. Even the shower murder sequence anticipates the intricate camera movement that ends in a close-up of blood mingling with shower water gurgling down the drain.

Presumably, Cavanagh enjoyed access to eight pages of handwritten notes by Hitchcock in which the director laid out precise camera movements and sound cues for certain key sequences. In the scene in the used-car lot, writes Hitchcock, "The CAMERA pans along a series of California plates." He emphasizes "the relief of the traffic cop's whistle" that breaks the tension when Mary's boss peers at her through the windshield of her stopped car, stolen money in her purse. And to describe Mary's car journey after stealing the money, Hitchcock writes:

> The long traffic-laden route along Route 99—the roadside sights—the coming of darkness. Mary's thoughts about Monday morning and the discovery of her flight with the money. The rain starts.

So assured and cinematic are his concepts that Hitchcock even inserted an intriguing bit of self-parody or foreshadowing here and there. In a scene in which Norman Bates prays for the swamp to gulp down Mary's car, a small plane buzzes overhead like a deranged fly. The moment simultaneously recalls the pursuing crop duster in Hitchcock's previous film (*North by Northwest*); refers to Mother Bates, who "wouldn't even harm a fly," in the last line of his present film; and anticipates the winged furies of his next (*The Birds*). In the precise notes to the sound editor that the director dictated months before he cut *Psycho*, Hitchcock would continue to insist on the insertion of the buzzing of the plane.

Hitchcock might well have puzzled over the deficiencies in Cavanagh's draft. Where were the self-confidence, insouciance, and black wit of the writer's TV work? There seemed no percentage in commissioning a rewrite. Without so much as a personal word of explanation to Cavanagh, Hitchcock cashiered him, to the tune of $7,166, on July 27. Michael Ludmer, to whom the director often delegated the responsibility of dropping writers, observed: "It was very difficult for Mr. Hitchcock to express his feelings. There was a *great* deal of input that Mr. Hitchcock gave a writer. He didn't know how to say, 'I'd like to tell you how I feel about these pages,' if there was a problem. He knew that a writer would be upset or disturbed if he were to find out that somebody else was coming on the script. So he would delegate the delivery of that message." Cavanagh was to write the scripts for several of the more well-received Hitchcock TV shows, including "Arthur," "Mother, May I Go Out to Swim?," and "Coming, Mama." He died at age forty-nine, in 1971.

On the rebound, MCA agents suggested to Hitchcock another

young client, Joseph Stefano, a thirty-eight-year-old former lyricist-composer. Exuberantly cocky, volatile, and streetwise, Stefano, who had only owned a television for two years, had harbored no writing aspirations outside of music. Then, he had watched a live telecast of *Playhouse 90*, at the time a leading showcase for promising playwrights, directors, and actors, and thought; "I can do that." Stefano recalled: "I wrote a one-hour teleplay and within two weeks, the boss of a secretary friend of mine had made a deal for me with [producer] Carlo Ponti. I'd never even *read* a screenplay. Somebody had to tell me about 'Long shots,' 'Exterior,' and 'Interior.' "

Stefano won respectable notices for his first produced screenplay for Ponti, *The Black Orchid*, a moonlight and Mafia soap opera, released by Paramount, starring Anthony Quinn and Sophia Loren. He also won awards for his own *Playhouse 90* script, "Made in Japan," also a relationship story. Still bemused today by how quickly things happened, Stefano said, "I was offered a seven-year contract at Twentieth Century–Fox without knowing who the hell I was as a writer or even knowing that much about films." Stefano's wife, then pregnant, had always wanted to live in California; with the security of the movie contract, the writer abandoned his music career and moved west.

Stefano grew so "miserable" with his first studio assignment, a Sam Engle production called "A Machine for Chuparosa," he asked his agent to secure a release from the contract with Fox. Fox agreed. The neophyte writer fretted that such an action might blackball him within the industry, yet the same studio immediately hired him to adapt a J. R. Salamanca novel, *The Lost Country*, as a vehicle for rising young actor Anthony Perkins. Perkins never made the movie. Elvis Presley did, as *Wild in the Country*, from a script by Clifford Odets.

Stefano hopped to MCA, where he was represented by Ned Brown, the very agent who had finessed the acquisition of *Psycho* for Hitchcock. Stefano presented Brown with a list of ten directors "who could teach me something." Meetings for Stefano with William Wyler and Otto Preminger had short-circuited when Lew Wasserman alerted Brown to Hitchcock's immediate need for a writer. Hitchcock rejected Stefano sight unseen, telling agent Brown, "My fear about Mr. Stefano is that, from the work of his I've seen, maybe he doesn't have a sense of humor." The director had lumped Stefano with what he termed "the Reginald Rose– 'Playhouse 90' *crowd*"—humorless, self-important types with Something to Say.

To Stefano's rescue came the formidable agent Kay Brown. Brown, among her many accomplishments, had steered David O. Selznick toward the acquisition of the Margaret Mitchell novel, *Gone with the Wind*, and toward Daphne Du Maurier's *Rebecca*. Brown had also negotiated Hitchcock's first American contract with Selznick and had influenced the director to hire playwright Samuel Taylor as screenwriter for *Vertigo*. "I hadn't done *anything* to support my writing for *Psycho*," Stefano said, "but my agents felt I was exactly what Hitchcock needed—someone who could do characterizations. They thought it was a very inferior book, a very sleazy kind of property. Hitchcock was strange about a lot of things. He only liked to work with people he knew and wasn't about to meet any new writer. Finally, there was enough pressure put on him by Lew Wasserman and everybody else, who kept saying, 'Just meet him, that's all.' "

Yet when Stefano read the Robert Bloch novel as a pre-interview preparation for Hitchcock, the writer was puzzled over the big lobbying effort on his behalf. "I was very disappointed," Stefano recalled. "Having loved all Hitchcock's work, I had in mind *The 39 Steps, Rebecca,* and *North by Northwest*, not some strange little pulp fiction. [*Psycho*] didn't even ring of a Hitchcock picture. I let [Hitchcock] know how disappointed I was as soon as we met."

"[Hitchcock] told me that he had a script by Robert Bloch that hadn't worked out," Stefano asserted. Bloch, who was living in Wisconsin at the time, today denies he wrote any such script. An intra–Revue Studios correspondence by Peggy Robertson dated December 19, 1959, confirms, "It is my understanding that Mr. Stefano has not been exposed to the James Cavanagh first draft screenplay. It is further my understanding that no synopsis, treatment, or material of the like has been written for this film other than the above two items."

But when they met, Hitchcock offered Stefano no suggestion that he saw in *Psycho* anything more than a chance to show the low-budget horror *schlockmeisters* a thing or two. Stefano said: "I told him part of the problem was that I really didn't like this man, Norman Bates. I really couldn't get involved with a man in his forties who's a drunk and peeps through holes. The other problem was that there was this perfectly horrendous murder of a stranger I didn't care about either. I just kept talking to him in the vein 'I wish I knew this girl,' 'I wish Norman were somebody else.' "

As to the writer's qualms about the central male character, Hitchcock pacified Stefano with a question: "How would you feel if Norman were played by Anthony Perkins?" The writer recalled: "I said, 'Now you're talking.' I suddenly saw a tender, vulnerable young man you could feel incredibly sorry for. I could really rope in an audience with someone like him. Then I suggested starting the movie with the girl instead of Norman."

A great screenwriting collaborator of Hitchcock's, Charles Bennett (*The 39 Steps*, *Young and Innocent*), once described the director as "literate" only to the extent that "he liked to read the dirtiest parts of *Ulysses*." Instinctively, Stefano played to the sexual imp that lay inside the director. Stefano recalled: "I told him, 'I'd like to see Marion shacking up with Sam on her lunch hour.'* The moment I said 'shack up' or anything like that, Hitchcock, being a very salacious man, adored it. I said, 'We'll find out what the girl is all about, see her steal the money and head for Sam—on the way, this horrendous thing happens to her.' He thought it was spectacular. I think that idea got me the job."

Neither writer nor director committed to another meeting beyond the first. Hitchcock seemed particularly wary about repeating his experiences with James Cavanagh. But Stefano felt that he had penetrated the Hitchcock armor. "He found that I was very funny and we had a lot of laughs together," said the writer. Soon after, the Hitchcock office arranged a second meeting, which

*In the final script, the name Mary Crane was changed to Marion Crane.

the director began by excitedly proposing: "What if we got a big-name actress to play this girl? Nobody will expect her to die!" Stefano observed: "He wanted somebody much bigger than Janet Leigh—someone I didn't think was terribly good. But once he mentioned Janet Leigh, the whole thing really began to get me: She was someone with no association with this kind of movie—a suspense-horror movie—and neither were Perkins, Hitchcock, nor I."

By mid-September 1959, Hitchcock had been sufficiently convinced: He hired Stefano, but only on a week-to-week basis. The arrangement was hardly secure for Stefano, but it gave Hitchcock a ready escape hatch if their collaboration failed to ignite. Yet, ignite it did, and the writer was eventually to receive $17,500 for his labors. But Stefano continued to harbor hopes that he and the director would expand, deepen, and glamorize the source material into what Stefano called "a real Hitchcock movie, where a lot of money is spent just because it's *there*." But, no. "When I asked him why he had bought the book, he said he noticed that American-International was making movie after movie for under a million dollars, yet they all made ten or thirteen million. Then I saw it: He had bought this tight little novel and had no intention of blowing it up."

Hitchcock completely scuttled the James Cavanagh first draft, and, according to Revue intraoffice correspondence, that draft was never shown to Stefano. "He told me there was no point in reading it," Stefano explained. "Even in [Robert Bloch's] book, I don't think Bloch was aware of some of the things he came up with, like the shower scene. But the dynamics of it *were* there. What excited me was the thought of taking this warm, sympathetic woman away from the audience and replacing her with Tony Perkins, not the Norman Bates of Bloch's book."

For his part, Hitchcock was more charitable toward Bloch and his novel. The director told writer Charles Higham in *The Celluloid Muse*, "*Psycho* all came from Robert Bloch. Joseph Stefano . . . contributed dialogue mostly, no ideas." Robert Bloch attributes Stefano's peckishness to simple turf rivalry. "It's a good thing Mr.

Stefano didn't adapt *The Bible.*" But it had long been Hitchcock's tendency to appropriate any good idea as his own. Hitchcock and Stefano held five weeks of daily story conferences at Paramount, beginning at 10:30 A.M., the hour to which the director agreed to accommodate Stefano's ongoing sessions with a psychoanalyst. According to the writer, "When it got down to 'Let's get some work done,' he was never very eager. He was very hard to pin down. I wanted him to tell me what he expected this movie to be like, but the preferred gabbing, gossiping, and he *loved* to laugh. I think he really got a kick out of me. He told me his last writer, Ernie Lehman [*North by Northwest*], was a worrier and a bitcher. But I was laughing all the time, thinking to myself, 'You didn't expect to be in movies in the first place and here you are working with Hitchcock.' "

For Stefano, keeping Hitchcock's quicksilver mind attuned to *Psycho* was an uphill battle all the way. According to the writer, when Hitchcock talked about the job at hand at all, it was usually to throw out "wild ideas" that he expected one to weave into the scenario. It almost seemed as if the director felt it necessary to "school" a writer in the world according to Hitchcock: his brand of wit, wisdom, flippancy, and power. Stefano said, "One of the easiest times for anyone to get in to see Hitchcock was whenever he was in conference with a writer. Lew Wasserman used to come in and they'd talk stocks and money, money, money!" Yet despite the director's quirky timetable, certain "givens" fell into line. "Purely for budgetary reasons, I knew he had decided to do the movie in black and white," Stefano explained. "And without too much conversation, we decided this was going to be a picture of Gothic horror, something he had not really done before."

Stefano perceived that the way to grasp Hitchcock's imagination was to conceptualize and verbalize the story in terms of visuals. According to Stefano, "He was not interested in characters or motivation at all. That was the writer's job. If I said, 'I'd like to give the girl an air of desperation,' he'd say, 'Fine, fine.' But when I said, 'In the opening of the film, I'd like a helicopter shot over the city, then go right up to the seedy hotel where Marion is spending her lunch hour with Sam,' he said, 'We'll go right into the window!' That sort of thing excited him."

Left to grapple with complexities of character on his own, Stefano found the freedom disarming and exhilarating. "I worked on a level of characterization that was probably unheard-of for what turned out to be a horror movie. In fact, I felt like I was writing a movie about Marion, not about Norman. I saw Marion as a girl getting on in years working at a dull job around un-delightful, unimpressive people. She is in love with a man who won't marry her because he has financial problems. The greatest thing about Marion is that she never stops to think 'Can I get away with this?,' which is exactly the way that someone performs an act of madness when they themselves are *not* mad. Once we got to the motel, the whole game changed for me. From then on, we were into manipulation of the highest order. Torturing the audience was the intention. Because there was no precedent for *Psycho* in Hitchcock's body of work, I went at it with an in-credible and surprising amount of freedom."

In other details of script construction, however, Hitchcock was the complete detail man. "We worked out the story piece by piece," Stefano observed. "He was very big on technicalities, like the elaborate business of the girl's trading in her car. He would say, 'I think we ought to see her get important papers when she goes to her house to pack up. A pink slip, and such.' He never wanted audiences asking questions. His theory was 'Think what the audience is going to ask and answer it as fast as possible.' "

To make certain Stefano got the details right, Hitchcock hired a Hollywood-based detective as a technical adviser. The Hitchcock office also had the screenwriter observe the style and manner of a used-car dealer, Ralph Cutright, at 1932 Wilshire Boulevard in Santa Monica. Stefano was also provided with data on every fore-seeable plot point, from the topography of Route 99 (including names, locations, and room rates of every motel) to details of the administration and physical appearance of real estate offices; from traffic citations and mother fixations to amateur taxidermy.

Stefano quickly found that no plot twist tickled Hitchcock more than predesigning the murder sequence. The writer recalled

Hitchcock's relish for the scene that would eliminate a sympathetic character—played by a star actress—*one-third of the way into the story.* "We had the longest discussion about laying out the shower murder," Stefano recalled. "Both of us wanted to know exactly what was going to be on film. I remember sitting on a couch at his Paramount office where we were working this particular day, discussing the murder in great detail. He rose from his desk, came round toward me, and said, 'You be the camera. Now, we won't have her really lying on the bathroom floor. We'll show him lift up the shower curtain . . . ' And Hitchcock acted out every move, every gesture, every nuance of wrapping the corpse in the curtain. Suddenly, his office door flew open behind him. In walked his wife, Alma, who rarely came to the studio. Hitchcock and I yelled, '*Aaaaaaaaagggghhhhh!!!*' The shock of the intrusion at that moment was so great, we must have laughed for five minutes!"

After the second week of story conferences, Hitchcock departed without explanation for a two-week commitment. "I had the feeling this was going to be my screen-test," Stefano recalled, chuckling. "He said, 'Why don't you start writing the scene with the girl and her lover in the Phoenix hotel?' So I wrote it, right to the point where she walks out of the hotel room. When Hitchcock came back, I handed him the pages and we went on talking. The next day he said, 'Alma loved it.' He never said *he* loved it, but he kind of made me feel if he didn't, I wouldn't have been at the meeting."

The director's *sangfroid* came as no surprise to the writer, who thought the Hitchcock staff "a strange organization." According to Stefano, "They weren't into compliments. It was like royalty. The compliment was that you were *invited.* Hitchcock was talking about John Michael Hayes one day—someone who had written several of his huge hits [*To Catch a Thief, Rear Window*, etc.]. Hitchcock said, 'Oh, he had *one* good line in *The Trouble with Harry* where Shirley MacLaine says, 'I've got a short fuse.' Right there, I said to myself, 'If you think you're going to get any applause, Stefano, forget it.'" Longtime Hitchcock collaborator, screenwriter Charles Bennett (*The 39 Steps*) summed up that quality in Hitchcock as "a character flaw." Bennett told journalist Pat McGilligan in *Backstory*, "And a very ungenerous character flaw, actually, because as I said, he is totally incapable of creating a story or developing a story. He has got good ideas—but he will never give credit to anyone but himself."

While attending to last-minute details on the foreign release of *North by Northwest*, Hitchcock dispatched a small crew to Phoenix, Arizona, to shoot additional "atmosphere" and research photographs. Stefano completed a first draft screenplay in three weeks and turned it in on December 19, 1959. Despite the screenwriter's cavils about the original novel, he clearly helped himself to the best of Bloch—structure, characters, atmosphere, tone—while enlivening the dialogue with gallows wit and deepening the characterization. Whatever Stefano had believed about Hitchcock in terms of being a "time-waster," certainly something of the director's influence informed the screenplay.

"He only asked me to change one scene and one word," Stefano recalled of Hitchcock's response to the script. "He didn't think a scene where the highway cop wakes the girl after she's been sleeping in the car was suspenseful enough. I had the cop as a handsome young guy coming on to her, preventing her from moving on. Hitch liked the idea during our discussions, but after reading the script, he wanted the cop to be more menacing. The offending word was in the first scene where the heroine is telling Sam she won't see him anymore and he makes a crack about writing each other 'lurid' love letters. Hitch said, 'I don't like "lurid."' I said, 'Do you think it's wrong for the character?' 'No, no,' he said, 'I just don't like the word.' So I said, 'If that's your only justification, I won't cut it.' " Stefano didn't. Surprisingly, neither did Hitchcock.

Although Stefano read the response of Hitchcock as satisfactory, the director was to streamline, to drop while shooting (or editing), many attempts by the writer to challenge the censors and to enrich the complexity of the characters, context, and texture. In the opening scene—the tryst between Sam and the heroine (called Mary in the script) in the Phoenix hotel room—

Stefano foreshadows the closing line of the movie ("Why, she wouldn't even harm a fly") by interrupting a long kiss with ". . . the buzzing and closeness of an inconsiderate fly." (The idea was cut.) The stodgy, unappealing Sam waxes eloquent about his and Mary's being "a regular working-class tragedy" and tells her: "You know what I'd like? A clear, empty sky . . . and a plane, and us in it . . . and somewhere a private island for sale, where we can run around without our—shoes on. And the wherewithal to buy what I'd like." (The lines were cut.)

In the scenes set in the real estate office as written by Stefano, the vulgar oil man, Mr. Cassidy, makes a blatantly sexual remark to Mary that was cut from the film. In the scene as written, Cassidy leers at Mary, saying, "What you need is a weekend in Las Vegas," to which she replies, "I'm going to spend this weekend in bed." The oil man retorts, "Only playground that beats Las Vegas." Stefano also tried to sustain the suspense of Mary's flight with the stolen money by having her stop at a gas station to fill up, only to flee when a pay phone jangles; but this was cut. And lengthier than in the completed film was the scene in which the highway patrolman ("his face dispassionate," although he is not described as wearing sunglasses) delays her.

In his description of Mary's harrowing car trip, which Hitchcock was to shoot like a heavily stylized descent into the underworld, Stefano several times describes quick cuts to the car wheels in the driving rain. Hitchcock was to shoot the sequence with intense subjectivity—never varying the point of view from that of the heroine. Stefano pokes a good deal of phallic fun at Norman. In the scene in which Mary arrives at "Mrs. Bates Motel" in a rainstorm, Stefano describes Norman's umbrella as dangling "limply and uselessly at his side." Later, Norman's elaborate, postshower-murder cleanup is continued with shots of him hosing away the tire tracks leading to the swamp. And following "An Extreme High Angle" that depicts Norman as he carts Mother's bloodstained shoes and skirt to the basement furnace, Stefano proposes a silent, long shot of the Bates house and chimney, from which an eerie plume of smoke rises. All were cut from the final film. But Hitchcock was also to insert (then later cut) the last image into the screenplays for *The Birds*, *Torn Curtain*, and also at least two unfilmed projects of the sixties and seventies.

Hitchcock also dropped from the script an elaborate visual pun in a montage sequence in which the rented car of Detective Arbogast continually bypasses Bates Motel as he questions other hotel owners. In a screenplay rife with allusions to the connection between food and sex, Hitchcock cut a line that Norman utters to Arbogast during the interrogation about Mary: "She had an awful hunger." Lost, too, were such touches as Norman tenderly caressing and hiding away a stuffed bird knocked off a lampshade during his conversation with Arbogast; a conversation in the hardware store between Sam and Lila played against a background display of carving knives; a grisly sight gag to occur when Sam leaves Lila in the store in search of Arbogast, "among some bathroom fittings a nozzle from a shower falls to the floor"; and an elegant camera move that begins in a medium shot on Sam and Lila talking in their motel room, glides past them to the flower pattern on the wallpaper, and ends in a big close-up of Norman's eye peering in at them. The latter shot was to have "echoed" the earlier, similarly voyeuristic moment when Norman watches Mary disrobe.

Throughout the screenplay, Stefano went to some pains to flesh out the characters of Sam and Lila, whom Hitchcock called mere "figures." If James Cavanagh had tried to trump up a flat-out romance, Stefano's more subtle attempts center on a slow thawing of the initial chill between Sam and Lila as they hunt for the missing girl. Coos Lila while she and Sam wait vainly for Arbogast to return from the motel, "Whenever I start contemplating the panic button, your back straightens up and your eyes get that God-looks-out-for-everybody look and . . . I feel better." Sam: "I feel better when you feel better." Before Sam hurries off to question Bates at the motel, Sam advises Lila, who wants to accompany him, to stay behind and "contemplate your . . . panic button."

In a scene late in the action, when the couple drive to the motel to investigate the disappearance of Arbogast, Sam mutters,

"I wonder if we'll ever see Mary again—alive." As Lila reminisces about how her sister sacrificed her own college career for Lila's, she says, "Some people are so willing to suffer for you that they suffer more if you don't let them." Sam mumbles, "I wouldn't let her lick the stamps," a reference to one of Mary's absurdly poignant lines in the opening scene in the hotel room. In the penultimate scene, when the psychiatrist explains Norman's illness, Lila "begins to weep softly, for Mary, for Arbogast, for the destroyed human beings of the world."

Hitchcock excised it all, convinced that the audience would tolerate Sam and Lila only so long as they propelled the resolution of the mystery. Stefano regretted the loss of the sentimentality, but Hitchcock clearly preferred Stefano's more subversive side. In that arena, Stefano prevailed. The script is shot through with obvious delight in skewering America's sacred cows—virginity, cleanliness, privacy, masculinity, sex, mother love, marriage, the reliance on pills, the sanctity of the family . . . and the bathroom. Stefano said, "I told Hitch 'I would like Marion [Mary] to tear up a piece of paper and flush it down the toilet and *see* that toilet. Can we do that?' A toilet had never been seen on-screen before, let alone flushing it. Hitch said, 'I'm going to have to fight them on it.' I thought if I could begin to unhinge audiences by showing a toilet flushing—we all suffer from peccadillos from toilet procedures—they'd be so out of it by the time of the shower murder, it would be an absolute killer. I thought [about the audience], 'This is where you're going to begin to know what the human race is all about. We're going to start by showing you the toilet, and it's only going to get worse.' We were getting into Freudian stuff and Hitchcock dug that kind of thing, so I knew we would get to see that toilet on-screen."

Despite the gusto with which he and Hitchcock took a meat-ax to American taboos, Stefano rejects the claims by Hitchcock critics and biographers that *Psycho* marked a darkening in the world view of the director. He said, "Hitchcock didn't think we were doing anything that was any different from his *last* movie or would be from his *next*. He didn't seem to think that this was coming from a 'new Hitchcock.' No matter what has been read into Hitchcock's state of mind, I don't think at any time he was making it he was knowingly or unconsciously reflecting any particular darkness from within. He simply had a script and he was shooting it."

Hitchcock accelerated his production plans and schedule while Stefano polished the script to the director's specifications. The writer delivered a slightly revised second draft dated November 2, 1959. Further modest alterations and refinements were turned in on November 10, November 13, and December 1. Following this, Stefano and Hitchcock convened for a day at the director's home to break down the shooting script. This stage of the development process had always been among the most rewarding, for Hitchcock. "My films are made on paper," the director often told the press. Stefano detailed the process by which Hitchcock created imagery from words. "From my master scenes, he'd say, 'Shall we have a close-up here of, say, a purse?' For the shower scene, we made the decision that you would never see the knife touch the body. I told him I thought there was a point beyond which we would lose the audience, since we *like* Mary, feel sorry for her, and know that she is going to return the money. He told me that Saul Bass, who had done the titles for him on other films, was also going to storyboard the shower scene." By early November, with that sequence in mind, Hitchcock had already sent the first script draft to Bass, the innovative graphic designer who had created title sequences for *Vertigo* and *North by Northwest*, among others.

Stefano recalled how Hitchcock enthused over the chance to manipulate sound to heighten audience involvement and to implicate them, with Norman Bates, as voyeurs. In the scene where peeping Norman watches Mary through the hole in the motel office wall, Stefano wrote, under the direction of Hitchcock: "The SOUNDS come louder, as if we too had our ears pressed against the wall." Stefano claimed that Hitchcock was also very open to suggestions for camera placement—so long as they fit within his overall vision. For instance, the writer said he proposed to Hitchcock that he modify the point of view for the second killing in the movie, the stabbing of Arbogast. "When we got to Arbogast going into the house and up the stairs, I said, 'If you only start pulling the camera up when the woman comes out of the room, I'm going to get suspicious why you're not showing her.' That phrase—'I'm going to get suspicious'—was my key to get him to change something. I said, 'When he starts to go upstairs, what if we go way up high like we're removing ourselves from what's about to happen? The audience *knows* what's about to happen to the detective anyway, so the upward movement would already be established when the mother runs out from her bedroom.' He said, 'That's going to cost a lot of money. I'll have to build a thing way up there.' The next day he said, 'It's worth it.' As much as he was concerned about keeping costs down, he wasn't about to do anything that would hurt or detract from the movie."

Writers from Charles Bennett (*The 39 Steps, The Man Who Knew Too Much*) to Raymond Chandler (*Strangers on a Train*) and from John Michael Hayes (*Rear Window, To Catch a Thief*) to Ernest Lehman (*North by Northwest, Family Plot*) have attested to Hitchcock's having been an exasperating collaborator. Stefano recalls only a single flare-up. "He wanted to cheat on something," the writer noted. "It was the scene where Arbogast comes to the motel and he and Norman talk, then Norman goes off to the house to put on Mother's clothes and kills Arbogast. Hitchcock wanted Norman to just go out the door [of the motel office], but I said, 'If we don't see him walking to put the sheets away, I'm going to be suspicious when we go up to the house.' Hitchcock muttered, 'Well it might be one of those things you might want to cut.' I said, '*Shoot it and don't cut it!*' I told him this wasn't going to be the kind of movie where he could get away with stuff like he had in the past."

Within hours, Hitchcock and Stefano had fully broken down the screenplay. Uniquely Hitchcockian was his insistence on turning the script into a virtual blueprint for production. Each scene was composed with the camera—frequently acting as the audience surrogate—in mind. In the third act of *Psycho*, Lila Crane (Vera Miles) is about to do what the entire audience was to hope/fear she will do: search the Bates house—alone. Explained Stefano: "He always thought about making the audience share the point of view of the character." From the screenplay:

EXT. REAR OF MOTEL—S. C. U. [CLOSE-UP]—DAY
    Behind the motel Lila hesitates. She looks ahead.
LONG SHOT—DAY
    The old house standing against the sky.
CLOSE-UP
    Lila moves forward.
LONG SHOT
    The CAMERA approaching the house.
CLOSE-UP
    Lila glances toward the back of Norman's parlor. She
    moves on.
LONG SHOT
    The house coming nearer.
CLOSE-UP
    Lila looks up at the house. She moves forward pur-
    posefully.
SUBJECTIVE SHOT
    The house and the porch.
CLOSE-UP
    Lila stops at the house and looks up. She glances back.
    She turns to the house again.
SUBJECTIVE SHOT
    The CAMERA MOUNTS the steps to the porch.
CLOSE-UP
    Lila puts out her hand.
SUBJECTIVE CLOSE-UP
    Lila's hand pushes the door open. We see the hallway.
    Lila ENTERS PAST CAMERA.

Once Hitchcock and Stefano had completed the breakdown, it
was all over but the shooting. "We had lunch and toasted the
project with champagne," said Stefano. "He looked very sad, and
said, 'The picture's over. Now I have to go and put it on film.'"
Despite their long hours of story conferences and kibbitzing, Stefano singled-out that particular moment as one of the few during
which Hitchcock let down his guard. But in another, after the
director had arranged a private showing of *Vertigo* at the writer's

request, Stefano believed he had at last glimpsed the man who hid behind the mask. "Here was this incredibly beautiful movie he had made that nobody went to see or said nice things about it," Stefano said. "I told him I thought it was his best film. It brought him to near-tears."

With the screenplay virtually ready to face the cameras, Hitchcock prepared to begin production in early December.

Note

A Note on Sources: The cornerstone for my research was the invaluable Alfred Hitchcock Collection of the Margaret Herrick Library of the Academy of Motion Picture Arts and Sciences, donated by Patricia Hitchcock O'Connell. The papers attest to Mr. Hitchcock as the compleat filmmaker but a frustratingly incomplete record-keeper. Nevertheless, the collection encompasses correspondence, production records, treatments, screenplays, and legal files for many post-1950s Hitchcock projects. I have also made use of The Billy Rose Theater Collection at the Library of Lincoln Center, New York, and of the American Film Institute Library, Los Angeles. The private collections of Frederick Clarke, Gary A. Smith, Paul Farrar, Sam Irvin, and Martin Kearns provided information and inspiration while supplementing material of my own.

For a general overview of a life in films, I found *Hitch* by John Russell Taylor and *The Art of Alfred Hitchcock* by Donald Spoto to be helpful. For analysis of the movie and others in the Hitchcock canon, one could hardly do better than *Hitchcock's Films* by Robin Wood and *Hitchcock—The Murderous Gaze* by William Rothman. The frame-by-frame breakdown book on *Psycho* by Richard J. Anobile was enormously useful for verifying visual memory.

Unless noted, most of my information on the making of the film stems from personal interviews with Mr. Hitchcock and his collaborators that I conducted from the winter of 1980 through the early spring of 1989. My first interview was with Hitchcock himself in January 1980 at his offices at Universal. I was promised twenty minutes of a great man's valuable time. An hour later, he was still waving away his assistant, as if he were having a wonderful time being asked questions he must have heard a thousand times. Although battered in body and spirit, Hitchcock was, by turns, brilliant, acerbic, pedantic, lost in reverie, gossipy, and frustrated by the projects that he knew he would never make. I will never forget his grace, nor his rare good manners. Three months later, Hitchcock was dead.

I particularly want to salute the artists who were associated with Mr. Hitchcock and the making of the film *Psycho.* They shared happy and painful memories, gracefully endured my endless fussing and clarifying, and, in some cases, reviewed early drafts for accuracy: Harold Adler, Jack Barron, Saul Bass, Robert Bloch, Robert Clatworthy, Helen Colvig, Margo Epper, Hilton Green, Virginia Gregg, Mrs. Joseph Hurley, Paul Jasmin, Janet Leigh, Michael Ludmer, John McIntire, Jeanette Nolan, Tony Palladino, Anthony Perkins, Rita Riggs, Marshal Schlom, Leonard South, Joseph Stefano, H. N. Swanson, Lois Thurman, and Lurene Tuttle.

I hope this book will underscore the fact that, even for a Hitchcock, filmmaking, like living, is nothing if not a collaborative art.

4

Early Reception

❖ ❖ ❖

❖ ❖ ❖

The following is taken from the June 17, 1960, *New York Times* review of *Psycho*. Certainly not all reviews were this negative, but Crowther was a well-respected reviewer, despite the fact that he seems to have seen a film that's not the *Psycho* we know. The piece indicates just how superficial movie reviews can be and also provides a baseline to measure against the serious criticism that follows.

BOSLEY CROWTHER ❖ Hitchcock's 'Psycho'
Bows at 2 Houses

You had better have a pretty strong stomach and be prepared for a couple of grisly shocks when you go to see Alfred Hitchcock's "Psycho," which a great many people are sure to do. For Mr. Hitchcock, an old hand at frightening people, comes at you with a club in this frankly intended blood-curdler, which opened at the DeMille and Baronet yesterday.

There is not an abundance of subtlety or the lately familiar

Hitchcock bent toward significant and colorful scenery in this obviously low-budget job. With a minimum of complication, it gets off to a black-and-white start with the arrival of a fugitive girl with a stolen bankroll at an eerie motel.

Well, perhaps it doesn't get her there too swiftly. That's another little thing about this film. It does seem slowly paced for Mr. Hitchcock and given over to a lot of small detail. But when it does get her to the motel and apparently settled for the night, it turns out this isolated haven is, indeed, a haunted house.

The young man who diffidently tends it—he is Anthony Perkins and the girl is Janet Leigh—is a queer duck, given to smirks and giggles and swift dashes up to a stark Victorian mansion on a hill. There, it appears, he has a mother—a cantankerous old woman—concealed. And that mother, as it soon develops, is deft at creeping up with a knife and sticking holes into people, drawing considerable blood.

That's the way it is with Mr. Hitchcock's picture—slow build-ups to sudden shocks that are old-fashioned melodramatics, however effective and sure, until a couple of people have been gruesomely punctured and the mystery of the haunted house has been revealed. Then it may be a matter of question whether Mr. Hitchcock's points of psychology, the sort of highly favored by Krafft-Ebing, are as reliable as his melodramatic stunts.

Frankly, we feel his explanations are a bit of leg-pulling by a man who has been known to resort to such tactics in his former films.

The consequence is his denouement falls quite flat for us. But the acting is fair. Mr. Perkins and Miss Leigh perform with verve, and Vera Miles, John Gavin, and Martin Balsam do well enough in other roles.

The one thing we would note with disappointment is that, among the stuffed birds that adorn the motel office of Mr. Perkins, there are no significant bats.

◆ ◆ ◆

Crowther, to his credit, was sensitive to the popularity of the film and went back to see it again. He finally noticed that something special was going on. He sent letters to Hitchcock apologizing for his review (see Rebello: 171). And, to make his apology open to his public, he put *Psycho* on his ten best list at the end of the year. Despite its brevity, his remarks indicate that the complexity and the importance of the film were beginning to grow.

BOSLEY CROWTHER ◆ *Psycho* Entry for "Ten Best Films"

Psycho . . . Old-fashioned horror melodrama was given a new and frightening look in this bold psychological mystery picture. Sensual and sadistic though it was, it represented expert and sophisticated command of emotional development with cinematic techniques. Aptly performed by Anthony Perkins, Vera Miles, and Janet Leigh.

reread

5

The Building of a Reputation

◆   ◆   ◆

◆   ◆   ◆

To understand *Psycho*, and its growing reputation as a major work of American film, we need to understand some basics of the auteur theory. Auteurism was developed by a group of French film enthusiasts, including future filmmakers such as François Truffaut and Jean-Luc Godard, who watched in day-long screening orgies American films that had been embargoed during World War II. They didn't understand English and therefore depended on the films' visuals. They discovered in a number of filmmakers—Howard Hawks, John Ford, and Alfred Hitchcock, among others—that no matter who wrote the film, starred in it, or what studio produced it, commonalities in visual and narrative structure could be discovered based on who directed it.

From this discovery came the notion that the director was the guiding force of a film, and from the close study of a director's work, an under-standing of how its meaning was created. Future French filmmakers Eric Rohmer and Claude Chabrol wrote the first full-length study of Hitchcock in the fifties. Many articles were produced, and the following was published in 1960, the year *Psycho* was released, in the influential French journal, *Cahiers du cinéma*. The article is filled with enthusiasm and soaring moral judgments—in fact one of the major discoveries of the French was that Hitchcock's film contained a strong moral structure. For Jean Douchet, Hitchcock creates a world full of light and dark, intermingled. With this understanding, he begins the close analysis of the film's form—the "form-force," as he keeps referring to it—that, along with his concentration on how Hitchcock creates audience response, would be further developed by others. And he is one of the first to note that the film reveals everything about itself even as it pretends to create a great horror-mystery. Incidentally, there is here, as there is in other essays, reference to the French filmmaker Jean Cocteau and his film *Orphée* (1949) in which motorcyclists in dark glasses appear as messengers from the underworld. Such is the appearance of the policeman who stops Marion on the road. Hitchcock knew his film history very well indeed.

JEAN DOUCHET ◆ Hitch and His Audience

This article is forbidden to those who have not yet seen *Psycho*. Which is not to say that others are obliged to read it. But it is impossible to examine the film without unveiling its secret. And knowing it will deprive the reader, the future spectator, of a major part of his pleasure. I know this from experience. In his last interview here, Hitchcock narrated his film from beginning to end to Jean Domarchi and me, and mimed it in an extraordinary manner. For more than an hour we saw *Psycho* being born, sequence by sequence and sometimes shot by shot. I say *born* advisedly, because this happened in October 1959 and Hitchcock started shooting in November. And now, in Paramount's small private screening room, we felt that we were seeing the film for the second time. We were deprived of some of the terror felt by the others who were there.

Now this terror is Hitchcock's first, if not entire, objective. Even in the least of his interviews he loves to reveal to us the point at which, for him, creation is based on an exact science of audience reactions. This is not a financial concern (he was actually convinced that *Psycho* would be a failure), nor is it for publicity reasons (though he makes admirable use of publicity, we know, since *North by Northwest*, what he thinks of it), but because he attributes a mission to "suspense" films. This mission is catharsis. The audience must "untrammel" itself on the psychoanalytical level, make confession on the logical level, purify itself on the spiritual level. So Hitchcock needs the active participation of the audience.

The proof? *Rear Window*. It is here that Hitchcock exposes his conception of cinema (which is cinema within cinema), reveals his secrets, unveils his intentions. In the film James Stewart, reporter photographer, is first and foremost a spectator. This is one of the reasons for our seeing him confined to his chair. Through him Hitchcock's intention is to define the nature of the spectator, and specifically the nature of the Hitchcockian spectator. The latter is a "voyeur." He wants to enjoy the spectacle. What he sees on the screen (and so what Stewart watches in the apartment on the other side of the courtyard) is the projection of his own self. This alone, *a priori*, can hold his interest. In one way or another it is himself that he sees. A spectacle which, after all, would soon become tedious if a precise aspect, a mystery, had not entirely captured his attention. Thereafter his intelligence fixes itself on an idea which grows into an obsession. Reasoning and deduction give way to *subjectivity*, to feelings of desire and fear. The more he desires or fears, the more his expectation will be fulfilled—and way beyond what he is hoping for. So strong is Stewart's wish for a crime to have been committed that the crime materializes and happens for him. In a Hitchcock film it is the spectator who creates the suspense; the suspense only meets the request for it. (Remember Doris Day, also a spectator, at the Royal Albert Hall in *The Man Who Knew Too Much*.) In other words, Hitchcock first excites the worst feelings of his audience and then, through his spectacle, authorizes them to be satisfied. The sense of horror which the audience experiences gives rise to other feelings, pure and noble feelings, which alone allow the first feelings to be cancelled out. Here cinema is not just therapeutic, it is a genuinely magic art.

Which brings us back to the *auteur*'s purpose. Hitchcock's intention is to unmask reality and show it to us in *triple* form. Triple like those three window blinds which are raised one after the other in the very first shot of *Rear Window*. The first reality is obviously that of the *everyday world*, immediately recognizable to the spectator. Which is why Hitchcock takes so much care with it. Since it serves as the fixed base of his structure, the director goes to considerable lengths to portray it with great attention to the truth. In his eyes falsehood is inadmissible. Still less the arbitrary. (We are far removed from Clouzot's *Les Diaboliques*.) Never, absolutely never, does Hitchcock cheat the audience. He sometimes—and willfully—diverts their attention (as he diverts Stewart, at the moment the crime unfolds, in *Rear Window*), but he always leaves them enough to work on. The spectator can, if he wants, reconstruct in his mind the events which have been unfolded before him. This is especially the case with *Psycho* where everything, down to the last detail, is clearly revealed. Nothing, then, is less justified than the charges of lack of verisimilitude which certain people have leveled at Hitchcock.

The second reality, the second blind, opens on the *world of desire*. For this is just the way that the apartment appears from the other side of the courtyard. Everything that happens in the everyday world—in Stewart's apartment—is inscribed there, projected as on a screen. Stewart's own apartment is duplicated there many times, peopled by forms which are themselves animated by the forces which gave birth to them. These forms-forces personify the secret thoughts, mental attitudes, and above all the desires of our hero. And in this world they have a real existence and active power. Like a huge mirror turned on the everyday, the world of desire produces a reverse image of its situations as well as its thoughts; the world of the couple of [Grace] Kelly and the (paralyzed) Stewart, as well the couple comprised of Raymond Burr and his bedridden wife; Stewart's latent desire to be rid of Kelly, which is effectively carried out by Raymond Burr. These forms-forces of desire constitute the fundamental component of every Hitchcock film. A psychoanalyst will see it as a representation of the feeling of guilt. Never, however, before *Psycho*, has our director provided so much evidence of it. Here the form is really nothing other than a form endowed with a terrifying force.

Finally, the third reality, the *intellectual world*. This is the main plank of the Hitchcockian oeuvre, the plumb line which connects the two parallel universes and allows them to communicate in this way. This is what the director relies on in all his films. So it is through the intermediary of this world that Stewart, confined in his everyday universe (which is why we never leave his living room throughout the film), can penetrate the world of desire. Inasmuch as he is a spectator, then, what does our hero see? What he believes to be the everyday world, and which is only his own reflection. But the world of desire soon reveals its true nature. A horrible act is committed there, which the hero has not seen but which he imagines. From then on his attention is roused, his intellect is placed at the service of his interest. If Stewart conducts his investigation by a logical process of induction and deduction, working from the slightest clues, his objective is scarcely a noble one. On the contrary. He seeks less to reveal the light than to penetrate the shadows, those shadows in which the killer wraps himself—though a cigarette betrays his presence. In short, he examines the objective facts only so that he may better gratify his own subjectivity, and to satisfy even more an unhealthy curiosity. (Seen in this light, the publicity dreamed up by Hitch for *Psycho* becomes a major constituent of the film: the audience must *want* to be afraid.) From then on he cuts off his right arm—lucid understanding. He finds himself as unarmed as a primitive, subject to the great ancestral fears. His reason wanders willfully into the irrational, surrenders—defenseless (like Janet Leigh under the shower)—to the all-powerful occult.

Faced with the menacing of the murderer, who has come from the world of desire, a sudden invader of his everyday world, Stewart sees his flashbulbs as an altogether ridiculous ally. The wholly material light is not enough to protect him. "We're all in our private traps," someone says in *Psycho*: the Hitchcockian spectator more than anyone else. Because Stewart, at the summit of his curiosity, wants the intellectual distance represented by the courtyard to be physically bridged by Kelly, he unleashes what occultists and magicians fear the most: the counter-shock. If the reader now really needs persuading that *Rear Window* is the Hitchcockian concept of cinema, let him recapitulate the above as follows. Stewart is like a projector; the apartment opposite, the screen; the distance which separates them, the intellectual world, would then be occupied by the beam of light. Remembering also that Stewart is from the beginning the spectator, the reader may conclude that the hero "makes himself his own cinema." But isn't that precisely the definition of "voyeur," the essence of morose gratification?

Well? Well, we must push on with the investigation of this intellectual world. First, the more this world is concentrated on an object of desire or fear, the more intense it becomes, and the more the force of that intensity animates the form it has created. At the same time the form is made explicit and the force is augmented. As in *Psycho*. Let us assume that Stewart comes down from the screen of *Rear Window* in order to sit himself in the theater, that he becomes each one of us—a spectator. His "voyeur's" appetite finds sustenance from the very beginning of *Psycho*. The camera indiscreetly enters a room where the blinds are drawn in the middle of the afternoon. And in this room is a couple on a bed, wrapped in an embrace which indicates a great physical attraction. At this point he feels frustrated. He wants "to see more." If John Gavin's torso just satisfies at least half the audience, the fact that Janet Leigh is not naked is taken badly by the other half. This aroused desire should logically find its conclusion at the end of Janet's journey. She will be naked, totally, offering herself totally. The sexual act performed on her will also be extreme. So the wish is gratified beyond all hopes.

But let's go back to the beginning of the film. The spectator's feeling towards Janet is at once one of desire and one of contempt. A woman who takes a room in a shady-looking hotel, in the middle of the afternoon and in her own provincial town, does not deserve respect. So he has no problem assigning to her his own worst instincts. Among others, his unconscious desire, and what in his own life he can't bring himself to do—theft. Back now in her office, Janet herself is present at an important transaction. The spectator, who is beginning to be bored by these banal scenes of professional life, wants something to happen. To be precise—and why not?—that Janet Leigh will take the money for herself. The transaction being irregular, there would be no proof, and the owner of the money is a really nasty type. Happily, her boss asks her to take the money to the bank. Now the sum involved is $40,000. Moreover, this happens on a Friday: the theft would not be apparent until the following Monday. Janet takes the money. And here she is, on the road.

A motorcycle cop stops her: a simple identity check. We are gripped by a feeling of anxiety. This feeling is soon increased: the cop follows her. What does he want? Have they already discovered the theft? By now we are very anxious for her to get away with it. We are with her all the way. But this altruistic feeling hides our own crime, which Janet Leigh has to commit on our behalf. Apparently sympathetic, it disguises an improper desire. A desire which will be gratified: the cop takes off.

(Why does he let her go? There are essentially three explanations. First, psychological: this woman seems very confused; moreover, she is pretty. It's normal for a cop—a man, after all—to hope that she will ask him for help. Well, she doesn't ask for help. Second, the logical explanation: as a traffic cop he is concerned about Janet Leigh's tiredness. He is professionally obliged to follow her, for fear that she will cause an accident. As it happens, she doesn't cause one. Finally, another explanation—the occult. The very appearance of the motorcycle cop, reminiscent of the motorcycle cops in Cocteau's *Orphée*, belongs to the domain of fantasy. He is at one and the same time conscience and the Angel of Order, dispatched for a last attempt at salvation. But he cannot save someone who does not want to be saved. If the reader-spectator is familiar with the notions of magic, he knows that the audience's wave of hostility prevents the Angel from accomplishing his mission. Hence, in Hitchcock's films, the extreme importance of the *call*, frequently symbolized by the telephone. Thus in *Rear Window*, Stewart, in sending Kelly to the killer's place, both provokes him and calls him. Inversely, the killer calls him on the telephone before he arrives. In *Psycho*, the fact that the sheriff, in the second part of the film, telephones Bates, throws a singular light on what he represents in the occult order of

things. We can only converse equal to equal, man to man, angel
to angel, or God to Satan (*North by Northwest*). On the other hand,
humans can call on superior powers, whether they are malevolent or benevolent: Teresa Wright in *Shadow of a Doubt*, Farley
Granger in *Strangers on a Train*.)

Salvation being rejected by us, and so also by Janet Leigh, she
is now prey to every kind of delirium, delivered up to the powers
of the night, can't bear the glare of the headlights. Her fatigue
makes us want her to stop. Hence our relief when she does stop
at the motel. But the strange, mysterious look of the place and
its proprietor gives us qualms. We sense danger, the more so
because Janet Leigh is alone in these sinister surroundings, alone
in her room, with the window wide open, as she looks for somewhere to hide her money (our money). And all she can do is
leave it lying there on the night table. From now on we have
everything to fear. To fear that the money will disappear while
she is eating. And because we have everything to fear, her conversation with Perkins seems too long to us. We want to see this
fear verified. Our desire to *see* is about to become even stronger:
Perkins, like us, is a voyeur and watches his guest as she undresses.
Is he going to rape her or rob her?

Neither one nor the other, but worse. Because our desire and
our fear still have nothing real to fasten on to, are still blurred
in our minds, the form which they assume is itself imprecise. A
sort of shadow, a kind of ectoplasm. But, exasperated by our
waiting, they are at the height of their intensity. And the force
that we have imparted to this form will be of awesome power.
So the form-force commits its outrage.

(It should not be thought that I am extrapolating. On the one
hand, I am only describing what we see, what every spectator
could have felt. On the other hand, I would point out that *Psycho*
was filmed in forty-one days. That scene which lasts a mere forty-
five seconds on the screen took six days to complete. Hitchcock
has told us about the immense difficulties he and his cameraman
[John] Russell faced in rendering this imprecise form. He wanted
no tricks; he wanted the effect to come directly from the lighting.

In short, he had an extremely precise idea for arriving at this imprecise form. Let us give him the credit, which he claims vigorously elsewhere, of knowing what he is doing and of shooting only what is strictly necessary.)

An outrage, then, at once crazed and fascinating. An outrage which by filial piety, Perkins attempts to efface. And while he is about this, we are entirely with him. We are involved in his sordid household chores; we accept that Janet Leigh, wrapped in a translucent shower curtain, really becomes what she was for us—a form. We are simply in a hurry for this business to be over. We are also afraid that a passerby, lost on this little traveled road, will discover the crime. That fear is increased when Perkins, having a quick look round the room to see if he has not forgotten anything belonging to Janet, does not see *our* money.

(Which proves that Janet found the best hiding place. "To appreciate *Psycho* you need a great sense of humor," says Hitchcock. Especially Hitchcockian humor which is, as we know, a way of inverting our desires; that is, of realizing them in a manner which contradicts our expectations. And is not inversion, moreover, our director's preferred system?)

But Perkins retraces his steps, sees the packet, and takes it. We hope that he will discover the money and keep it—in short, that the murder will have a material justification. But as he throws it into the boot of the car, with the body and the victim's other things, we feel relieved somehow. Perkins heaves the whole thing into the slimy, stagnant water of a swamp. The car sinks halfway. Let it disappear, we think. At last it sinks completely, definitively. We heave a sigh of relief. The darkness—or our subconscious—has, we believe, swallowed up forever our complicity in the theft.

But for this we have become accomplices in a crime. We have climbed a rung on the ladder of guilt. I don't think it would be useful to continue describing the film in detail. What we need to grasp above all is the way Hitchcock's imagination works: how Hitch uses the spectator for the internal progression of his film, how he plays on his fears and desires. The spectator has only to analyze his reactions to the arrival of the private detective. He knows why the form-force, looming for the second time, will be precise, though still mysterious. After this ordeal he has only one wish: to flee. To flee this motel and its inhabitants. But the mechanism which he himself has set in motion can no longer be stopped. From now on he is paralyzed, glued to his seat as he approaches the limits of fear. The more so when he discovers that the presumed murderer has been dead for ten years. Now comes the total rout of his logical mind, the collapse of his intellectual world. From here on, for the spectator, every thing becomes an object of terror. The simplest thing he sees, however banal, is enough to scare him. Each new scene is an instrument of terror. There is only one possible instinct left to him: prayer and blind faith. He hopes with all his heart that Vera Miles, Janet Leigh's sister who has come looking for her, will be saved. These noble and wholly disinterested sentiments, along with a fear which has reached its highest point, necessarily cause the form-force to reveal at last its true face to the light. It is vanquished.

Hence the necessity, after this testing voyage to the end of the night, to the end of the world of desire, to return to our everyday world. This task can only fall to the intellectual world, but one deprived of all passion, detached from subjectivity, disencumbered by morbid curiosity. In short, scientific reasoning. This explains the psychiatrist's speech. Released now, the spectator can contemplate the object of his terror, that form-force which seems, like a bird of the night, impaled and pinned to the wall. And it excites a great pity in him—a pity which it tries to refuse while seeming to provoke. ("Let them see what kind of person I am. I'm not even going to swat that fly. I hope they are watching. They'll see. They'll see, and they'll say, 'Why, she wouldn't even harm a fly.'") Our pity may be the last chance of salvation for that form-force which seems forever damned, the chance to emerge from the shadows, like the car pulled by a huge chain from the black waters of the swamp.

In this way, following the example of *Psycho*, and by being situated uniquely in the audience's viewpoint, it becomes easier to understand the multiple relations in Hitchcock's work between the three realities. If the spectator belongs to the world of the everyday, it is quite clear that the screen conceals the world of desire. Is it not the property of the screen to be peopled uniquely by forms animated by forces? These forms, though intangible, are possessed of a reality. If, then, the spectator finds on the screen an exact reflection of his everyday universe, it communicates with him immediately. If he feels that appearances have not been faked to "get" him, he can't "disconnect." He is caught up in a phenomenon of fatal allurement. The more so since, on the screen, Hitch intends to enact what the spectator wouldn't dare to do in his everyday life. The spectator is involved more and more intensely with the forms which are charged with assuming his impulses and his secret dreams. He no longer looks objectively at everyday appearances, but receives them subjectively. There is, however, no intrinsic difference in these appearances; it is the spectator who transforms them, changes their illumination. Here the screen finally becomes for him the only reality. His supreme goal is to penetrate it.

The ideal vehicle for linking these two worlds and allowing them to communicate (spectator with screen, the everyday world with the world of desire) is obviously the intellectual world. For Hitchcock, it is clearly a matter of assigning to it the role of transmission. And the term *vehicle* is really the only one which can take account of all those trains, planes, cars, skis, boats, bicycles, wheelchairs, etc., which haunt his universe. We experience them not only as a sign of the passing from one world to the other, but above all as a sensation. As a sensation of allurement, of a slide which nothing can stop. They even give the impression of fatality. The reader will immediately recall the multiple variants which Hitch likes to introduce on a theme which is so close to him. But perhaps never has he so well and so completely "dreamed" as in *Psycho*. Janet Leigh's long and remarkable car journey allows the material and intellectual passage from one world to another: from objectivity to pure subjectivity. Generally, in Hitchcock, the human body is the first of the vehicles (hence the condemnation of dance, which gives the body its fatal seductive slide—the Stork club in *The Wrong Man*, the *thé dansant* in *Vertigo*, or the waltzes of the merry widows in *Shadow of a Doubt*).

And, by extension, a vehicle which encloses a being becomes that being's new body. This is why Janet Leigh, in changing her car, is expressing a profound desire to change her body, her personality. She wants to save a love, pure in itself, from the sordid material circumstances which surround it. But far from wanting to fight to give that love a noble status, she is only looking for purely external expedients. Far from trying to transform herself, she believes that her wish will be granted by changing her material shell.

So if I believe that occultism is at the base of Hitchcock's work, this is not because I am fascinated by the esoteric, nor even that I think it is fundamental to the auteur. It is simply the method of understanding which gives the artist's imagination its greatest opportunity to dream. Moreover, since this doctrine does not contradict the other systems of understanding, it allows an extremely varied vision of the world, one which is adapted to the creator's true temperament. It is certainly true that, in commenting on Hitchcock, we can be satisfied with psychoanalysis. Nevertheless, I don't think this is enough to explain the invention of the forms and their internal dynamics.

Hitchcock's work always depicts some form of duel between Light and Shadow—between, in other words, Unity and Duality. The very first shot of *Psycho*, after Saul Bass's abstract titles, reveals an immense stretch of landscape round a very ordinary-looking town, shot in an extremely harsh light. Here, it seems, all must be immutable—a sense of eternity. Titles specify the place, time, and date. In opposition to this light, the second shot establishes an absolute blackness in which we are engulfed along with the camera until a room is revealed, then a bed and lovers embracing. In two shots Hitchcock states his proposition: *Psycho* will speak to us of the eternal and the finite, of being and nothingness, of life and death—but seen in their naked truth. Nothing must please in *Psycho*, which is the inverse of *Vertigo*. This latter film was constructed on seduction, hence on disguise, the dressing up of appearances, the appeal of the images—on its attraction, in other words. Here, all is founded on harshness (and no such detail is spared us), on faces without makeup, on the shock of the montage (a *cut* montage, cutting like a knife). This journey towards death must only frighten, and frighten by its *hardness.*

Note

This essay was translated by David Wilson.

✦ ✦ ✦

Robin Wood's *Hitchcock's Films* was originally published in 1965 and was the first serious book-length study of Hitchcock in English. Wood's strong preoccupation was to prove (and it did need proving back then) the seriousness of Hitchcock's work—hence the references to literature, Shakespeare in particular. The essay on *Psycho* in his book begins to plumb the depths of the film and continues the strong analyses that follow Douchet's groundbreaking work. The reprint of the book does not substantively change the original essays.

ROBIN WOOD ✦ *Psycho*

... function
Is smother'd in surmise, and nothing is
But what is not.
—MACBETH

But if you look at the matter from a theoretical point of
view and ignore this question of degree you can very well
say that we are all ill, i.e. neurotic; for the conditions
required for symptom-formation are demonstrable also in
normal persons.
—FREUD, *Introductory Lectures on Psycho-Analysis*

You have to remember that *Psycho* is a film made with
quite a sense of amusement on my part. To me it's a *fun*
picture. The processes through which we take the audience,
you see, it's rather like taking them through the haunted
house at the fairground.
—HITCHCOCK, interview in *Movie 6*

Psycho opens with a view of a city. The name of the city appears followed by a precise date and a precise time, as the camera swings over the rooftops and apartment blocks. It hesitates, seems to select, tracks in towards one particular block, hesitates again before all the windows, seems to select again, then takes us through one slightly open window into a darkened room. Arbitrary place, date and time, and now an apparently arbitrary window: the effect is of random selection: this could be any place, any date, any time, any room: it could be *us*. The forward track into darkness inaugurates the progress of perhaps the most terrifying film ever made: we are to be taken forwards and downwards into the darkness of ourselves. *Psycho* begins with the normal and draws us steadily deeper and deeper into the abnormal; it opens by making us aware of time, and ends (except for the releasing final image) with a situation in which time (i.e., development) has ceased to exist.

The scene we witness between Marion Crane (Janet Leigh) and Sam Loomis (John Gavin), while carefully and convincingly particularized in terms of character and situation, is ordinary enough for us to accept it as representative of "normal" human behavior. A leading theme emerges, unexceptional both in itself and in the way in which it is presented, though it subtly pervades the whole scene: the dominance of the past over the present. The lovers cannot marry because Sam has to pay his dead father's debts and his ex-wife's alimony; "respectable" meetings in Marion's home will be presided over by her (presumably) dead mother's portrait. From this "normal" hold of past on present, with its limiting, cramping effect on life (the essence of life being development), we shall be led gradually to a situation where present is entirely swallowed up by past, and life finally paralyzed. That the lovers are meeting surreptitiously, doing things that must be concealed from the outer world, provides a further link (still within the bounds of normality) with Norman Bates. And in both cases the "secrets," normal and abnormal, are sexual in nature.

Everything is done to encourage the spectator to identify with Marion. In the dispute between the lovers, we naturally side with her: Sam's insistence on waiting until he can give her financial security annoys us, because it is the sort of boring mundane consideration we expect the romantic hero of a film to sweep aside, and we are very much drawn to Marion's readiness to accept things as they are for the sake of the relationship. This is in fact the first step in our complicity in the theft of the 40,000 dollars. It is Sam's fault that Marion steals the money, which has no importance for her. It is simply the means to an end: sex, not money, is the root of all evil. Indeed, the spectator's lust for money, played upon considerably in the early stages of the film, is aroused only to be swiftly and definitively "placed": the fate of the money, after the shower murder, becomes an entirely trivial matter, and Hitchcock by insisting on it evokes in us a strong revulsion.

Our moral resistance is skillfully undermined during the office scene. The man with the money—Cassidy—is a vulgar, drunken oaf; he has plenty more; his boast that he "buys off unhappiness," that his about-to-be-married "baby" has "never had an unhappy day," fills us with a sense of unfairness even as we realize how far his boast probably is from the truth: whatever he is, Cassidy does not strike us as a happy man.

The whole fabric of the film is interwoven with these parent-child references: even Marion's fellow office-girl has a prying mother, and Marion's room is decorated with family photographs which look down on her as she packs. Cassidy's relationship with his "baby" takes us a step into the abnormal, because it is highly suspect: she will probably be better without the 40,000 dollar house, which is clearly a symbol of her father's power over her. That Marion will also be better without it is a reflection we do not allow ourselves, any more than she does. By minimizing our moral opposition to the notion of stealing 40,000 dollars, Hitchcock makes it possible for us to continue to identify with Marion, involving ourselves in her guilt as easily and unthinkingly as she herself becomes involved. There is no clear-cut moment of decision: she takes the money home, changes, packs her suitcase, but the money lies on the bed and she constantly hesitates over it: her actions tell us that she has committed herself, but she doesn't consciously accept that commitment. We are able to commit acts we know to be immoral only if we inhibit our conscious processes: Macbeth never really knows why he "*yields* to that suggestion whose horrid image does unfix his hair ...," but the yielding itself involves the paralysis of his conscious moral fac-

ulties. So it is with Marion: the decision having gripped her
(rather than been taken), she necessarily forfeits her powers of
conscious will. She drifts helplessly, and we drift with her.

Her inability to control her actions rationally is illustrated in
numerous incidents. As she drives, she imagines voices, conversations: Sam, her boss, Cassidy. She knows Sam will be horrified,
will reject the money (she cannot finish the imaginary conversation with him); yet she drives on. Her boss notices her as her
car is held up by traffic lights, and she sees him notice her; yet
she drives on. Everything she imagines stresses the impossibility
of getting away with it and the uselessness of it anyway; yet she
drives on. A suspicious policeman sees her changing cars, and she
knows that *he* knows what her new car looks like, and what its
number is, and that she is throwing away an irretrievable 700
dollars pointlessly; yet she goes through with the exchange.
Throughout the journey Hitchcock uses every means to enforce
audience-identification—the staging of each scene, the use of subjective technique, the way in which each subsidiary character is
presented to us through Marion's eyes, Bernard Herrmann's music and Hitchcock's use of it, all serve to involve us in Marion's
condition. With her, we lose all power of rational control, and
discover how easily a "normal" person can lapse into a condition
usually associated with neurosis. Like her we resent, with fear and
impatience, everything (the policeman, the car salesman) that
impedes or interferes with her obsessive flight, despite the fact
that only interference can help her; just as, two films later, Marnie will be helped only by events that are entirely contrary to
her wishes, everything she wants being harmful to her. As Marion
drives on (after the exchange of cars), we share her hopelessness
and her weariness. The film conveys a sense of endless journey
leading nowhere, or into darkness: as the imagined voices become
more menacing, darkness gathers. Driving through darkness, she
imagines Cassidy learning of the theft of the money: "I'll replace
it with her fine soft flesh": Marion's verdict on herself, hideously
disproportionate to the crime, will find its hideous enactment.
Rain begins to fall on the windscreen before Marion—before us.
She pulls up at the Bates Motel, which seems to materialize

abruptly out of the darkness in front of her. She has by her actions penetrated the shell of order, and like Macbeth plunged herself into the chaos-world, which finds here its most terrifying definition.

The confrontation of Marion and Norman Bates (Anthony Perkins) is in some ways the core of the film: the parallel made between them provides the continuity that underlies the brutal disruption when Marion is murdered. It is part of the essence of the film to make us feel the continuity between the normal and the abnormal: between the compulsive behavior of Marion and the psychotic behavior of Norman Bates. In the "parlor" behind his office, surrounded by Norman's stuffed birds and paintings of classical rapes, they talk about "traps." Marion is brought face-to-face with the logical extension of her present condition. Norman tells her, "We're all in our private trap. We scratch and claw, but only at the air, only at each other, and for all of it we never budge an inch": he is defining the psychotic state, the condition of permanent anguish whence development becomes impossible, a psychological hell. The parallel between the two is clinched when Norman says to her, "We all go a little mad sometimes. Haven't you?"

It is her perception of Norman's condition that gives Marion her chance of salvation, which she takes. In answer to his question, she says, "Sometimes just one time can be enough. Thank you." She decides to return the money the next morning. The decision this time is clearly made: she has regained her freedom of will, her rationality. The scene prepares us for the transference of our interest from Marion to Norman. We see Marion under the shower, and her movements have a ritualistic quality; her face expresses the relief of washing away her guilt.

It is not merely its incomparable physical impact that makes the shower-bath murder probably the most horrific incident in any fiction film. The *meaninglessness* of it (from Marion's point of view) completely undermines our recently restored sense of security. The murder is as irrational and as useless as the theft of the money. It also constitutes an alienation effect so shattering that (at a first viewing of the film) we scarcely recover from it.

Never—not even in *Vertigo*—has identification been broken off so brutally. At the time, so engrossed are we in Marion, so secure in her potential salvation, that we can scarcely believe it is happening; when it is over, and she is dead, we are left shocked, with nothing to cling to, the apparent center of the film entirely dissolved.

Needing a new center, we attach ourselves to Norman Bates, the only other character (at this point) available. We have been carefully prepared for this shift of sympathies. For one thing, Norman is an intensely sympathetic character, sensitive, vulnerable, trapped by his devotion to his mother—a devotion, a self-sacrifice, which our society tends to regard as highly laudable. That he is very unbalanced merely serves to evoke our protective instincts: he is also so helpless. Beyond this, the whole film hitherto has led us to Norman, by making us identify with a condition in many ways analogous to his: the transition is easy. After the murder, Hitchcock uses all the resources of identification technique to make us "become" Norman. He is a likeable human being in an intolerable situation, desperately in need of help and protection yet by the very nature of the case unable to obtain it. As he cleans up after his mother's hideous crime, the camera becomes subjective; they are our hands mopping away the blood. At the same time we cannot forget Marion; the intense anguish aroused in the spectator arises, as usual, from a conflict of responses. Our attention is directed repeatedly to the last lingering trace of Marion which Norman almost overlooks: the money, become now a mere squalid bundle of paper, an ironic reminder of her life, her desires, her relationship with Sam.

Psycho is Hitchcock's ultimate achievement to date in the technique of audience-participation. In a sense, the spectator becomes the chief protagonist, uniting in himself all the characters. The remainder of the film is inquiry into the sources of the psychological hell-state represented by Norman Bates: a descent into the chaos world. The other characters (Sam, Lila, Arbogast), perfunctorily sketched, are merely projections of the spectators into the film, our instruments for the search, the easier to identify with as they have no detailed individual existence. Each stage in the descent adds to the tension within us: we want to know, and we dread knowing, we want the investigators to find the truth and put an end to the horrors, yet we have involved ourselves in those horrors through our identification with Norman. One is struck (bearing in mind the care with which Hitchcock always selects his players) by close physic resemblances between certain characters. That between Vera Miles and Janet Leigh can be easily explained: they are sisters: but what of that, still more striking, between Anthony Perkins and John Gavin? As they face each other across the counter of Norman's office, we have the uncanny feeling that we are looking at two sides of the same coin; and the scene in question, which seemed at first mere suspense, useful only in its plot context, becomes one of the most moving of the film. The two men look at one another, and we look at them, and we realize suddenly that they are interchangeable: each seems the reflection of the other (though a reflection in a distorting mirror), the one healthy, balanced, the other gnawed and rotted within by poisoned sex. Similarly, Vera Miles is the extension of Janet Leigh, and what she sees is, potentially, inside herself. The characters of *Psycho* are *one* character, and that character, thanks to the identifications the film evokes, is us.

Lila's exploration of the house is an exploration of Norman's psychotic personality. The whole sequence, with its discoveries in bedroom, attic, and cellar, has clear Freudian overtones. The Victorian *décor*, crammed with invention, intensifies the atmosphere of sexual repression. The statue of a black cupid in the hall, the painting of an idealized maiden disporting herself at the top of the stairs, a nude goddess statuette in the bedroom, are juxtaposed with the bed permanently indented with the shape of Mrs. Bates's body (the bed in which, we learn later, she and her lover were murdered by Norman), the macabre cast of crossed hands on her dressing table, the stifling atmosphere of stagnation: one can almost *smell* it. The attic, Norman's own bedroom, represents the sick man's conscious mental development: strange confusion of the childish and the adult, cuddly toys, grubby unmade bed, a record of the "Eroica" symphony; the unexplained nature of all this carries the suggestion that what we see are mere superficial hints of underlying mysteries, a suggestion confirmed by the clasped, untitled book that Lila never actually opens (a Bates family album?) [In fact she does open it; we are never shown what is inside, as Wood points out in a note to a later reprint of the article, and refers to the various possibilities of the act: does Lila look shocked? Does the book contain pornography?—ed.] Consequently we accept Norman more than ever as a human being, with all the human being's complex potentialities. The cellar gives us the hidden, sexual springs of his behavior: there Lila finds Mrs. Bates. It is a *fruit*-cellar—the fruit is insisted upon in the mother's macabre joke about being "fruity": the source of fruition and fertility become rotten.

Our discovery of the truth, of course, partly changes our attitude to what has gone before. It adds, for example, many complexities to our understanding of the shower murder, which we see now as primarily a sexual act, a violent substitute for the rape that Norman dare not carry out, and secondarily as the trapped being's desire to destroy a woman who has achieved the freedom he will never achieve: a point that gives added irony to the fact that it is her awareness of Norman that gives Marion that freedom. What it cannot do is remove our sense of complicity. We have been led to accept Norman Bates as a potential extension of ourselves. That we all carry within us somewhere every human potentiality, for good or evil, so that we all share in a common guilt, may be, intellectually, a truism; the greatness of *Psycho* lies in its ability, not merely to *tell* us this, but to make us experience it. It is this that makes a satisfactory analysis of a Hitchcock film on paper so difficult; it also ensures that no analysis, however detailed, can ever become a substitute for the film itself, since the direct emotional experience survives any amount of explanatory justification.

The effect of forward tracking-shots in the film (from the opening right through to Lila's exploration of the house [and toward Norman in his jail cell—ed.]) is to carry us always further inside or into darkness. All the time we are being made to *see*, to see more, to see deeper: often, to see things we are afraid to see. Hence the insistence on eyes, into which the camera, our own eyes, makes us look, to see the dark places of the human soul beyond. And hence the dark glasses of the policeman: he is the only character whose eyes we never see, because it is he who is watching Marion, and hence ourselves. By the end of the film, Hitchcock has placed us in the policeman's position: we watch Norman Bates as the policeman watched Marion, and he is as conscious of our gaze as Marion was of the policeman's. On the other side of the cinema screen, we are as inscrutable, hence as pitiless, as the policeman behind his dark glasses. We may recall Norman's remark about "institutions" in the dialogue with Marion: ". . . the cruel eyes studying you." Norman is finally beyond our help. Much of the film's significance is summed up in a single visual metaphor, making use again of eyes, occurring at the film's focal point (the murder of Marion): the astonishing cut from the close-up of the water and blood *spiraling* down the drain, to the close-up of the eye of the dead girl, with the camera *spiraling* outwards from it. It is as if we have emerged from the depths *behind* the eye, the round hole of the drain leading down into an apparently bottomless darkness, the potentialities for horror that lie in the depths of us all, and which have their source in sex, which the remainder of the film is devoted to sounding. The sensation of vertigo inspired by this cut and the spiraling movement itself, are echoed later as we, from high above, watch Norman carry his mother down to the fruit cellar.

The cellar is another clear sex symbol. And what Vera Miles finds there at the end of the quest are once again eyes: the mocking "eyes" of a long-dead corpse as a light bulb swings before its face: the eyes of living death, eyes that move without seeing, the true eyes of Norman.

The psychiatrist's "explanation" has been much criticized, but it has its function. It crystallizes for us our tendency to evade the implications of the film, by converting Norman into a mere "case," hence something we can easily put from us. The psychiatrist, glib and complacent, reassures us. But Hitchcock crystallizes this for us merely to force us to reject it. We shall see on reflection that the "explanation" ignores as much as it explains (the murder as symbolic rape, for example). But we are not allowed to wait for a chance to reflect: our vague feelings of dissatisfaction are promptly brought to consciousness by our final confrontation with Norman, and this scene in the cell, entirely static [actually, the camera moves—ed.] after the extremes of violence that have preceded it, is the most unbearably horrible in the film. What we see is Norman, his identity finally dissolved in the illusory identity of his mother, denounce all the positive side of his personality. "Mother" is innocent: "she" spares the fly crawling on Norman's hand: it is Norman who was the savage butcher. Thus we witness the irretrievable annihilation of a human being. The fly reminds us of Marion, who wasn't spared: the act constitutes a pathetic attempt at expiation before the pitiless eyes of a cruel and uncomprehending society. For a split second, almost subliminally, the features of the mother's ten-year-dead face are superimposed on Norman's as it fixes in a skull-like grimace. The sense of finality is intolerable, yet it is this that makes our release possible: we have been made to see the dark potentialities within all of us, to face the worst thing in the world: eternal damnation. We can now be set free, be saved for life. The last image, of the car *withdrawing* from the dark depths of the bog, returns us to Marion, to ourselves, and to the idea of psychological liberty.

Psycho is one of the key works of our age. Its themes are of course not new—obvious forerunners include *Macbeth* and Conrad's *Heart of Darkness*—but the intensity and horror of their treatment and the fact that they are here grounded in sex belong to the age that has witnessed on the one hand the discoveries of Freudian psychology and on the other the Nazi concentration camps. I do not think I am being callous in citing the camps in relation to a work of popular entertainment. Hitchcock himself in fact accepted a commission to make a compilation film of captured Nazi material about the camps. The project reached the rough-cut stage, and was abandoned there, for reasons I have not been able to discover: the rough cut now lies, inaccessibly, along with vast quantities of similar raw material, in the vaults of the Imperial War Museum. But one cannot contemplate the camps without confronting two aspects of their horror: the utter helplessness and innocence of the victims, and the fact that human beings, whose potentialities all of us in some measure share, were their tormentors and butchers. We can no longer be under the slightest illusion about human nature, and about the abysses around us and within us; and *Psycho* is founded on, precisely, these twin horrors. For Hitchcock it was a "fun" picture, and a streak of macabre humor ("Mother . . . what is the phrase? . . . isn't quite herself today") certainly runs through it. Is it, then, some monstrous perversion? Many have found it so, and their reaction seems to me more defensible than that of those (must we include Hitchcock himself?) who are merely amused by it (". . . make us think twice about stopping at any building looking remotely like the Bates motel . . ."). David Holbrook, for example, remarks (presumably with *Psycho* in mind, since his book appeared in 1962), "Of course, if we live in the world of detective stories and Hitchcock films we may take all this sordidness in a light-hearted spirit as a snuff-like piece of stimulation. But if we are responding to poetry and drama our senses should be sharpened . . ." (*Llareggub Revisited*). Yet this seems to me a short-sighted and insensitive verdict: if one is responding to *Psycho*, one's senses should be sharpened too. No film conveys—to those not afraid to expose themselves fully to it—a greater sense of desolation, yet it does so from an exceptionally mature and secure emotional viewpoint. And an essential part of this viewpoint is the detached sardonic humor. It enables the film to contemplate the ultimate horrors without hysteria, with a poised, almost serene detachment. This is probably not what Hitchcock meant when he said that one cannot appreciate *Psycho* without a sense of humor, but it is what he *should* have meant. He himself—if his interviews are to be trusted—has not really faced up to what he was doing when he made the film. This, needless to say, must not affect one's estimate of the film itself. For the maker of *Psycho* to regard it as a "fun" picture can be taken as his means of preserving his sanity; for the critic to do so—and to give it his approval on these grounds—is quit unpardonable. Hitchcock (again, if his interviews are to be trusted) is a much greater artist than he knows.

◆ ◆ ◆

Hitchcock was British and began his film career in England (actually, he began his apprenticeship as an art director for films in Germany), so it is not surprising that the British should have written extensively on Hitchcock. Raymond Durgnat's *The Strange Case of Alfred Hitchcock, or the Plain Man's Hitchcock*, is one of the early full-length studies of the director and, like Robin Wood's book, lays important groundwork for future scholars. He pays close attention to the form of the film, and, like Wood, his analysis of the ways *Psycho* plays on Marion's eye and the shower drain sets the tone for the George Toles essay, " 'If Thine Eye Offend Thee . . . ,' " which appears later in this book.

Durgnat calls on many other films in the course of his analysis, taking *Psycho* out of its isolation and indicating that originality depends on tradition. He is particularly observant in placing the film in "the old dark house" tradition, not only of horror cinema, but back to the eighteenth-century Gothic novels that influenced them. He also wrestles with the problem raised in many of the essays contained in this volume, arising from Hitchcock's comment that *Psycho* was a "fun" picture, indeed, a joke. Finally, he, like Wood, writes about a quality of Hitchcock's work that was widely discussed in early criticism: the notion of "complicity," the fact that the audience is placed in a false identification with truly evil characters, such as Norman Bates.

Hitchcock was on Durgnat's mind throughout his scholarly life. His full-length study of *Psycho*, appropriately titled *A Long, Hard Look at "Psycho,"* was published posthumously.

RAYMOND DURGNAT ◆ *Psycho*

Hitchcock claims *Psycho* is primarily a fun picture—"you see it's rather like taking them through the haunted house at the fairground." Most of Hitchcock's work answers to this description, and *Psycho* is a *potpourri* of *Charley's Aunt, Bluebeard, Sweeney Todd, Oedipus Rex* with additional dialogue by Sigmund Freud, and *The Laurel and Hardy Murder Case.* All of which doubtless precipitated the initial critical reaction of distaste and revulsion, although second

85

thoughts, by a younger generation of critics, reasserted Hitchcock as an earnest moralist and a filmmaker of some finesse.

The camera climbs towards a window like any other window. Documentary-style, a subtitle states time and date; but it really means: Here and Now, at this moment, without warning, imperceptibly, destiny entered these lives. On a hot day, during their lunch-break, in an impersonal hotel bedroom, Marion Crane (Janet Leigh) and Sam Loomis (John Gavin) are half-naked and necking. The nightmare begins at noon. The heat, the bleached feel of the visuals, the half-naked-ness, the time, evoke an atmosphere of unsatiated sensuality (indeed, the heavy petting of so many of Hitchcock's American films, from *Notorious* to *North by Northwest*, suggests a frustrating coldness, even, intercourse with neither orgasm nor emotional relief). In a very matter-of-fact way the lovers are discussing the man's divorce and the money they need if they are to marry. The general situation—half-stripping at lunchtime and then talking about cash—is vaguely offensive; yet they seem decent people, we accept and care about them. This ambiguity pervades their whole relationship. In some way Sam seems petulant, weak, unworthy; in others, Marion seems prim, tough, less concerned with unconditional love than with—respectability? Are they in love or only convinced they are? At any rate, we're not especially anxious for them to get married. In default of the money, she is tempted to break off the affair, and we are sufficiently disquietened to watch with something between curiosity and concern, rather with an eagerness for them to get married and live "happily ever after."

Marion returns to the sane, shallow, superficial people of the office where she works. It's not long before sex and cash are intertwined again. A fat client makes a rather coarse and vulgar attempt to flirt with her, brandishing a fat bankroll in her face. The other office-girl, a plain and silly creature, is naïvely jealous of these gross attentions. "I expect he saw my wedding ring." Her self-consoling remarks rubs salt in Marion's wound. We agree with her feeling that she is too pretty, efficient, sincere in love, to deserve to be worse off than this other girl. The fat customer brags that he wouldn't miss the money if it were stolen, and

Marion's boss absolutely insists on entrusting it to her. Such smug, imperceptive responses all round reinforce our feeling that Marion has as much right to this excess money as its actual owner. These pinpricks accumulate into a kind of obsession and reinforce the confusion between her respectability (or pride) and her love (or sensuality). The money seems to offer a solution to all these "raw edges" of feeling. Her theft is (so to speak) an impulse born of converging obsessions, which suddenly click into place forming an irresistible urge. It is also a tribute to her daring, her strength of passion; there is an element of moral *hubris vis-à-vis*. There is also an element of *hubris vis-à-vis* her lover, as if in acting so boldly where he has been so weak she is taking over the initiative—and is not going to be thanked for her devotion. Soon she is driving hard away from town, tormented not so much by conscience as by fear. We can't believe she'll get away with it, especially as criminals never do in American films. We hope she will, and there is still a get-out: the theft won't be noticed until Monday morning, she can always return the money. Will she go on to decide to return it, but lose it? Will someone else steal it from her? Will Sam betray her, by his weakness, some-how?

A big, brutal-looking motorbike cop with dark glasses trails her, suspiciously. His menacing figure recalls the lawbreakers of *The Wild One* and the motorcyclists of *Orphée* who ran men down in the name, not of justice, but of a law above the law, the brutal Will of destiny. He is "the law," but he has a special, *personal* brutality of his own. Is he really following her, or is she only imagining he is? The psychological pressures complicate and intensify. To shake him off, she exchanges her car at a garage run by a very obliging character, apparently the very antithesis of the cop. The cop is saying, "I remind you of punishment: turn back!" the garagehand, "I make crime pleasant and easy, go on." She acquires a white car—the color of her underwear in the necking scene, the color of innocence and dissatisfied sensuality; but all her precautions are of no avail. The cop still tails her, a terrifying dark angel sent to give her a last chance. Or sent simply to torture her, to diminish her chances: for without him she has a weekend in which to repent. There is danger of, as it were, rape-by-justice. We sigh with relief when at last she shakes him off.

She is beyond the reach of the law—or fear—now. But—where is she? The rain pours down across the windscreen, blurring lights and creating a wavering landscape. She is in what in *Orphée* is called *la Zone*, the no-man's-land between reality and the nightmare. The cop was both danger and safety. It is almost as if he were sent, after all, not to turn her back, but to make her drive on. The theological notion of double predestination provides a clue, "God sends sinners a chance to repent *in order that* by rejecting it, as he knows they will, they will damn themselves more thoroughly than ever." But as she reasons with herself, she is beginning to realize the futility of her theft—Sam is too sensible to accept the money. . . .

The rain forces her into a motel, managed by Norman Bates (Anthony Perkins). Norman is an engagingly naïve country youth, very honest, unconcerned with making money, almost a symbol of rustic virtue and country contentment. The whole film hinges on his sensitivity and charm—we tend to like him whatever his faults. His friendliness is all the more reassuring in contrast with the sinister atmosphere (the stuffed birds of prey, the Victorian house just behind the motel, where his petulant, tyrannical old mother lives). He seems tainted by the atmosphere, but the over-obvious horror clichés shift our suspicions from Norman to the atmosphere; they camouflage the inevitably stilted presentation of his relationships with Mrs. Bates; they contrast with the slick, modern, informal style of the film as a whole. Mrs. Bates comes from Norman's childhood, and it's fitting that she should exist in an aesthetic idiom now considered childish—she would feel quite at home in James Whale's *The Old Dark House*.

Marion calls Norman's bird-stuffing a rather morbid hobby and says Norman resembles the dead birds of prey. Hitchcock plays fair with his audience, even while misleading us. True, he lets us believe in Mrs. Bates—but so do Marion, and Norman. Maybe, as the psychiatrist says later, Norman was never entirely Norman, he faintly knew the truth about Mrs. Bates—but then again Mrs. Bates is very stilted, we only half-believe in her.

Norman cheerfully admits to his faults of character; he is a very reasonable, modest guy. Gradually Marion realizes that she is his superior, that, if unhappy, she is self-possessed, whereas his "contented" acquiescence in looking after his domineering mother has something weak and helpless. His wisdom about money and the example of his servitude help to free her from the power of her impulse. She realizes that what she stole was not love but only money, an attempt to avoid her problems. Norman is almost a sacrificial victim whose tragic example frees her.

But he is not a hopeless case. We feel that she owes it to him to return the favor. We want him to be freed from his horrible mother for he is a decent fellow. There is something dissatisfying in Marion's decision simply to return, alone, to the everyday, with its little degradations, its mutually exclusive choices—while leaving Norman here, unhelped. A sort of bewilderment percolates through the audience at this weird, premature "happy ending." We are, so to speak, in another "zone."

The film elaborately establishes Marion's search for a hiding-place for her cash. The search seems to turn her indifference to Norman into an entrenched cynicism for he isn't the sort of lad to steal it. As she undresses, Norman watches through the peephole. We laugh very uneasily at his avid voyeurism, but it does not quite put him in our bad books. For he has been lonely and dominated by his puritanical mother; and his spying on Marion represents a movement towards normality and freedom, which we want for his sake. This is almost a dissatisfying love scene (like necking for lunch). The erotic overtones are juicy, and please us. And we are pleased to feel the story moving again.

The "movement towards" Marion is intensified—with a vengeance—when Mrs. Bates with a knife upraised charges in and stabs her to death in the shower. The murder is too erotic not to enjoy, but too grisly to enjoy. Its ferocity and pornography are opposed; we are shocked into violent protest and horror, yet they force on the average spectator a rapid, hysteric, moral oscillation between protest and enjoyment. There is a Hays Code [the Hollywood self-censoring rules that preceded those of the Motion

Picture Association of America] sort of moral in the air: "Look what thieving necking girls get," but her fate is also ironically unjust: for she had just resolved to return the money.

If the Peeping Tom episode is a "weak" yet eerie version of the hotel scene, the murder is a sarcastic exaggeration of it—her sensuality's satisfied now, all right. We feel guilty about enjoying this film, but we have to admit we're having our money's worth of fun and fear.

Mom would be a convenient scapegoat; but we are headed away from complacent hatred back into something subtler and far more uncomfortable by Norman's distress at her crime and his concern for her. In the next sequence, he begins mopping-up operations in the bathroom, the action of an exceptionally dutiful son. The presence of Marion's naked corpse is both erotic and extremely uncomfortable. The film offers us a "first-person" experience answering the question which so often occurs to crime fans, "Would I be able to get down to the practical details of clearing up the corpse and the blood?"—a thought which appalls many people more than that of the actual killing. The answer the film gives is, "A sensitive and dutiful son like Norman can— therefore, so could you, if you really had to." We watch Norman doing it, and the feeling that we could too is gratifying to the worse side of our nature, but upsets the other.

Although there is a quietly disturbing contrast between Norman's usual sensibility and his matter-of-fact practicality on this particular chore, we feel that in this way he was on the edge of being "liberated" by his interest in Marion, that she slew Marion so as to keep him, and that in covering up for Mom, Norman is turning the other cheek, manifesting the equanimity and charity of a saint. The spectator's moral purity is being outflanked at both ends—by morbid, pornographic interest and by a sympathetic pity for charming Norman.

Not that indignation and disgust are lulled asleep. On the contrary. For example, there is a very precise mix between a C.U. [close-up] of the plughole down which our saintly voyeur is swabbing the blood and a C.U. of Marion's open eye staring at us as if to say, "What about my feelings? Why don't you interview the dead?" She's peeping back at us from beyond the grave, from down the drain, with protest and indignation, eternal and colossal—or surprise and fear—or just nothing. This visual rhyme is not just a piece of sadistic wit but a little essay in metaphor; it never does to interpret visual effects too definitely, but, e.g., the plughole is like an eye socket, the eye ("Window of the soul" as they say) is just a mushroom out of a black hole. There is a sense of total nothingness and if the "joke" provides a little hysteria which relieves the horror faintly it insinuates a subtler unease: we must be mad to be laughing at a joke like this.

Norman chews candy as he watches the white car sink beneath the very black surface of the swamp behind the house. As the film uses psychoanalytical ideas it's appropriate to use them on the film—the bathroom scene, very glossy and white, and devoted to the theme of cleanliness, is followed by a scene in which everything disappears into a black sticky cesspool. Norman has pulled the chain.

When the car sticks instead of sinking, we are alarmed, but when at last it disappears we heave a sigh of relief. Thank goodness! Norman is a good boy (despite the candy), it would be wrong to punish him, Marion's a corpse, it's no use crying over spilt blood, bury her quick, tidy up, get her out of the way! But when Norman tosses in the thick wad of cash, which he thinks is just an old newspaper, a cry of shock and regret is wrested from the audience. That valuable money, what a waste! Norman's saintly indifference to Mammon hurts us. We want to forget Marion probably because her murder shook us up so much. But the money had become "what she died for, what she hid," that is, virtually a substitute identity. Its derisive disappearance creates hysteria as again the narrative seems to "end."

Sam Loomis discusses Marion's disappearance with her sister Lila (Vera Miles). The visuals are gray and scruffy. The setting is Sam's wife's ironmongery [hardware] store where callous chit-chat about insecticides is overheard and pitchfork prongs are visually prominent. The drab everyday is full of trivial or latent cruelty. The meeting of lover and sister is hostile, but their disputes are ironically complacent compared with the terrible truth. Lila seems more sensible, more adult than Marion, and perhaps more righteous—but also worried, subdued. A private detective, Arbogast (Martin Balsam), insists on introducing himself and tells them that Marion has absconded with the money. They refuse to believe him. They detest his coarse, obnoxious approach—so do we, and, like Sam and Lila, feel he must be up to some dirty game. His cynicism doesn't fit Marion's case—although, in a sense, it is justified.

As he tracks Marion down to Norman's mansion we half-want him to fail—for Norman's sake, and because he may be up to some cynical scheme of his own. . . . Just before he confronts Norman we realize that he is completely, admirably honest. In the battle of wits between Norman and Arbogast we sympathize with them both—Marion *must* be avenged, Arbogast is tough enough to uncover the truth; and yet Norman's motives are selfless, and perhaps Mrs. Bates will be more than even Arbogast bargains for. As he climbs the stairs towards the old lady's room, we realize clearly that his pushful cynicism, hitherto his strength, is now his weakness. He is formidable, and physically is probably Mom's match, but he is too naïve to be looking for whatever he'll find— and Mrs. Bates comes tearing out of her room with the super-speed of the superstrong insane and with repeated jabs of her knife sends him tumbling backwards down the stairs, dead, just like that. Is Mom invincible?

Another car sinks into the swamp, the narrative "ends" at another nihilistic moment.

The whole plot, which has twice ended so disastrously, starts again, as Sam and Lila come to investigate the disappearance of the investigator who came to investigate the disappearance of . . . Probably by now most spectators have guessed that Mom = Norman. But we can't be sure, in such a film. The only thing we can be certain of is the imminence of violent death—again. What matters is not whether we know, but whether Sam and Lila find out—or get killed. They might. Heroes and heroines do, in this film. And if they do find out, what will happen to Norman— saintly accomplice of two—at least—crimes . . . ?

The determined, but prosaic and therefore perilously naïve,

couple call on the local sheriff (John McIntire) who explains that
Norman is eccentric but harmless, that Mom has been dead and
buried these ten years past, and so on. But we heard Norman
persuade Mom to hide in the cellar, and we saw Mom come
tearing out of her room to kill Arbogast. The sheriff's clue is so
wrapped up in complacency and ignorance that instead of clarifying our suspicions it confounds them further. The sheriff's suggestion opens up astounding new avenues of depravity: "If Norman's mother is still alive, then who's the woman buried up there
in Green Lawns Cemetery?"[1] If they believe what the sheriff says,
they will never go to the old house, and then how can Marion
and Arbogast be avenged? But *if* they go there....

Sam keeps Norman talking while Lila sneaks into the house
to explore; clearly the most dangerous game to play, especially
with a possible Mom waiting for her. As we can't make up our
mind whether the danger is coming from in front of her (Mom)
or from behind her (Norman), we're no longer thinking very
coherently, and as we can't make up our mind what we want to
happen to Norman, we yield to a helpless hysteria.

Norman grows more anxious and angry as Sam brutally presses
him; he struggles to keep his temper, to quieten his tormentors'
suspicions, while keeping Mom from breaking out in himself (if
you know) or (if you don't) bravely protecting his Mom or (if
you're not sure) both or neither or which? The scene almost shifts
our sympathies round—such is Norman's sincerity—to: "brutal
smug adulterer bullies sensitive kid into despair." After all,
whether Norman is weak or maniac or both, he probably believes
in Mom, he is only trying to obviate another climax, another
killing, he is frantically on the side of peace.

Lila explores the house. Amidst the tension there is an unexpected intellectual interest, and pathos. Norman's rooms are a
picture of his mind and everyday life. There is the record-player
with the classical LP (so out of place in this Gothicy house), there
are the fluffy childhood toys which are presumably still played
with. Norman is weaker-minded, more sensitive, than we thought,

---

1. Well might he ask.

which makes him more pathetic (and more surprising—menacing?). Norman, mad with suspicion, rushes from the motel into the house as Lila takes refuge in the cellar—where, we know, Norman puts Mom in times of stress. And Mom does exist, there she is, horribly old, evil and withered, at a closer look she's dead and withered, but still grinning malevolently, she's a ghost, and when Lila turns, there's *another* Mom, grinning malevolently, very much alive, knife upraised. There aren't no Moms, there are two Moms, then the second disintegrates, the wig slides off, it's Norman. It's not simply the surprise that shocks; it's the intensity of terror and the obscenity of the disintegration. In rather the same way, when Mom came tearing out of her room at Arbogast, she had the notoriously terrible strength of the insane, and a visible virility quite obscene in an old lady; the explanation doesn't explain *that* away; it intensifies its impact because illusion and explanation coexist.

We are relieved to hear that everything is going to be comfortably explained for us by the police psychologist (Simon Oakland). As soon as we see him we begin to dislike his brash, callous, know-all manner, he puts our backs up as Arbogast did. We expect the clichés: poor mixed-up kid, it was all the fault of stern, possessive, puritanical Mom. But gradually we realize he's not saying this at all. It was Norman who was jealous, who imagined that his (for all we know) normal Mom was a promiscuous Mom and murdered and embalmed her and then imagined she was a jealous puritanical Mom and then lived out two false characters— nice normal Norman and nasty Mom. So much for rustic contentment. Norman was never, we gather, entirely Norman, i.e., even when he was being charming and we felt sorry for him, he knew deep down what he was doing. The psychologist's explanation takes away our explanation: what we thought was "deep," the "solution," is merely the topmost level of nastiness. He restores terror, guilt, injustice. Up till now Mom's gruesome appearance has been in accord with her character: "Well, if she's dead, she asked for it, look at how she messed up her tender and devoted son." Now all this is reversed, the coconut-faced corpse was once a sunny, apple-cheeked mother. The boy has literally turned her into his fantasy of her.

But if the psychologist, brutal and cynical, is the most intimate of private eyes, the joker is still to come. All we've had has been an intellectual, rational explanation. Now we see Norman sitting against a blank, white, hygienic wall. He is in full-face close-up, his madness is rammed into the cinema. Briefly our entire world is his face, the thoughts behind it, *his* world. We have little else with which to identify. An utter flatness, whiteness, simplicity, in short, eternity. He is cackling to himself, in Mummy's voice. She is jubilant because she is outwitting them all, pretending to be a sweet old lady who won't even hurt a fly. Mom has just killed Norman and disguised herself as him.

The Chinese sage wrote: "Now I do not know whether I was then a man dreaming I was a butterfly or whether I am now a butterfly dreaming I am a man." With Norman it's flies. His ricocheting self-punishment is so total that—well, we can hardly pity him, for there's no one left there to pity. And he or she or it seems to think it is escaping punishment, which is very immoral of him or her or it; but a nausea *like* compassion makes itself felt. We are too thoroughly satisfied to hate.

The appearance of Mom's face under the madman's, and then of a skull under Mom's, has a climactic brutality, but also simplifies, liberates us from the baffling maze of malevolent Nothings which our sensitive boy has become. Needless to say, it is a simplification on the most nihilistic level: are any of us realer than our skulls? There follows a shot of the police lifting Marion's car, wrapped in chains, from the swamp. There is no "decent obscurity." And Nothing to the nth degree has killed real people whom we sympathized with. But we too hoped the car would sink (just as we hoped Marion would get away with the cash). We too have been accomplices after the acts—futile acts.

People leave the cinema, chuckling incredulously, groggy, exhilarated yet hysterical, half-ready to believe that everybody in the world is as mad as Norman. A cathartic indulgence in pornographic murder is succeeded by an embarrassed humility, an unsentimental compassion towards insanity. The entire film is a prolonged practical joke in the worst of taste. If it weren't in bad taste, it would not be cathartic, embarrassing, or compassionate.

It is not just a sick joke, it is also a very sad joke. Because it is outrageous, it exhilarates, but it is a very depressed film as well. The byplay with the money is strange and disturbing. It is produced as a weapon of seduction by a repulsive but normal male. Its victim resents the implied insult but yields to the money. The money, she felt, would enable her to find, all at once, respectability, sensuality, love. It becomes the last clue, a substitute-identity, an anti-soul. Marion who hoped to avoid choice, and sacrifice (the *hubris* of American optimism), is reduced to a nude body, a car, bankroll.

Everything piles up in the swamp—and is dredged up again. The film is not just a sick joke and a very sad joke, but a lavatory joke. It is a derisive misuse of the key images of "the American way of life": Momism (but it blames son), cash (and rural virtue), necking (and respectability), plumbing, and smart cars. The reality to which Sam and Lila return is not a joyous one, but a drab shop of insecticides, pitchforks and—in addition—a vision of horror. The plot inevitably arouses in the spectator a feeling that Lila and Sam could eventually, possibly, consolingly, fall in love. But there is no hint of it in the final image. Each is still alone. This is the sanity that balances the diabolical nothing which is the human soul. Marion, striving for everything, lost everything. Only Norman has defied society and superficiality and found "rest." Only Norman has found himself, and lost himself.

Like many films, *Psycho*'s aesthetic method is not that of providing enlightening information about its characters; it provides just enough to confuse us; it works by luring the audience into becoming the characters, sharing and living out their experiences within them in carefully determined patterns. The characters tend to be alone on the screen. Even the conversations are filmed mainly in alternating close-ups. The close-up both enlarges (intensifies) and isolates (blots out the rest of the world). While each character is speaking the spectator sees, feels, becomes him and only him. The next shot wrenches him into becoming the *antag-*

onistic character. Our sympathies alternate rapidly—our feelings are poured into so many molds which are distended or smashed by contradictions, revelations, twists. Simple as the characters are, in principle, they are, because well acted, convincingly real. The atmosphere is hypnotic, the events so outrageous and managed with such brinkmanship of taste, the hints, allusions, and subversive shifts of sympathy are managed with such sly tact, its constant emotional collisions are so quick, subtle, and drastic, that the "sketchiness" of the characters no more invalidates them than it invalidates the plays of Racine.

In its powerful vagueness, it works on the spectator not unlike music. It is planned, felt out, in terms of varied motifs, of emotional chords and dissonances, of patterns. Hitchcock has a very refined sense of sly or brash emotional discords, of how to modulate and combine them. The coarse customer, the cop, Arbogast, and the psychologist are incarnations of the same force—unpleasant common sense. The trusting boss, the garageist [used car salesman], the local sheriff, Norman himself all agreeably further evil. The woman in the iron-monger's who is determined to kill insects painlessly is mirrored in Norman's final crone-voiced cackle that he won't even hurt a fly (is absurd squeamishness the hypocritical form of homicidal mania?). Norman, in conversation, unwittingly frees Marion of the compulsive theft which Sam inspired in her. But Sam bullies Norman like the cop bullied Marion.

Lila is a more reasonable, but "joyless" double of Marion. Sam loses Marion to Norman, but Norman is destroyed by Sam and Lila. Lila, in a sense, is Marion "come back"—a parallel to the "second Mom" in the basement. As Lila roams through Norman's rooms, she is almost the substitute mother, the young woman who is kind and normal will therefore destroy him. Norman and Sam are both dark-haired, faintly resemble each other. Norman killed his mother because he thought she had a lover; and is destroyed by a young adulterer and his mistress's sister. The three penetrations to "the truth about Norman"—Marion's, Arbogast's, the young couple's—are like three movements in music—the first two themes are contrasted (a sensual theme involving a girl, an unromantic theme involving Arbogast, the third combines them—a young couple who aren't quite romantically connected).

All these patterns, like inversions of certain emotional chords, result from the film's simplicity of form, but they are like haunting harmonies placed on a simple, yet eerie melodic line. The cutting has a quick, ragged, Stravinskian rhythm.

The minor quirks and sins (adultery, a "thing" about insecticides) of the normal world are the tips of the horns of the real reality, concealed beyond, or below, the "zone." In *Psycho* nothing that isn't disturbing or tainted ever happens, and to enjoy it (as most people do) is to stand convicted, and consciously convicted, of a lurking nostalgia for evil (i.e., of thoroughly enjoying it in fantasy). Norman's big mistake is that he let his fantasies enjoy him. The film is a practical joke: it convicts all the spectators of Original Sin. One does not so much watch, as participate in it, as one might in a religious ritual involving the confession and a— well, one cannot say that absolution is granted. On the contrary, we have to take what comfort, or discomfort, we can from the implied complicity.

Hitchcock may have had a Jesuit education, but surely *Psycho* isn't a Christian film; it has a Dionysiac force and ruthlessness, one might call it a Greek tragi-comedy.

It comes very close to a certain existentialist preoccupation, in so far as it portrays the ravages of emotional inauthenticity which reduce a human soul to a total, complex facticity in depth which it feels is pure freedom but which is merely *le néant* [nothingness]. One postulates the comparison with the same reserves as in the case of *Vertigo*. Hitchcock approaches the same themes from several opposite directions (fundamentalist and Freudian). The disintegration of personality represents an intensification of the themes of *Vertigo* and *North by Northwest*.

The perfection of the film's mechanism is illustrated by the unusual degree of unanimity and mutual complementarity, displayed by various exegeses (the above, reprinted from *Films and Feelings*; Jean Douchet's initial article in *Cahiers du Cinema*; Robin Wood's in *Hitchcock's Films*, David Thompson's in *Movie Man*, and

Leo Braudy's in *Film Quarterly*). While the usual variety of moral, metaphysical, and psychological systems can be read into it, the full experience of the film is clearly a matter of our involvement with highly specific experiences and attitudes whose interpretation normally involves a variety of conventionally separate disciplines (ethics, sociology, cultural anthropology, depth psychology, etc.). Hence the difficulty of "interpreting" the experiences within films in intellectually coherent terms, although fortunately a considerable diversity of ideological interpretation may coexist with a considerable unanimity of dramatic involvement. And this agrees with Hitchcock's taking great care over the variety of disparate cultural backgrounds to be found within the U.S. market. Hence it isn't too difficult for Hitchcock's films, like many others, to be ideologically equivocal yet adequately intersubjective as between the artist and a variety of spectators.

6

Psycho's Music

◆   ◆   ◆

◆   ◆   ◆

There has, in general, been very little written on film music, if perhaps for no other reason that the disciplines of music analysis and film analysis rarely come together in one person. But the fact is that music is an integral component of film, even before the advent of sound, when a piano or full orchestra accompanied the film in the movie house. In a few instances, some directors and composers have had a close, ongoing, working relationship. Think of John Williams and Steven Spielberg.

But no more important relationship has existed in American film than the one between Hitchcock and Bernard Herrmann (the cantankerous composer who came to Hollywood with Orson Welles and scored *Citizen Kane*). Royal Brown's book on film music is one of only a handful of books that treat music and the cinematic image, and his treatment of the Hitchcock-Herrmann artistic relationship is detailed and profound—something Hitchcock himself deigned to recognize, when, in the interview earlier in the book, he talks about the stabbing of Arbogast in musical terms, as Durgnat does the structure of the whole film.

Brown demonstrates how the very structure of the music itself works together with the visual structure of the film. Brown's analysis is sometimes quite technical. However, if you play piano or guitar, his musical notation should be clear. But even if you don't know musical notation, you will see how closely music and image go together, so closely that, listening to Herrmann's music to any Hitchcock film will instantly bring the images of that film to mind.

A few definitions and explanations will be helpful: Brown refers often to the relationship of music and image in the Russian film, *Alexander Nevsky* (1938), directed by Sergei Eisenstein and composed by Sergei Prokofiev. Eisenstein went so far as to create a chart that shows a vertical correspondence between the score, the images, and the abstract patterns in both that occur in one sequence of the film. (The chart can be found in Eisenstein's *The Film Sense*.) Timbre refers to musical tonality. Diachronic and synchronic are ways to visualize meaning-making structure in music, film, language, etc. Diachronic structure is vertical, like chords in music. Synchronic is horizontal, the melody. Diagetic or diegesis refers to the entire fictional world created by a film.

ROYAL BROWN ✦ Herrmann, Hitchcock, and
the Music of the Irrational

[Hitchcock] only finishes a picture 60%. I have to finish it
for him.
—BERNARD HERRMANN

. . . It would seem that contact with the Hitchcockian universe, in which almost every moment of seeming rationality seethes with undercurrents of irrationality, provided [Bernard] Herrmann with the impetus to develop certain devices and to carry them further than he had previously done. One reason for this might be the musical nature of Hitchcock's cinematic style. Certainly, one of the keys to the Hitchcock touch would have to be con- sidered the manner in which the entire body of shots of a given film follows a prearranged plan, so that any one particular shot, much like the "normal" musical chord . . . , has meaning only when considered in the context of the shots surrounding it and,

more broadly, within the temporal elaboration of the entire artistic conception. In this sense, Hitchcock, though always extremely attentive to the narrative elements of his films, comes
closer to a director such as Eisenstein through the creation of a
musically structured cinema. . . . But where Eisenstein worked
closely with his composer to integrate the music (and sounds)
into the film's overall quasi-musical structure, Hitchcock, working separately from his composer, came up with a more dialectical
film/music relationship in which, paradoxically, the synchronicity
of the musical score functions more like that of the single image.
In a way, it is as if the correspondence between music and image
elaborated by Eisenstein for *Alexander Nevsky* were reversed in
Herrmann/Hitchcock, with the visual image seemingly more carried forward by diachronic time than the musical one.

Although Herrmann, with his nonthematic devices, had already been heading toward a more nearly pure film-music genre
that would not cut across the grain of inherently cinematic procedures, the composer obviously sensed that he would have to
further stifle Western music's natural tendency to organize itself
into diachronically elaborated blocks in order not to gild the lily
of Hitchcock's ingeniously organized filmic totalities or to cut into
their effectiveness by setting up conflicting movements. Thus, for
example, Herrmann began to rely even less on the types of dramatic shifts from major to minor mode that one can find in
numerous romantic composers such as Tchaikovsky, and in
countless film scores. Instead, he devised a chordal language that
simultaneously has major and minor implications. With this, and
with the long stretches where no harmonic resolution takes
place—so that the harmonic colors stand even more strongly on
their own and so that the viewer/listener remains suspended—
Herrmann created a *vertical* synchronicity that sets up a strong
opposition to Hitchcock's *horizontally* created synchronicity. And,
of course, the immediacy of effect in the music fortifies and
stresses the deepest emotional content of individual shots or sequences. . . .

By the time he finished *The Wrong Man*, Bernard Herrmann had
already done for Hitchcock what he had not previously been able

to do and was to do only once again: he had scored more than two films for the same director.[1] As for Hitchcock, the director found himself in the happy position of having assembled "his own little group, which included his cinematographer Robert Burks, his camera operator Leonard J. South, his television cameraman John L. Russell (who was also the cinematographer for *Psycho*), his editor George Tomasini, his composer Bernard Herrmann, his personal assistant Peggy Robertson, his costume designer Edith Head, and a number of actors with whom he felt thoroughly at home."[2] The presence of Saul Bass, who did the titles for *Vertigo*, *North by Northwest*, and *Psycho*, did not hurt matters either. One has to think that the establishment of a solid rapport with many of the most important artists and artisans who can contribute to the realization of a film helped bring Hitchcock to the peak he reached in his next three films, *Vertigo* (1958), *North by Northwest* (1959), and *Psycho* (1960). One also has to feel that the opportunity to become immersed over a period of time in the style and manner of a great artist such as Hitchcock helped Herrmann not only to produce what most would consider to be his masterpieces as a film composer, but also to pen music that gives the impression of being not only an inseparable part of the films for which it was composed but also an extension of Hitchcock's personal vision.

Not surprisingly, the music for *North by Northwest*, a comic-thriller respite between the tragedy of *Vertigo* and the horror of *Psycho*, does not immediately strike the listener as offering a typical Herrmann/Hitchcock sound. Indeed, Herrmann designated as "Overture" the fandango (a quick, Spanish dance) that opens *North by Northwest*, whereas the initial music for *Vertigo* and *Psycho* is entitled "Prelude." To the listener, *North by Northwest*'s overture appears to be a kind of set piece easily separable from the body of the film, whereas *Vertigo* and *Psycho*'s preludes seem inextricably attached to the cine-musical action that follows the title sequences. And yet the delicate balances between music and film obviously perceived by both Hitchcock and Herrmann dictated an interesting reversal. Both the *Vertigo* and *Psycho* preludes, which

segue into new musical cues heard behind the post-title sequences, reach a brief point of resolution on D (more solid in
Psycho than in *Vertigo*). Herrmann did write a snappy, two-chord
conclusion to bring the *North by Northwest* overture to a decisive
conclusion in A major (the overture opens in A minor). But it
was obviously felt that the overture as originally scored separated
the title sequence too much from the film, all the more so since
there is no musical segue from the title to the ensuing New York
City shots. Therefore, the overture's final two chords, although
performed on all recordings made of the work, were cut from
the film, so that the music—and therefore the film—remains
unconsummated, suspended on a sustained seventh chord that
never resolves, a device used fairly frequently in the early days of
film scoring. It is as if the visual/narrative "music" takes over from
the music per se. . . .

Unlike *North by Northwest*, *Vertigo* and *Psycho* immediately establish
the type of harmonic color discussed above through the pervasive
use of the "Hitchcock chord" [elsewhere, Brown defines this as
"a minor major-seventh chord in which there are two major and
one minor third. (It should be noted that this type of chord
frequently appears in modern jazz, an idiom that has often been
heard by traditional musical ears as definitely belonging to the
domain of the irrational)"]. In *Vertigo*, this tetrad, formed by adding a major third above a root-position, E-flat minor triad, is first
heard as a repeated series of contrary-motion arpeggios played in
an extremely resonant configuration of high strings, winds, harp,
celesta, and vibraphone. The figure is heard throughout much of
the prelude (see figure 6.1). The identity of this chord is rein-

FIGURE 6.1. Bernard Herrmann, *Vertigo*.

forced, twelve measures into the prelude, by an unbroken, sustained presentation of it in midrange brass (see figure 6.2). The strings-only music in *Psycho* presents an identically structured chord—this one built up by adding a major third above the root-position B-flat minor triad—in the upper register, while the lower register configuration stresses more the augmented nature of the chord. . . . This chord, repeated five times in a characteristic rhythmic pattern, becomes a motif of sorts for the first third of the film (as do several other of the obsessively repeated figures from the prelude; see figure 6.3). Near the end of *Psycho*, just before Lila Crane (Vera Miles) touches Mrs. Bates's mummified body, the high violins sustain a chord on C-sharp-A-F that suggests the "Hitchcock chord" with the root missing. . . . The very nature of these chords, with their simultaneously minor/major aura, immediately throws the viewer/listener off the rationalized center of normal Western tonality into a more irrational, mythic domain in which oppositions have no implications that will be resolved by the passing of time, but exist only as two equal poles of the same unity. Both *Vertigo*'s and *Psycho*'s preludes maintain this framework by having their respective "Hitchcock chords" act as a focal point, continually repeated throughout the nearly three-minute length of the former and the 1'50" length of the latter. The preludes for both films conclude on a D unison. The dreamier *Vertigo* prelude, marked *Moderato assai*, accompanies Saul Bass's dazzling succession of slowly turning, colored, geometrical

FIGURE 6.2.

FIGURE 6.3.

whorls that appear against a black background and that have their point of departure in a woman's eye. In the music, the D on which the prelude concludes is almost constantly present, both as the top note of the "Hitchcock chord" and from time to time in the bass. In measures 3–5, for instance, unisons beneath the arpeggiated figure of figure 6.1 move from D to C, suggesting the harmonic relationship between the prelude (in G minor) and the ensuing "Rooftop" sequence (in C minor) and then, in measures 6–9, they move from a lower E-flat back to D. Whereas *Vertigo*'s prelude suggests tonality, it generally lacks the sense of harmonic movement characteristic of Western music and instead creates a sense of stasis that can be seen as a part of the feminine stereotypes (darkness, passivity) of the title sequence and its imagery, not to mention the whole Orphic bent of *Vertigo*'s narrative and structure. Indeed, Herrmann will later use a similar technique . . . to suggest not only the painting of Carlotta Valdez, but also the apparent reincarnation of the Spanish woman in Madeleine: Carlotta's "theme" initially plays in parallel major thirds over a repeated D, the characteristic habañera rhythm of which . . . provides the audience with a musical point of reference for Carlotta's "Hispanicity." The repeated D in a habañera rhythm will likewise dominate the "Nightmare" sequence.

In *Psycho*'s prelude, the "Hitchcock chord" is repeated so often and at such musically strong moments that it seems to be not only a point of departure, but a point of return as well. The prelude also goes beyond any other Hitchcock music, Herrmann-scored or otherwise, in its array of jarringly dissonant chords, the bitonality of which reflects on the film's ultimate narrative theme. But the lack of harmonic movement is counterbalanced by a frenetic rhythmic drive—the prelude is marked *Allegro (Molto agitato)*—that goes beyond even *North by Northwest*'s opening fandango in intensity.[3] In fact, the *Psycho* prelude proceeds at such a headstrong pace that it can move in and out of almost conventional resolutions without the audience ever getting a chance to relax on them. Thus, the prelude's first motif, which starts off as a simple breaking up of the "Hitchcock chord," strongly suggests the key of D minor by transforming the D-flat of the "Hitchcock

chord" into a leading-tone C-sharp (see figure 6.4). This potential
of *Psycho*'s particular "Hitchcock chord" to be utilized as a rather
kinky cadence chord is borne out by the end of the prelude, in
which a differently voiced version of the opening chord, repeated
a number of times in groups of four in the high violins, finally
gives way to a single, pizzicato, unison D, thus creating something
not unlike a 5→1 cadence with the fifth (A) as the top note and
the D-flat/C-sharp leading tone prominent in the chordal construction. In contrast, *Vertigo*'s "Hitchcock chord" floats above a
potential G-minor tonality that is never fully realized. Even the
prelude's final unison on D, instead of "resolving" to G, simply
drops down one step into the C-minor of the ensuing "Rooftop"
cue. *Psycho*'s slightly more conventional resolution, however,
seems to second the much more linear movement of the black-
and-white, horizontal lines of Saul Bass's title sequence, not to
mention the more phallic orientation of *Psycho*'s particular brand
of violence.

But, although the prelude, like any good prelude, in many
ways sums up the entire work to follow it, it at least comes to a
point of rest, which is more than can be said of *Psycho*'s conclusion,
as we shall see in a moment. Hitchcock immediately picks up on
this in the film's first shot by giving the audience an excessively
precise orientation in time and space, something he almost never
does (*Notorious* is the only other example): over an aerial shot of
Phoenix, Arizona, superimposed titles give us the name of that
city along with the date (Friday, December the eleventh) and even
the time (2:43 P.M.). To accompany this and the descent implied
by the aerial shot, Herrmann segues from the prelude to a descending series of ninth chords, the openness of which strongly
contrasts with the prelude's more claustrophobic chordal lan-

FIGURE 6.4.

guage. Here is a perfect example of a kind of vertical montage, with the downward tracking-in of Hitchcock's camera paralleled by the initial downward movement of Herrmann's ninth chords. But where Hitchcock's Peeping Tom camera sets up a quasi-musical "active expectation" of shots to come, Herrmann's parallel chords—and the repeated two-note figures that interrupt them—evoke a kind of claustrophobic, no-exit stasis. Further, the key that can be felt in the chords of this "City" cue and that is suggested in their spelling in the score, which has no key signature, is A-flat minor, a key which with its seven flats and the tritone relationship of its tonic note to D is about as far from D minor as it is possible to get. Thus Herrmann, in his post-title music, and Hitchcock, in his presentation of what seems to be a very ordinary lovers' tryst, set up a marked polarity between the night world of the title sequence and the day world of "The City."

The separation of these two worlds will, of course, end when Marion Crane (Janet Leigh) and Norman Bates (Anthony Perkins) come together in a seemingly accidental way that is actually set up to be felt as strongly fatalistic, as is Thornhill's falling into the paths of the villains in *North by Northwest*. Once this meeting occurs, the two worlds become inseparable, as Hitchcock suggests by the film's penultimate shot, in which a few frames showing the face of Norman's mummified mother are double-exposed in the dissolve that leads into the film's final shot of Marion's car being dragged up from the quicksand. Herrmann, in turn, resorts to bitonality for the film's final chord: over a D unison in the bass (the last note of a motif that will be discussed further on) we hear a chord that brings together the A-flat minor of "The City" with the D of the prelude (see figure 6.5). Where both *Vertigo* and *North by Northwest* arrive at their conclusions accompanied by tonal,

FIGURE 6.5.

even major-mode, resolutions on the music track, *Psycho*'s final chord refuses to resolve and remains bitonal and bipolar, just as the finale of the film—which follows the psychiatrist's smug explanations with (a) the shot of Norman/mother in his/her prison cell, which ends on a sick joke; (b) the double exposure of Mrs. Bates's mummified head; (c) Marion's car rising phoenix-like from its swampy grave—refuses to consummate the war between the rational and the irrational waged throughout. It should also be noted that... Herrmann's *Psycho* music... manifests a certain more modern musical logic, here on the level of the score's harmonic language, by bringing together in the final chord the two keys that open the film.

Unlike the *North by Northwest* overture, both the *Vertigo* and *Psycho* preludes also contain passages that have themes of sorts. Indeed, in *Vertigo*'s prelude, following a series of rising trills in the woodwinds and strings, the arpeggiated figure, while continuing, suddenly abandons the "Hitchcock chord" configuration and switches to a series of more open, broken ninth chords in a manner recalling the transition from *Psycho*'s prelude to the "City" cue. These chords' top notes, D-C-B-E, form the backbone of *Vertigo*'s principal "love music," which is, in fact, how this twice-heard segment is labeled on the cue sheet (these same four notes are also played, not always in sync with the above, in the orchestra beneath the arpeggiated figure). Further, the harmonization of these notes in the broken chords of the arpeggiated figure is identical to the harmonization, in unbroken chords, of the principal love theme. Thus is Herrmann able, with the two contrasting portions of *Vertigo*'s prelude, to suggest the two sides of the hero's "vertigo."

Herrmann likewise breaks up the *Psycho* prelude's obsessively repeated chords and motifs with a theme brought back at three different points and labeled "*Psycho* Theme" on the cue sheet. As a theme (as opposed to separate motifs expanded in harmonic sequences), it is paradoxically more developed and self-contained than anything to be found in *Vertigo* or *North by Northwest*. Working chromatically around the key of D minor, the twelve-bar theme, which offers no rhythmic variety, starts off in E-flat minor, modulates to E minor, and finally ends up on an F beneath which a form of the "Hitchcock chord" can be heard alternating with another chord, thus acting, as I have already suggested, as a point of return as well as a point of departure. Unlike *Vertigo*'s love theme, which appears throughout the film and is linked to a very specific element of the narrative, the "*Psycho* Theme" remains an inseparable part of the prelude music and is heard only within that context when it appears twice more during the first third of the film. . . . As far as *Psycho*'s prelude is concerned, one has the impression that the limiting of its reappearances, in various forms and with or without the "theme," to the first third of the pic-ture—the last time it shows up is as a brief snippet starting with the figure in figure 6.4 as the detective Arbogast (Martin Balsam) begins his search—corresponds with the "red herring" nature of the film's initial action. For while the *Psycho* prelude has a much more ominous cast to it than *North by Northwest*'s, like the latter its fast-moving, frenetic pace also suggests the flight and pursuit that are what the opening of *Psycho* seems to be about. Once the shower scene abruptly changes that impression, the remaining music takes on a much more static quality and the prelude is forgotten—save in the brief Arbogast cue—except in the subtlest of ways, including the occasional appearance of forms of the "Hitchcock chord."

Other types of film/music interactions contribute as well to the way in which the viewer/listener reads *Vertigo*, *North by North-west*, and *Psycho* and their subtle, subtextual implications. It has often been remarked, for example, that Herrmann's music for *Psycho* offers a rare example of a film score composed for strings alone. As composer/musicologist Fred Steiner has noted, "Such a device imposes strict limits on the available range of tone colors."[4] A quotation Steiner gives from a Herrmann interview shows that the composer obviously intended the restriction of tonal color as a musical equivalent of Hitchcock's exclusion of spectrum colors in favor of blacks, whites, and all the various grays in between: "I felt that I was able to complement the black and white pho-tography of the film with a black and white sound."[5] In this instance, then, one might suggest that *Psycho* offers an ongoing, vertical counterpoint between what might be referred to as visual and musical timbral structure. If, as Steiner points out, the use of black-and-white photography and of strings-only music can actually be considered as enhancing the expressive potential rather than limiting it, the music and photography also have the effect of giving the audience even fewer than the usual number of links with normal reality onto which to grasp, since *Psycho* offers neither the usual array of colors associated with everyday objects (and it must be remembered that by this point in film history more and more Hollywood films were being shot in color—*Psycho* was Hitchcock's last black-and-white film, and only the second one since *I Confess* in 1952) nor the usual diversity of instruments of the symphony orchestra in general and the film-score orchestra in particular.

. . . Another way in which *Psycho* cuts its audience off from normal reality is by its total avoidance of diegetic music. The absence of any music coming over a radio, phonograph, or what have you, has the function of heightening the effect of the film-music convention whereby the appearance of nondiegetic music generally "means" that something out of the ordinary is happening or is about to happen. Since *Psycho* has no diegetic music to somewhat "rationalize" music's very presence in the film, the nondiegetic music gets an even stronger weighting on the side of the irrational. It is as if Norman hears only this "unseen" score. This sets *Psycho* apart from the much more open *North by Northwest*, which not only makes spectacular use of large orchestral forces, it also contains a substantial amount of diegetic music. Indeed, *North by Northwest*'s first post-title musical cue is cocktail lounge music played on violin and piano in the Plaza Hotel. As it happens, this particular song, the McHugh/Adamson "It's a Most Unusual Day," serves as an ironically lighthearted presage of things to come. . . .

If, as I have already mentioned, the general tendency of Herrmann's motifs and occasional themes—and his harmonic progressions—is to move downward, both the *Vertigo* and *Psycho* scores contain prominent passages of parallel upward and downward movement (which, paradoxically, can be elaborated only in the music's horizontal movement) as well as passages of mirrored contrary motion. In terms of the affective impact on the listener, the effect would seem to be quite similar to that of the major/ minor ambiguity that has already been observed. In *Vertigo*'s opening motif (see figure 6.1), the down-up motion of the top line is opposed by the up-down motion of the bottom. In the ensuing rooftop sequence the chromatic string ostinato that runs beneath the brass octaves keeps the triplet figuration (considerably sped up) and presents a mirrored up-down motion. The relationship between this type of up-down tension and *Vertigo*'s narrative and structures should be apparent. All of *Psycho* can ultimately be seen as a series of descents (from Marion's compromised position in her love affair—the opening hotel-room shot even shows her lying down with John Gavin's torso towering over her—and her stealing of the money to the sinking of her car in the quicksand) counterbalanced by attempts, figurative or otherwise, to rise again (Marion's termination of the sexual trysts, her repentance over the stolen money, the final resurfacing of the car from the swamp, not to mention the psychologist's bringing of everything into the "light" of psychoanalytic rationality).

There is one example where music and cinematic movement complement each other to create a striking example of vertical montage in the audio-visual structure. In the sequence where Lila climbs the hill towards the imposingly gothic house where she hopes to find Mrs. Bates, Hitchcock, using crosscutting, alternates objective shots of Lila with subjective shots (her point of view) of the house. At the same time the camera continues to track in towards the house, which becomes larger and larger in the frame (ultimately being replaced by the front door), and to backtrack with Lila's movement forward in the objective shots (which might be said to represent the house's point of view), thus bringing closer and closer together the house and the person the audience is certain will be the next victim there. On the music track Herrmann starts with a sustained F in the violins over another sustained F four octaves lower in the cellos and basses. Just above the bass note the cellos (later the violas) play a four-note motif that rises a semitone at the end. Herrmann then proceeds to slowly bring down the violin line in half steps while, in contrary motion, the bass line and the four-note motive rise in half steps (see figure 6.6). This pattern repeats a total of twenty-four times during the fifty-two-second "Hill" cue until the violins and the first notes of the motif both reach a common F-sharp as Lila and the house also come together. The music then resolves on—what else?—a D–A-sharp–F-sharp chord, the "Hitchcock chord" minus the root. Hitchcock's montage here obviously goes beyond the classic shot/reverse-shot pairing, since the alternation is repeated too many times (twenty-one shots during the musical cue) without the intervention of any other kind of shot, and since much of the alternation works in even segments around two seconds in length. The director here establishes via the editing a rhythm that stands apart from the scene's considerable narrative implications. Herrmann's music, rather than mimicking the rhythm of the editing, creates a musical correspondence, working within its own temporal elaboration, of the movement established over the block of shots. Whereas both the visuals and the music also burst with overtones and undertones of suspense, the "vertical" effect of a musico-visual counterpoint, somewhat broader than what one finds in Eisenstein, cannot be denied. Once again, what Hitchcock accomplishes in the horizontal movement of the editing Herrmann suggests more vertically thanks to the simultaneity afforded by the textures of figure 6.6. And if the composer did not work hand in hand with the director to produce this vertical montage, the artistic qualities of the director's work obviously sufficed, even without a planned aesthetic, to inspire the composer. . . .

Finally, the three notes alluded to before (figure 6.5) form an

FIGURE 6.6.

extremely important motif, which Herrmann has called the *real Psycho* theme, that not only plays an extremely important role in the film but that also has a strong importance in Herrmann's overall musical vision. First heard during the cue labeled "The Madhouse," during which Marion suggests to Norman that he should perhaps put his mother in a home, this slow-tempo motif is formed of a rising minor seventh and a falling minor ninth, the latter an especially dissonant interval to the Western ear (a rising minor ninth that opens the last movement of [Anton] Bruckner's Ninth Symphony casts its somber shadow over the entire movement to follow; see figure 6.7). It has been noted by Graham Donald Bruce[6] that these three notes represent a distortion of a much calmer motif associated with Marion Crane. Repeated a number of times in a descending chromatic sequence during the initial hotel-room sequence, Marion's motif likewise contains three notes in a rising-falling pattern; in this case, however, the interval is a very consonant fifth in both directions, thus forming a calm and static figure that begins and ends on the same note. As Bruce indicates, the opposition of these two three-note motifs seems to support the line, "We all go a little mad sometimes," and to delineate Norman's madness and Marion's sanity as two sides of the same irrational/rational coin, a characteristic Hitchcock theme. More deeply and more darkly, the similarity between Marion's motif and the madness theme also perhaps suggests the manner in which patriarchal culture views madness as a manifestation of the feminine. It is also interesting to note that the madness motif has its roots far back in Herrmann's musical career. . . . The motif, and in fact the entire "Swamp" cue, come straight out of the composer's 1936 Sinfonietta for strings, which provides *Psycho* with some of its other music as well. Another form of the madness theme is associated with a generalized violence that follows one man's attempts to

FIGURE 6.7.

"subdue the beast": at the very end of Herrmann's cantata "Moby Dick" (1936–38), a solo clarinet plays an F, rises to a D-flat (a minor sixth rather than a minor seventh) and then gives way to a contrabassoon playing a C below the F (the minor ninth) as Ishmael speaks the line, "And I only am escaped alone to tell all this." In his 1950 opera, *Wuthering Heights*, Herrmann has the clarinets play a rising minor seventh from E-flat to D-flat, but then drop a semitone to the C below D-flat, rather than the C below the E-flat, as the servant Ellen catches Heathcliff by the arm. She then leads him to a mirror and sings the following: "Do you mark those two lines between your eyes? And those thick brows, that instead of rising, arched, sink in the middle? And that couple of black fiends, so deeply buried, who never open their windows boldly, but lurk, glinting under them, like devil's spies?"[7] Such might be a description of Norman Bates. Herrmann, at the end of his career, brought back the motif one final time to suggest how he saw the psychotic "hero" of Martin Scorsese's 1975 *Taxi Driver*, which was to be the composer's last film score. *Taxi Driver*, released after Herrmann's death, is dedicated to his memory.

Psycho was to be the last great Herrmann/Hitchcock collaboration. . . .

Notes

1. In 1962 Herrmann did the music for a third Henry King film, *Tender Is the Night*, eight years after his last King collaboration. François Truffaut later used the composer for two successive films, *Fahrenheit 451* and *The Bride Wore Black*. It is quite probable that Herrmann would have become the official suspense-film composer for Brian De Palma who, after *Sisters* and *Obsession* (both Hitchcock tributes), would have involved the composer in *Carrie*; Herrmann's death in December 1975 cut short the fruition of that potential tandem.

2. John Russell Taylor, *Hitch: The Life and Times of Alfred Hitchcock* (New York: Pantheon, 1978; rpt. New York: Berkeley, 1980), 266.

3. The tempo used in the film— $\decrescendo = 160$ —is considerably faster than what one hears on either Herrmann-conducted recording, which is around $\decrescendo = 132$.

4. Fred Steiner, "Herrmann's 'Black and White' Music for Hitchcock's *Psycho*," *Filmmusic Notebook,* 1, no. 1 (Fall 1974), 28–36 (part I), and 1, no. 2 (Winter 1974–75), 26–46 (part II). The quotation is from part I, 31.

5. Steiner, "'Black and White' Music," part I, 32. The interview quoted is by Leslie Zador, "Movie Music's Man of the Moment," *Coast FM and Fine Arts* (June 1971), 31.

6. Graham Donald Bruce, *Bernard Herrmann, Film Music and Film Narrative* (Ann Arbor, Mich.: UMI Research Press, 1985).

7. From the libretto adapted from the Emily Brontë novel by Lucille Fletcher, included in the CD by Unicorn/Kanchana UKCD 2050/52/52, 20.

7

Psycho and the Gaze

◆　◆　◆

◆　◆　◆

G aze theory" is essential to the understanding of films because both
films and their audience are constructed through the way the camera
looks at the characters, the characters look at each other, and—usually by
means of editing—we are asked to look at both. Hitchcock was a master of
the gaze. His films are largely structured on the interchange of looks, and he
is especially fond of the kind of "tracking" gaze, in which we see a character
walking, intercut with a tracking shot of what or who the character is
walking toward. A good example of this in *Psycho* occurs when Lila walks
up the steps to the Bates house, and we will see visual examples of this in
the last chapter. But we have already seen reference made to more profound
use of the gaze in the film, particularly Hitchcock's literal play on eyes:
Norman's eye peering through the peephole at Marion; her blood swirling
down the shower drain that dissolves to her dead eye, which the camera
turns and tracks away from in order to gaze at the money that the dead eye
is "seeing." Finally, of course, there is "mother's" empty eye sockets. Toles's
essay, one of the best written on the film, analyzes the eye and the gaze with
extraordinary insight.

The reader should note that Toles makes reference to the nineteenth-century American gothic poet and story writer (who also invented detective fiction) Edgar Allan Poe and to Georges Bataille, the twentieth-century French writer of essays and fiction that dealt with the erotic and the sadistic—much like Hitchcock.

GEORGE TOLES ◆ "If Thine Eye Offend Thee...":
Psycho and the Art of Infection

> I took from my waistcoat-pocket a penknife, opened it,
> grasped the poor beast by the throat, and deliberately cut
> one of its eyes from the socket! I blush, I turn, I shudder,
> while I pen the damnable atrocity.
> —EDGAR ALLAN POE, *"The Black Cat"*

Once all the narrative surprises of Alfred Hitchcock's *Psycho* have been discovered and its more obvious emotional provocations understood, I find that the most potent sources of my uneasiness while viewing it are still unaccounted for. Discomfort with this work is, in my experience, an endlessly renewable response; it is like a slowly spreading stain in the memory. The film feels as stifled and stifling as the indecipherable mind of its protagonist, Norman Bates. Not only does *Psycho* contain no point of release for the viewer—it also remains unclear what precisely the viewer expects (or needs) to be released *from*. *Psycho* offers a number of gestures of release—a snarling tow chain craning a vehicle out of a swamp, Marion's slowly upraised arm as she sits in the tub after the shower stabbing—which turn out to be no release at all. In the latter episode, for example, Hitchcock caresses us, in the dying woman's presence, with a hope of recovery, then immediately crushes it out as Marion extends her arm beseechingly *to us* (why don't you *do* something?), clutches the shower curtain and collapses to the floor. Marion's gesture to save herself answers our felt need, then instantly turns that need against us. Part of Hitchcock's complex achievement in the film is gradually to deprive us of our sense of what "secure space" looks like or feels like.

Psycho properly belongs in the company of such works as Edgar Allan Poe's "Berenice" and Georges Bataille's *Histoire de l'oeil*. These narratives, in addition to achieving their respective forms of pornographic intensity by impersonally rendered shocks, also attach the same obsessive significance to the *eye* as metaphor. Metaphor rather than object: the eye asserts its value and power chiefly through its "migration toward other objects," as Roland Barthes has suggested in his essay on Bataille's *Histoire*.[1] The true content of the narratives has much less to do with the fate of characters than with the fate of an image—the eye—as it undergoes repeated metamorphoses. Perhaps because the eye seems to represent identity simultaneously at its point of fullest concentration and maximum vulnerability, it naturally functions, in works so deeply concerned with aggression, as the principal locus of metaphoric transformation and exchange. The eye, after all, is the ultimate goal for any act of violation; it is the luminous outward sign of the private soul one wishes to smudge with depravity. But the eye is also profoundly linked with repression, and here it becomes threatening to the violator as well. Everything from the realm of experience that has proved damaging to the self, that has inflicted psychic wounds, has been channeled through the eye. Inevitably, the eye will be the vehicle of recurrence. The "invader," whatever his harsh business, always breaks in through the same eye window.

In Poe's "Berenice," there is an effort to limit the eye's potency by treating it as though it were inexpressive to the point of blankness. "The eyes [of Berenice] were lifeless, and lustreless, and seemingly pupilless, and I shrank involuntarily from their glassy stare to the contemplation of the thin and shrunken lips."[2] The narrator flees from the overwhelmingly oppressive presence of the eye, persuading himself in the process that the eye cannot see whatever it is that the narrator himself is afraid to see, that is, what he is struggling to repress. In his desire to avoid Berenice's gaze, however, he begins to fix his attention on her mouth, which instantly acquires the characteristics of a substitute eye. The mouth becomes an organ of intellection, whose teeth are oddly endowed with the eye's "sensitive and sentient power." As Daniel Hoffman has pointed out, Poe requires us to consider, perhaps for the first time, the ways in which "mouth and eye resemble each other. Each is an orifice of the body, surrounded by lips or lids which seem to open and close by a will of their own. Each is lubricated by a fluid of its own origin, and each leads inward ... toward the mysterious interior of the living creature."[3] The eye and mouth also take on the attributes of the "opening" that most frightens the narrator (and, in all likelihood, the author as well), and that forms the content of his repression: the vaginal orifice. The mind has made the latter unthinkable by confusing its properties with the mouth's. The vagina, too, is furnished with teeth that demand to be removed ("long, narrow, and excessively white, with the pale lips writhing about them"). In "Berenice" the eye's transformations can be construed entirely as an effort to block the passage of forbidden material to the conscious mind. With the sort of hideously perverse logic that we encounter in Poe's most distressing tales, the eye must turn into the thing it dreads in order to be spared the sight of it.

Georges Bataille's *Histoire de l'oeil* may appear, at first, to offer a less suitable analogue for the workings of *Psycho* than Poe's "Berenice." Hitchcock resembles Poe in his relentless preoccupation with repressed material. The spread of a massive, buried hurt or wound seems, as in Poe, to paralyze Hitchcock's narrative from within, finally rendering all of its wary, questing-for-order surface activity beside the point. Bataille, by contrast, foregrounds his horror, coolly displays it in a naked state, and plays with it at close range, like an intimate. The sordid and vicious so fully define the surface action of *Histoire* that the reader can't easily feel that this surface is potentially a screen for something worse. Bataille's story, nevertheless, strikes me as blocked in much the same way that Poe's and Hitchcock's are. His central overdetermined image—the eye, once again—feels like the only solid thing, the only living variable in a world of copulating phantoms. (The characters dwell in "a world so frail that mere breath might have changed us into light."[4]) Eyes and their metaphoric substitutes—eggs, a saucer of milk, a bull's testicle—are visually "there" for us in a way that nothing else is. Bataille imagines a world in which the eye, divorced from a specific personality and body, can pursue a life of pure objecthood, witnessing with pristine detachment acts of staggering vileness. Even when the eye becomes the focus of these acts (to be caressed, licked, pissed upon, punctured), it somehow always seems to float free in the end, aloof and intact. Bataille's repeated emphasis on the slicing and spilling open of eyes has the quality of a magician's demonstration: however mutilated the ceremonial object appears to be, it is perfectly restored in an instant. Though continually assaulted, the "eye" of the narrative can never go blind.

Punishment inflicted on the eye is not only a means of severing someone's ties with the world (as in the case of Oedipus); it can also be a way of reducing one's consciousness to the status of an object, so that one must learn to deal with consciousness entirely in object terms. The torture of the eye can mark a refusal of inwardness. One can't get past the literal eye, Bataille insists. Nothing stands behind it. Bataille's psychic strategy is to make his inner world so ossified and remote that no living experience, no emotionalized thread of memory can adhere to it. When Bataille addresses us in what we are meant to accept as his own voice, in the final section of *Histoire de l'oeil*, he disturbs us more thoroughly than at any point in his previous litanies of the monstrous. He recounts memories of his childhood—an utterly frozen landscape—as though they belonged to someone else. His hideous family ordeals are assigned the same value, and given precisely the same sheen of obscenity, as the events of the preceding narrative. Bataille's language refuses at every point to possess what it touches: it is truly a dead language. One finds it almost inconceivable that it could have been formed from the inside, that a life could speak through it.

Tonally, Bataille's endeavor to empty himself through indifference approximates (in function and effect) the austere, insulating wit of Hitchcock's *Psycho*. The best account of Bataille's attraction to the possibilities of indifference occurs in a passage from his

study of Manet's paintings: "Manet's was *supreme indifference*, effort-
less and stinging; it scandalized but never deigned to take notice
of the shock it produces. . . ."[5] The stuff indifference is made of—
we might say its intensity—is necessarily manifested when it enters actively into play. It often happens that indifference is revealed as a vital force, or the vehicle of a force otherwise held in
check, which finds an outlet through indifference.[5] The stuff of
indifference is made of—we might say its intensity—is necessarily
manifested when it enters actively into play. It often happens that
indifference is revealed as a vital force, or the vehicle of a force
otherwise held in check, which finds an outlet through indifference. Bataille's *Histoire* aspires to show us the paradoxical vitality
of an indifference without limits. This indifference might be said
to commence at that hypothetical point in the life of an endless
scream when the sound is so customary that it is no longer
worthy of notice. Personal pain is generally regarded as the one
area of experience to which insensibility cannot extend. If, like
Bataille's forever entranced character Marcelle, we were to become so lost to our feelings that we had no way of "telling one
situation from another," we would still be alive to the shock of
physical torment. It is this last bastion of aliveness that Bataille
desires to level out. What *Histoire*'s narrator reports are agonies
without personal dimensions, sensations that mimic those of mis-
ery but that somehow exist in a flat, becalmed state. By granting
pain a significance, by making any form of emotional concession
to it, we only increase its power over us. Let us rather do life the
appropriate disservice of denying to all of it the force of a lasting
impression. Indifference alone rescues us from the humiliation of
engagement.

Wit is Hitchcock's less conspicuous means of announcing *his*
indifference, his refusal to be engaged or soiled by his transactions
with suffering. The persistent presence of wit in *Psycho* should not
be mistaken, in the calmness of its operations, for a mitigation of
brutality. *Psycho*'s wit is hard and deeply ingrown; it stays well
below the surface of action, strangely unavailable (on a first viewing) to characters and audience alike. It is only with Norman's
final speech that the director's mode of joking seems to merge

with the awareness of a figure within the film's world. When the mysteriously mocking voice of "Mrs. Bates" at last reaches us, we cannot avoid the feeling that in its paradoxically "vacant" depravity it is the one voice we have heard that genuinely expresses the film's tone: "It is sad when a mother has to speak the words that condemn her own son." Bataille once wrote that "decent people have gelded eyes. That's why they fear lewdness." Mrs. Bates, whose sockets are both full and hollow, directly scrutinizes us (the viewers) with the gelded eyes of decency. She speaks quietly to us of a mother's duty to put an end to a bad son while we are confounded by the sight of her effortlessly inhabiting the lost son's body. (Yet another case of a character's gaze turning into the image it is forbidden to see.)

One is not really permitted to go anywhere with this image, or with the speech that accompanies it. Everything about them is sealed in, like the dead eye "soaked with tears of urine" that peers out of Simone's womb near the close of *Histoire*. We are almost beyond the language of "implications" here. Mrs. Bates's speech, imposed on Norman's rigid features, is offered as the impenetrable punch line of the joke that is *Psycho*. In the widest possible sense, we are left in the dark.

For Hitchcock, who is as sedate and comfortable in his chair as Mrs. Bates is in hers, wit always has the right to assert its innocence. It provides the inner life with a means of guarding itself absolutely in the very act of unveiling. Wit opens a place for the self to stand, composed and invulnerable, at a vast remove from any sense of pain that could damage it or spoil its game. Wit allows one to punish to one's heart's content, in the manner of Mrs. Bates, and yet remain blameless. It is the public guarantee that a crime or sin (regardless of appearances) has not quite been committed. The underlying content of art that compulsively seeks out some form of "joke container" for the expression of disorder may be understood as "the holding back from things," a phrase Sanford Schwartz has recently applied to the early paintings of de Chirico. "The pictures are about waiting, keeping oneself clean and untouched. The undercoating of nightmarish dread in them comes from someone who fears making a certain move."[6]

The fear of making a move is pervasive in Hitchcock's work, but it achieves special prominence in *Psycho*, where neither the characters nor the imagery seem to possess any alternative to immobility. Perhaps it is the complete dissociation of authorial self from an imagery that is struggling to express it that gives to *Psycho*, "Berenice," and *Histoire de l'oeil* their "infected" character. The normal poetic activity of making metaphors becomes precarious in these works because images have somehow lost the capacity for internal growth. An image cannot build beyond itself, provoking new connections with the "world at large" when it is entirely cut off from the impulse, desire, or need that called it into being. Instead of widening its range of associations, it can only replicate itself obsessively, craving the origin that is denied it, futilely attempting to burrow inward. The artist can neither separate himself from his dominant image nor see it plainly enough to penetrate it. Art that lacks all mobility, as this art does, can only fester in the place where it's stuck—and hence communicates by infection, spreading the mess that can't be gotten rid of to whatever it touches. Bataille, Poe, and Hitchcock cannot—in the works we're examining—give their oppressive metaphors any outward, public meaning except that of shock; but they are equally blocked from carrying the "eye" image inside. It is the interior, above all, from which this image is in flight. Like Scottie Ferguson, standing traumatized at the edge of the Mission Bell Tower in the final shot of Hitchcock's *Vertigo* (1958), unable to take a single step forward or back, these narratives can only articulate the hopeless stasis that has engendered them.

Having made some progress in establishing the nature of the metaphor we are concerned with, I will try to show how it operates in the shower murder sequence of *Psycho*. Once more we are confronted with a narrative situation in which a vicious, morally appalling act (murder this time), that would seem to demand our full emotional engagement, is subordinated to an eye's encounter with visual analogues. Why are we encouraged to notice, while Marion Crane is being stabbed, that the shower rose, Marion's screaming mouth, and finally the drain into which her

blood flows all correspond, at some level, to the victim's con-
gealed eye? In a culminating extreme closeup, this eye contem-
plates us with the alert fixity of death, while a false tear, formed
by a drop of shower water on Marion's face, announces that
emotion (of any kind) has no further part to play here. The tear
might as well be a fly: nothing is but what is. Why does Hitchcock
linger so long over this image, and why does the match cut
between the drain and the corpse's eye seem so conclusively to
define the imaginative center of the film?

Oddly enough, Marion does not appear to lose her place in
the world of *Psycho* after being brutally slain. Instead, one has the
feeling that she has at long last *found* her proper relationship to
that world. When Hitchcock's camera seems to emerge from the
darkness within the drain *through* Marion's eye, and then eases back
further to reveal her twisted head insensibly pressed against the
floor, the camera comes as close as it ever will to caressing the
object placed in front of it. We are being invited—before we have
had any chance to recover our equilibrium—to participate in the
camera's eerie calm by looking at things in the ways that the
camera instructs us. How *evenly* dead this girl is. How perfectly
and compliantly she harmonizes with the other blank surfaces in
her environment. Turbulence has surprisingly given way to an
order, a settled view, that nothing can put a stop to.

The camera elects to remain in a room that is temporarily
deprived of any human presence. Its purpose in doing so is to
tranquilize this setting by invoking an aesthetic response to it.
The fearful disarrangement of the bathroom space that horror
has just visited is not simply curtailed, it is denied. By the time
Norman rushes into the motel room, discovers the body, and
turns away from it in panicky disbelief, his response is already
disproportionate to ours. His anxiety subtly registers as an over-
reaction. Norman's agitated gestures fly in the face of the hypnotic stillness and order that the gliding camera of the previous
scene proposed as normative, reasonable.

For a number of years now, the standard means of justifying
the shower murder to viewers who find it repellent has been V. F.
Perkins's argument that Hitchcock's skillful montage succeeds in

"aestheticizing" its cruelty.[7] After all, we never actually see the knife penetrating Marion's flesh; we are only required to imagine it. Clearly this line of defense needs to be reexamined. There seems to be an underlying assumption that an aesthetic effect automatically acts as a cleansing agent, or as a guarantee of moral discretion in the creative process. But as we have seen in the case of "Berenice" and *Histoire de l'oeil*, even the most unsavory, abhorrent imagery can be made to yield a powerful aesthetic impression.

Before drawing any conclusions about the formal lucidity of Hitchcock's conception of the shower sequence, one would do well to consider the massive weight that this episode achieves within the total narrative structure. In Robert Bloch's potboiler novel, from which *Psycho* was adapted, Marion's death—far from being the central action in the plot—is matter-of-factly reported in a single, terse sentence. If it is appropriate to point out that Bloch made nothing of an event that Hitchcock responded to with astonishing imaginative intensity, it is also appropriate to inquire why Hitchcock made so much of it. Does it seem either dramatically feasible or fitting that a female protagonist whose status in the narrative never rises above that of pitiable victim should be disposed of in so extravagant, prolonged, and visually intoxicating a fashion? Is Marion's shabby, useless death a proper occasion for a virtuoso set piece? Surely an abbreviated, less conspicuously artful presentation would honor the victim more, if the *meaning* (in human terms) of what transpired figured at all in the artist's calculations.

The consequence of Hitchcock's aestheticized rendering is, instead, to enlarge the minutiae, in the manner of a pornographer prowling around flailing torsos, seeking out details to close in on. Hitchcock wants to make the act of slicing wholly *legible*, as opposed to merely averting his gaze. Hitchcock designs the stabbing to be as salaciously riveting as possible. We are meant—in fact, positively encouraged—to *see it all*, both what he shows and what he refrains from showing. The blanks that his editing leaves can only be filled in one way. Marion's degradation is increased immeasurably by our awareness that nothing in the moment-to-moment scrutiny of her ordeal is random or accidental. The entire murder feels densely inhabited by the director himself. What are we to make of his calm determination to extract a kind of classical shapeliness and beauty from this broad, unbeautiful pour of chaos?

It is impossible to understand the vision that *Psycho* as a whole is expressing in any terms other than those used in the shower sequence. But, as I hope to have demonstrated, Marion's murder refuses to accommodate any of the humanized or aesthetically dignified meanings one would be inclined to project onto it. I am sure that Hitchcock was not trying to deceive us when he said that the shower sequence had *no* meaning, as far as he was concerned. He placed it in that strangely aseptic realm of "pure cinema," where images, like poems, should not mean but be. For an image simply "to be," in Hitchcock's terms, it must be acknowledged as something with no depth—the screened image is both literally and ontologically flat. As Garrett Stewart has suggested in his essay on [Buster] Keaton's *Sherlock, Jr.* [1924], the most formidable illusion of movie space is that we seem to be looking into a frame "past which is recess and perspective."[8] Hitchcock's style is predicated on the belief that the *surface* of a screened image is absolute. It never yields to anything "within." The only interior it has is supplied by the mind of the spectator.

For Hitchcock the passage of material from life to the cinema involves an immediate (and total) subtraction of unmanageable elements. Film is not a medium for introspection. Disordered activity of any sort has no place there. Hitchcock conceives the act of building a patterned sequence of images as a means of asserting control over a "problem" without ever being required to *examine* it. In designing a series of shots, the mind can limit itself to lateral motion. There is no need to "look down," to probe past the image surface. One can always substitute further complications of formal arrangement for the distasteful messiness of analyzing one's position. Joseph Stefano, the screenwriter of *Psycho*, memorably described Hitchcock directing a nude model in the shower sequence. He stood on a platform above the shower in his dark business suit, "a model of rectitude and composure. One sensed that Alfred Hitchcock does not stand in front of naked women, and that he has precisely this feeling about himself, so that for him she was not naked, and that was that."[9]

Arranging a composition for the camera is the way to demonstrate that its content is manageable. And the only level on which this content has to be seen and accounted for is the level of form. It is possible, therefore, for Hitchcock to work in the very midst of obsessive fears and unacceptable desires, yet not be confronted by them. His negotiations with obsession are never carried on from the inside. He has only to "frame" his anxiety, flatten it into an image, for it to be held in place. Viewers, of course, as he well knows, will very likely "dirty" themselves as they imagine the experience that he has at no point felt obliged to touch. They cannot keep the images at a regulated distance (and handle them with the proper delicacy) because they did not control the process that brought them into being. Control, as always for Hitchcock, is to be understood here as ability not to internalize. However much he may be stirred by his proximity to the extremes of sadism in the shower killing, he is persuaded that the search for visual order is a permanent safeguard against fixation, and that he can endlessly brood upon the separate details of the action while keeping his perceptions chaste. Hitchcock's decision to link the "eye" throughout the shower sequence with as many other ovals as possible derives from his conviction that any painful subject can be stabilized if one locates a point of concentration apart from the "thing itself." There is invariably something distinct from the business of suffering to claim one's attention.

But eyes and eye surrogates, as the examples of Poe and Bataille make clear, are never resting places. In fact, the three Hitchcock films that seem to me the purest (and most extreme) embodiments of his imaginative concerns (*Rear Window* [1954], *Vertigo*, and *Psycho*) make an affliction of the eye their ascendant theme. *Vertigo*'s credits present us with a masklike female face in which only the nervously moving eyes betray any distress. The camera then proceeds to move into one of these eyes, passing mysteriously through the pupil and coming out "behind" it—thus marking a path to which Hitchcock will return in *Psycho*. Only in the latter he reverses his direction, as the dark drain "proposes" a withdrawal from an eye that is dead. Interestingly, all of the eyes that matter in *Psycho* are counterparts of this dead eye—cruel, staring, or frozen, they seem to hold only one expression. And eventually we discover that this single, ominous look, forever resurfacing like a figure in a nightmare, has belonged from the outset to Norman Bates.

Earlier, I suggested that Norman's voice at the end of *Psycho* is the only authentic voice we hear in the film. He is simultaneously revealed—at that instant when he finally meets the camera's gaze and looks directly at us—as possessing the only acceptable pair of eyes. The man whose stare has become an awful and limitless conjunction of emptiness is *Psycho*'s one true seer. The hobby of this seer, one recalls, was taxidermy, which allowed him to conduct studies of birds to find out how eyes "die" (or, as in his mother's case, fail to die—transformed into living wounds that the son must try to heal). The film as a whole is equally concerned with the process by which eyes surrender their identity (or life) to Norman. By a spectacular feat of absorption, Norman ultimately manages to contain the entire world of the film in his pitiless glare.

Psycho's next-to-last image is a dissolve of Norman's face into the mummified features of his mother; for a moment he seems to peer through the empty sockets in which his eyes are now imaginatively sealed. The dissolves could continue almost indefinitely, however, because Hitchcock's key imagery in the film is nearly all constructed on the same principle: Mr. Lowery's accusing glance that launches Marion's flight by car; the policeman's sunglasses looming gigantically over her as she wakens from sleep; Marion, throughout her nocturnal journey, peering toward us anxiously from behind the wheel of her car as we share her thoughts. (At one point, when imagining Cassidy's threat to replace his stolen money "with her fine, soft flesh," she smiles in close-up, and her expression hauntingly anticipates Norman's final, mocking look.) Following Marion's introduction to Norman, we are shown the silent company of stuffed night birds that "watch" Norman in his parlor, one of whose wings are extended so that it appears forever in passage toward its prey; when Marion has left the parlor, we see Norman's eye, in mammoth close-up, intently fixed upon his hidden peephole—a large, dark, circular gouge in the wall with a single point of light at the center. (The hole-eye linkage clearly prepares us for the comparison of eye and drain.) And as the shower sequence commences, there is a close-up of a toilet bowl flushing down a torn scrap of paper that Marion doesn't wish anyone to see. By this juncture, as we have already observed, the eye is fully available for complex metamorphic exchanges with other objects. The toilet bowl, like the drain, is yet another visual sign for the eye evacuating its contents.

Once Marion is dead, and Norman sets about eliminating all traces of her presence, two additional eye metaphors emerge. Thus Hitchcock completes the series that began with Norman at his peephole by circling back to him and, in effect, showing how Marion's eye has resolved itself into his. There is an overhead close-up of the circular rim and black interior of Norman's pail as first his bloodied cleaning rags and then the mop with which he has cleaned the sides of the tub are thrust into it. Here, and in the more potent image that soon follows—the top of Marion's car forming a ghostly white spot in the middle of an encircling swamp—the hollow eye of the drain is replaced by more clotted and retentive ovals: eyes filling up rather than emptying, but only with unwanted things. Norman contrives to make whatever disturbs him disappear from sight, but, instead, like the vehicle suspended in the swamp, the objects of his anxiety look back at him.

Norman relates to his field of vision as though it were somehow interchangeable with the field of consciousness. (In this respect, he resembles Hitchcock.) The successful manipulation of perception is taken to mean that the mind is under equally strict direction. Life, for Norman, has gradually been reduced to an endless tidying up of his barely manageable visual space. His is forever devising fresh hiding places for his mother's (and his own) garbage. Anything that his mother judges depraved (i.e., anything provoking strong desires in Norman—and mother always knows) must be dropped from the perceptual frame. "Out of sight, out of mind" is the chief article of faith in the Bates household. If one thinks about it carefully, one realizes that the dramatic situation in *Psycho* literally dictates that Norman and his "mother" can never see the same things at the same time and never see them in the same way. They are constantly vying for possession of the same visual field; whoever "sees" at a given moment is empowered to make an interpretation, but the meaning of the visual field alters radically as control of it shifts back and forth. The question that I feel is necessary to consider is, Where does Norman's vision go, where does his knowledge and desire hide during those intervals when he is not permitted to absorb what his eyes perceive?

Norman's extreme but eminently logical solution to his impossible filial bind is to learn how to see and do the things that are forbidden to him without actually seeing anything. That is to say, the fact of his presence and involvement in acts that are literally unthinkable for him is "dropped from the frame." As his mother blindly wields the knife, Norman's eyes are somewhere else, trying to stay focused on what is decent. It is doubly imperative then that he do a thorough cleaning job when "something bad" happens because he must expunge the event from both public *and* personal view. As Norman desperately suppresses his own powers of vision, he comes to believe that the work of seeing has been taken over by the inert forms that fill his landscape. His closed world has truly become a beast with a thousand eyes, whose sole end is to keep him under surveillance.

Norman's perception is restricted to the order he manages to maintain within his frame. Beyond that increasingly close-at-hand point where order ceases, he encounters a blank wall. But the various "holes" he has filled for the sake of order—the swamp, the fruit cellar, the parlor with its mounted birds, his mother's corpse—have sprouted eyes whose awareness is rooted in that ugly disorder Norman has gone to such pains to eradicate. The blank space where Norman's vision tapers off is the place where theirs begins: "they" can see further because "they" can see into things. And because Norman's carefully limited outer world has become hopelessly confused with his inner world, he expresses any form of looking as a violation. As he tells Marion in his parlor, he knows what it feels like to have "cruel eyes" studying him. His survival, however, depends on his ability to keep the perception of this undifferentiated other split off from his own. He cannot allow himself to imagine, even for a moment, what it is those alien, impenetrable eyes might know about him.

This aspect of Norman's predicament helps to explain the omnipresence of mirrors and reflections in *Psycho*. Beginning with Marion's decision to steal forty thousand dollars, which she arrives at while looking at herself in the mirror, almost every interior scene prominently features a mirror that doubles as a character's image, but that *no one* turns to face. In Marion's case, as James Naremore points out in his valuable *Filmguide to Psycho*, the ability to confront her own image is lost after the theft.[10] This is one of the many ways in which Marion's surrender to her "nameless urge" serves to draw her ineluctably into Norman's frame of reference. After Marion is repeatedly shown attended by reflections of herself that she does not acknowledge (in the bathroom of the used car lot, at the motel registration desk, and in the motel room itself), the pattern is given a sudden, disquieting twist. While Marion is stationed in profile beside the motel's dresser mirror, Norman stands in for the reflection in the following series of shots. In Hitchcock's shot-countershot cutting between Norman and Marion, we notice that the profile views of the two facing figures are perfectly symmetrical. Norman occupies the extreme right-hand side of an imbalanced frame, Marion the extreme left-hand side in alternate shots: mirror images.

Norman's imprisonment in the midst of steadily more ominous reflections is shadowed forth in Marion's situation at the motel. In the world of *Psycho*, whenever one picture of the self cracks or is denied recognition, another more dangerous image must form in its place. Inside the crack, so to speak. Marion refuses to look at herself, so Norman will look for her. He will reflect her life by making it into a likeness of his own, although he doesn't understand (any more than she does) what this will entail. Once this life mirroring has commenced, it proceeds on a number of levels. Norman seems to stand in for Sam Loomis, Marion's lover, as well as for her (the physical resemblance of the two men has been noted by many critics). The last, frustratingly inconclusive meeting of the two lovers is replayed in a more somber key by Norman and Marion.

Sam Loomis, who is not strong enough to act upon his love (or whose love is not strong enough to require action), gives way to an even weaker Norman, whose emotional energies have been strangled and for whom "falling in love" can only mean what it means to Scottie Ferguson in *Vertigo*: falling into the void at one's center. Norman's eye for beauty is really an incurable appetite for nothingness. And yet strength of a certain kind exists in Norman. He is sufficiently strong to punish a *desire* for love that has no right to assert itself (mother says so) and nowhere to go. Unlike Sam, he will carry things through to an end point; if Marion can only threaten and confuse him as an image of love, she can be made to reflect him in some other way that will allow for a completing action.

Marion had stolen the money, as she sees it, because she chose to stake everything on love. She flees by car through the night, driving, she imagines, toward her love, but at some point in her journey passes "through the looking glass" and ends up facing Norman instead, a ghastly inversion of that love. Then Hitchcock, having revealed the things that prevent love from becoming what it wants to be in the world of this film, discloses what is left for it to become. "On the right hand could slide the left glove," as Robert Graves wrote in his poem "The Terraced Valley." "Neat over-under."

Norman's "courtship" of Marion revives, in ghostly fashion, many of the gestures, conversational topics and objects of attention present in *Psycho*'s opening love scene—whatever filled the intervals between Sam and Marion's dispirited, unsatisfying embraces. The meal that Marion "didn't touch" in the hotel (and that Mrs. Bates wouldn't permit her to touch in the intimate precincts of her household) is finally completed with Norman in the motel parlor. Both Sam and Norman are given a moment where they throw open a window in response to the felt pressure of Marion's presence—Sam, out of discomfort with her talk of marriage; Norman, in his embarrassment at being alone with Marion in her bedroom. (The sudden, rasping sound of the venetian blinds as Sam jerks them up matches the sound and motion of the shower curtain being torn open.) Marion counters Sam's suggestion that they leave the hotel together by pointing out that he hasn't got his shoes on. These are the joking terms of their final separation. Sam remains behind, and we last observe him standing motionless, staring down at his stockinged feet. Just before Norman leaves Marion's motel room to go up to the house to arrange for their private supper, he registers his guilty delight at her acceptance of his invitation by stammering instructions to get herself settled "and—and take off your wet shoes." The removal of her shoes will serve to hold her there in the bedroom until his return—that is to say, in this particular bedroom, the site of all his secret erotic investigations. For Norman, requesting a woman to take off any article of apparel signals a daring advance in intimacy; the mention of shoes is his nervous, shorthand approach to "Why don't you slip into something more comfortable—and revealing?"

Later, in the parlor, Norman picks up the thread of Sam's earlier talk about "traps." Sam had described his life as a confinement within the "tiny back room" of his hardware store. (After Marion's death, Hitchcock provides a long-shot view of Sam at his desk in this room, from a camera positioned in the main doorway of the store. This shot neatly matches the hallway perspective of Norman seated at the kitchen table of the Bates's mansion directly before the shower scene. The mammoth interior of this house visually dwarfs him; the only spaces that he feels free to occupy in his own person are "out-of-the-way" rooms behind the main living area.) Sam had also complained to Marion about having constantly to "sweat for people who aren't there." In the parlor scene, Norman vastly extends the scope of Sam's plight. "We scratch and claw, but only at the air, only at each other. And for all of it, we never budge an inch." There is no distinction to be made between "the air" and "each other." We want the world to at least double itself for us when seen through eyes of love, but it remains intractably single (whatever our delusions to the contrary). We are always much "further out" than others think, to paraphrase a line of British poet Stevie Smith, "And not waving but drowning."[11] The only movements we make that are truly answered are those we see in our mirrors. And this, too, is empty space; we are forever thrown back on ourselves, possessors of nothing.

The only fully spontaneous moment Sam and Marion have together—one in which Marion's desperation is as much in evidence as her attachment to her lover—occurs when she runs toward Sam for an extended embrace in front of the large screen of a closed venetian blind. The next time Marion is placed before such a screen, it has become a shower curtain. Now it is Norman who is coming toward *her*, to be joined with Marion in a different kind of embrace. Touching and caressing have, of course, been the subtracted element in Norman's halting variation on Marion's assignation with Sam. He has only managed to touch her nakedness with his eye. At last he presents himself to her without barriers—on her side of the curtain screen—and enacts his "violent feeling" for her in the only way possible for him.

From Marion's standpoint, the shower (prior to the attack) is both a moral cleansing and an act of self-restoration. Afterwards, she will once again be able to meet her own gaze in the mirror. But as we have seen, Norman has replaced the image she turned away from. Having lost sight of herself once, while in the grip of compulsion, she is denied any chance to find her way back. In the course of her journey to Bates's motel, she has had to escape from one distrustful, accusing face after another. "Who are you and what are you doing?" is the unspoken question in every conversation. And Marion could not begin to formulate an answer. Everything conspires to turn her world inside out. In this condition, she at last lights upon the sympathetic image of Norman Bates, someone whose look she is not afraid of. He offers to keep her company in the darkness. As she listens to him divulge the story of his barren life, he becomes more troubling, but at the same time she begins to recognize herself in his tormented presence (or thinks she does). She sees him as the instrument of her salvation: "This could be my life; I must not let it be." Having reached this understanding, Marion turns away from Norman, just as she withdrew from the uncomfortable figure regarding her in her mirror at home. But she is forced to confront this dim, hovering reflection one more time in the shower episode.

In Hitchcock's exceptionally demanding metaphoric scheme, where the eye is the faculty for "unseeing" and mirrors are present only so that they can be avoided, the shower murder, as I've previously argued, is the point of greatest metaphoric blockage, and consequently, greatest pressure for release. It is the place where Hitchcock, like Bataille and Poe (but equally like Norman and Marion), can neither separate himself from the image, nor see it plainly enough to penetrate it. Hitchcock goes to such extreme lengths to create the impression that Norman and Marion and Marion and Sam mirror each other because the world of *Psycho* is traumatically fixated; it has no capacity for enlargement. Everything in it seems to be formed at the point of rupture in Norman's vision—the blocked passage between his public self and "lost" private self. This is the point at which *nothing* can ever be seen or taken in. In his brilliant study of metamorphosis in literature, *The Gaping Pig*, Irving Massey suggests that "trauma, like art, develops at the point where imitation replaces action. . . . We mimic what we cannot fight off."[12] The shocks in *Psycho* all seem to erupt from within, as they do in dreams, where characters form and reform under the pressure of a single image, and where all movement leads to the same place. ("And for all of it, we never budge an inch.")

I have already compared the shower curtain to the screen of the venetian blind in the hotel room. (And recall that Hitchcock's camera, anticipating Norman's shadow slowly advancing behind the curtain, introduced itself in *Psycho* by entering like a phantom behind the venetian blind and probing the dark opening of an eye-like window. This first descent into a vacant eye is the action that brings the film's world into focus.) The curtain also invites comparison with a mirror. Norman's dark silhouette serves as a mirror for Marion when she whirls to face it because all the unresolved elements in her experience seem to converge in it with hallucinatory force: the car windshield wiper making "knife strokes" against the rain; the policeman's huge, disembodied head in dark glasses startling her awake that morning; the swooping owl in Norman's parlor; Norman's visible desire for her; his anxious, lonely eyes suddenly turning rigid and glowering as he leans forward in his chair; her fear of being captured and exposed; and ultimately, ending at the place where she (and the film) began, her own body lying motionless (on a bed/bathroom floor), eyes fixed upon a man looming over her: Sam/Norman. Marion's recognition—that this death is meant for her and not anyone else, that all her confused strivings have been directed to this goal, which imitates her life and which she fends off like a traumatic recollection—solves nothing, of course. It simply places her squarely on the hopeless ground she is doomed to occupy: "Now I know where I am." This is more than the viewer can say as the film's action comes to a dreamlike halt with the death of its apparent subject, and then—inexplicably—continues.

When Hitchcock's camera finally relinquishes its hold on Marion, after fully expressing its fascination with her immobility, it moves out of the bathroom and over to Marion's night table, where her stolen money lies in a newspaper. The camera registers uncertainty about what its subject should now be; it does not appear to know what it's looking for. This is an uncertainty shared by all of *Psycho*'s remaining characters.[13] Once Marion's theft, her guilt, and the money itself have been eliminated as concerns of the film, Hitchcock contrives to keep the subject of *Psycho* physically absent and morally indefinable. It is pushed out of everyone's reach. No one, including Norman, is in possession of what is withheld. To the extent that it can be identified at all, *Psycho*'s "issue" becomes the silhouette behind the curtain—an image poised to shatter at the eye's moment of contact with it, like the double reflection that startles Marion's sister Lila during her search of Mrs. Bates's bedroom. (As Lila turns to accost the woman behind her, what she discovers is her own distraught face in the looking glass.) *Psycho*'s missing subject is perhaps best described as a figure glimpsed but never quite seen: a dim outline in a lighted upstairs window; the spectral imprint of a rigidly coiled form on a mattress. On a first viewing, we chiefly feel it as a threat of recurrence that is under no one's control.

The various subjective filters through which the search for answers is carried forward (Arbogast, Lila, Sam) seem to know less and less about the quality of dread that fills the air. Our only link with these characters is the act of searching, but they are only able to search for things that we know are not there. (Marion rolled up in a curtain; the money rolled up in newspaper.) They futilely retrace each other's steps and imitate each other's actions, without ever having the sense of what their eyes need to connect with. In effect, they are all the same character, existing only to pass through the rooms of the motel and house, exposing themselves to the disturbing features of a landscape that will never be made clear. This composite searcher belongs to the "inside world" as surely as Norman Bates does. From Norman's side of the mirror, it is the strangers' search which poses the danger of uncontrollable repetition: it is the shadow of *his* trauma that seems to draw nearer with Arbogast's and Lila's furtive movements through his domain. They are closing off his mental exits, sealing him in. The only place for him to hide from the object of his dread is within the object itself: "Hold me, Mother; hold me tight. I'm afraid to go to sleep." As long as mother is there to protect him, the dark places can't be opened. To quote Massey once again, trauma "may be a thought that has never been killed, that has never been set off from the self."[14] Norman's murders are attempts to eliminate a thought that must not take form. Killing is, paradoxically, the deepest place of forgetting.

It remains to inquire why so many of the films made by Hitchcock in this period place the problems opposing the characters so fully in the realm of mind, but out of the mind's reach. Hitchcock's customary starting point in a film project was a situation in which *outer* circumstances had somehow passed out of one's control. The emphasis shifted decisively in *Vertigo*, where inner circumstances become the unmanageable factor. As anyone who has studied Hitchcock's style is aware, the basic building block in his narrative structures is always the "reacting look" of his characters. Major scenes are typically conceived as an intricate juxtaposition of glances with various objects and figures to which the perceiver has a clearly defined emotional relation. Hitchcock generates suspense by uniting the viewer's gaze with a character who, for some reason, is prevented from seeing his situation whole. Characters are menaced either by details they've failed to see or by the sheer mass of what they do see. The audience generally has no difficulty in reading a character's look because they know what to make of the objects set before him; they understand why the character finds those things important.

In *Vertigo* Hitchcock is no longer dealing with "transparent" reactions. The precise nature of Scottie Ferguson's relationship to what he sees is in doubt from the beginning. *How* his eye sees becomes vastly more important than the information it is given to process. His perceptions reflect a mounting internal strain and distortion; there has been a poisoning at the source. The camera in Vertigo repeatedly performs hypnotic circling movements around its subjects so that everything comes to be seen in the light of Scottie's disorder. Circling also defines Scottie's problematic visual relationship with the objects that seriously engage him: they form a vortex for the eye. He stands helpless under their spell. For example, Scottie discovers that he is in love with Madeleine as he stares himself into a haunted state. Being in love means not being able to look away, being so utterly lost to the properties of one image that no other is in any meaningful sense visually alive. Whatever is associated with the beloved is hyper-fetishised—which is to say, rendered static, immutable. If Madeleine would return his love, she can only prove the genuineness of her feeling for him by remaining forever the same, exactly as he first saw her.

Scottie has been immobilized by a profound emotional shock in the film's opening scene (a policeman attempting to rescue him as he hangs suspended from the side of building loses his balance and plunges to his death). Scottie attempts to free himself from this trauma by exchanging his fear for what he takes to be love, but the only form of love he is open to is one that will reproduce or imitate the conditions of that original shock. He requires a love that will not participate in the dangerous flux of reality—that will stay frozen, suspended, at a fixed distance. The cure for vertigo, he believes, is to make something in his world stand perfectly still. There is no need to question his own im- mobility in the presence of one who is compelled to share it. Naturally, a love with trauma at its base must eventually find its way back to that trauma. Both of Madeleine's declarations of love to Scottie are quickly followed by the sight of her falling from the tower of the Mission Dolores. Madeleine's plunge to annihi- lation is at once an absolute barrier to love and its only possible expression. The vision of her descent possesses Scottie completely. The real reasons for Scottie's continual resubjection to the image that blinds and paralyzes him are not those manufactured in the external plot. What numbs the viewer, finally, in *Vertigo* is that all of its mysterious occurrences seem called into being by a terrible inner necessity. To meet the demands of Scottie's love, Madeleine must literally fall through the hole of his gaze. It is only there, where love empties itself and dies, that he is able to see her.

In *The Birds* [1963] it might appear that Hitchcock has returned to the realm of purely external aggression, but an examination of its structure reveals that the terms of inquiry are a further elaboration of those in *Vertigo* and *Psycho*. Once again, and in a most daring manner, Hitchcock effects a strange separation be- tween his characters and a subject that resists formulation, per- haps even widening the gap that we feel in *Psycho*. As so many critics complained at the time of *The Birds*'s release, the painstak- ingly elaborated network of psychological relationships that is Hitchcock's primary focus for roughly the first half of the film has only the most tenuous pertinence to the bird invasions that dominate the second half. The latter seem to function more as an interruption than as an extension of the film's thematic con- cerns. Furthermore, one is not convinced that the birds have any role to play in the elucidation or working through of the char- acters' difficulties. They appear to be there for their own sake, and Hitchcock consistently baffles our efforts to make anything of them.

I would argue that, like the "dead eye" in *Psycho*, the birds are
a metaphor caught in transit—one that can only repeat itself
because it has no capacity for growth or conversion. The birds
are the "forgotten" image in Hitchcock's world, the shadow behind the curtain ("so vacillating and indistinct an outline") that
cannot quite be seen for what it is or truly named. For that reason
it is empowered to translate everything (at any moment) into its
own dark language. Only once in the course of the film does
Hitchcock provide us with direct visual evidence of the worst that
the birds can do: in a lake of silence, the camera executes three
harrowing jump cut moves toward the corpse of Dan Fawcett,
whose pecked-out eyes have become rings of blood. The "shock
that has no end" is the secret quarry of *The Birds*. By the end of
the film, each of the surviving principal female characters—Melanie, Lydia, and Cathy—has been steeped in a trauma that she
will never be able to decipher. The child, Cathy, is obliged to
stand by a window and watch, stunned, as the protector who
had just pushed her to safety behind the door of her own house
(a gesture which costs her her own chance of entering) is swiftly
mutilated. Lydia, upon her discovery of Dan Fawcett's corpse,
rushes from his house in a daze and struggles, for what seems an
eternity, to find a word or a scream that can be fitted to what
she has beheld. No sound will come forth, and thereafter her
main activity in the film is to listlessly survey the contents of her
household, waiting for them to resume their former connection
to her, or hoping perhaps to stare them back into some form of
sense. Melanie, who is subjected to a long, tremendously savage
attack near the film's conclusion, offers us, as one of her last
gestures, a "clawing of the empty air" in front of her in a desperate attempt to stave off a horror she can still see. *The Birds*,
then, is also about the process of being caught in spaces from
which there can be no mental advance.

In *Psycho* Hitchcock's camera can never complete its search for
"Norman Bates" because from the very outset it is so firmly fused
with the object of its quest. The camera eye, in effect, is seeking
to uncover itself, recalling once more the moment when Lila is

trapped between the two facing mirrors in the Bates's mansion. It is in this sense that *Psycho* demands consideration as a *personal* film. Both the proclivities and areas of withdrawal in Norman's mode of vision—in fact, his whole strategy of structured avoidance—faithfully reproduce Hitchcock's own method of screening the world, where exposure is always an act of concealment. The landscape of *Psycho* is one that no one inside the film knows how to look at, and the camera merely reinforces the characters' arrested gaze. In no other Hitchcock film does the camera close in on so many objects that refuse to disclose their significance. The nearest thing to a penetration of the interior is Lila's exploration of the Bates's house, but here, as before, whatever the inquiring eye approaches seems instantly to escape what it designates. Moreover, like the front door of the Bates' dwelling, which appears to move toward Lila as soon as it looms into view, the space seems sentient, as though a living thought were trying to remember itself through these objects (the bronzed hands; the flower-patterned sink; the imprint of the bed; Norman's dolls and stuffed animals; and the untitled book that Lila prepares to open as the house search ends). Lila's function in this episode is like that of the silent menial at the close of Poe's "Berenice," who merely points at the objects that need to be seen until they are recognized and can "freeze" the eye that knows them. But in *Psycho* there is no final shock of recognition. Everything we have witnessed in the film ultimately appears to have been pulled through the hollow sockets into which Norman's face dissolves in the last scene. In the strikingly simplified visual field of *Psycho*'s conclusion, there is only a rigid form against a blank screen. The psychiatrist's explanation that has just ended has no more to do with what we now see than Marion's money had to do with her as she lay on the bathroom floor, her eye firmly fixed on nothing. All movement has subsided except for that of the steadily advancing camera. When Norman meets its gaze, the camera halts, as though transfixed by its own reflection. The image dissolves to reveal a half-submerged object, coated with filth, rising toward us from the swamp; and here *Psycho* ends.

Notes

1. Roland Barthes, "The Metaphor of the Eye," in *Critical Essays*, trans. Richard Howard (Evanston: Northwestern University Press, 1972), p. 239. See also Roland Kuhn, "The Attempted Murder of a Prostitute," in *Existence, A New Dimension in Psychiatry and Psychology*, ed. Rollo May, Ernst Angel, and Henri F. Ellenbarger (New York: Basic Books, 1958), pp. 365–425.

2. Edgar Allan Poe, "Berenice," in *The Complete Tales and Poems* (New York: Modern Library, 1965), p. 645.

3. Daniel Hoffman, *Poe Poe Poe Poe Poe Poe Poe* (New York: Doubleday, 1972), pp. 234–35.

4. Georges Bataille, *Story of the Eye*, trans. Joachim Neugraschel (New York: Urizen Books, 1977), p. 56.

5. Georges Bataille, *Manet*, trans. Austryn Wainhouse and James Emmons (Cleveland: Skira, 1955), p. 82.

6. Sanford Schwartz, "Reflections (The Mystery and Melancholy of a Career)," *New Yorker*, 28 June 1982, p. 93.

7. V. F. Perkins, *Film as Film* (Baltimore, Md.: Penguin, 1972), p. 106.

8. Garrett Stewart, "Keaton through the Looking Glass," *Georgia Review* 33 (Summer 1979): 365.

9. John Russell Taylor, *Hitch: The Life and Times of Alfred Hitchcock* (New York: Pantheon, 1978), p. 256.

10. James Naremore, *Filmguide to Psycho* (Bloomington: Indiana University Press, 1973), p. 36.

11. Stevie Smith, "Not Waving But Drowning," in *The Norton Anthology of Poetry*, rev. ed (New York: W. W. Norton, 1975), p. 1097.

12. Irving Massey, *The Gaping Pig: Literature and Metamorphosis* (Berkeley & Los Angeles: University of California Press, 1976), p. 8.

13. For a discussion of a similar search in Poe's "The Purloined Letter" (nearly as famous as that in *Psycho*), see Jacques Lacan, "Seminar on 'The Purloined Letter,' " *Yale French Studies* 41 (1972), pp. 38–72.

14. See Massey, *Gaping Pig*, p. 6.

8

Psychoanalytical Approaches

◆   ◆   ◆

◆   ◆   ◆

Psychoanalytical theory has had an enormous influence on film studies, especially when refigured through the work of a French psychiatrist, Jacques Lacan. Like Freud, Lacan focused on the oedipal cycle, but he politicized it to a certain extent and pointed out its foundation in, and repetition of, the masculine, patriarchal order. He developed metaphors for the oedipal process that made his theories especially attractive to film criticism. Simply put, Lacan spoke of the Oedipal process as the child's inevitable entry into the world of language—the language of the father, the dominant male voice. In his narrative, the child begins in a state of oneness with its mother, a fullness of self and security, a world of images that Lacan calls the Imaginary. This is figured in the metaphor of the mirror, where the child sees him or herself next to the mother, separate but together—just like the moviegoer sees herself reflected, for better or worse, in the fullness of a film's "reality." But the Imaginary is also imaginary; it can't exist; its fullness must be fragmented as the child takes a final step into the world of the father, the world of language, the Symbolic realm of law and societal order—which stands in and outside of the Real, a not-too-well-defined term that indicates a world that is ongoing, infiltrated, yet free of the control of the Symbolic.

This all sounds like the narrative of *Psycho* itself, except for its last part. Norman is unable to leave the Imaginary, the world of his mother. And this is the core of Robert Samuels's argument. He starts with the Freudian notion that all humans are bisexual and that heterosexuality is a culturally demanded move—what happens when we enter Lacan's Symbolic order. He explains that Norman never left the Imaginary of mother and child and in fact absorbed mother. Norman is always half, half mother, half Norman, a bisexual who has left both the Real and Symbolic realms behind, folded in on himself, and become psychotic. Samuels also expands on the commonly accepted notion of Hitchcock's misogyny, his hatred of women, and shows how this film—along with all his others—shows this fear and a resulting diminishing of women, until, in *Psycho*, she is cut to pieces and buried in the swamp.

A few specialized words are used here: "Signifier" is the visual or verbal part of a cluster of meanings called a "Sign" (the other part of the cluster is the Signified, which is the complex, often ambiguous, always culturally determined set of meanings triggered by the Signifier). "Object (*a*)" is a Lacanian phrase that refers to the remainder of the "Real" in an individual that resists the Symbolic and becomes an object of desire— perhaps of escape. The "Other" is any thing, any person, any sexual orientation, any ethnic identity unacceptable to the culture and therefore placed outside the "Symbolic" and demonized. The "fluidity of the feminine" is a concept developed by a number of feminist critics who have noticed that throughout the history of literature and film, women are associated with liquid, with flow, with a kind of insubstantiality that makes it easy for patriarchy to, in effect, bottle them up.

For another view of women in Hitchcock's films, I would recommend Tania Modleski's *The Women Who Knew Too Much*. Modleski, while not denying Hitchcock's misogyny, shows that his women characters have more substance than they have been given credit for. It is Lila Crane who makes the ghastly discovery in the Old Dark House.

Finally, Samuel's introduces the concept of the postmodern that Linda Williams will expand on in her essay. Here he takes it to mean the atemporal and ahistorical.

ROBERT SAMUELS ◆ Epilogue: *Psycho* and the
Horror of the Bi-Textual Unconscious

Throughout this work, I have focused on the relationship between Lacanian psychoanalysis, feminist theories, and Queer Theory. In this interaction, we have learned that many feminist and
psychoanalytic concepts and structures depend upon a heterosexist model of sexual difference that equates masculinity with the
Symbolic order and femininity with the Real. The result of this
process is that the unconscious becomes "heterosexualized." I
have countered this heterosexual logic by developing the theory
of bi-textuality.

This notion of a polyvalent foundation of sexuality and textuality is derived directly from Freud's early theory that the unconscious is inherently bisexual. In one of the most crucial
passages in the *Three Essays on the Theory of Sexuality*, Freud argues
that heterosexuality, and not homosexuality, is the form of desire
that has to be constructed and explained: "All human beings are
capable of making a homosexual object-choice and have in fact
made one in their unconscious. . . . Thus from the point of view
of psychoanalysis the exclusive sexual interest felt by men for
women is also a problem that needs elucidating and is not a self-
evident fact."[1] Due to America's cultural homophobia, this foun-
dational argument by Freud has been repressed, and thus a major
part of his theory has been neglected.

One reason why the homosexual and bisexual aspects of the
unconscious have been ignored is due to the disorienting aspects
of bi-textual desire. Multiple forms of sexuality and textuality
upset the clear binary logic of sexual difference. The bi-textuality
of the unconscious also threatens the heterosexual control of the
Symbolic order. Our culture is therefore grounded on the repression of the unconscious and the need to avoid any encounter
with the Real of bi-sexuality. In Hitchcock's *Psycho*, this horror of
the Real and the bi-textual becomes associated with the fear of
psychosis.

I would like to argue that *Psycho* represents Hitchcock's own retrospective look back at his previous films and an anticipation of some future movies. I will argue that almost every scene and symbol in this film either directly cites or plays off of another scene or symbol from an earlier film. The central films and themes that I have been discussing throughout this book can be summarized in the following list: the effaced female subject (*The Lady Vanishes*), the masculine horror of the feminine (*Spellbound*), repetition and the Real (*Rebecca*), feminine fluidity and be-hind sight (*Notorious*), internalized abjection (*Marnie*), sublimation and melancholia (*Vertigo*), homoerotism and the gaze (*Rear Window*), and the maternal super-ego (*The Birds*). I would like to posit that *Psycho* circulates these different images and themes in a postmodern way that renders all questions of temporality and intentionality problematic. More so, the bi-textual themes and impulses, which Hitchcock merely Symbolizes or hints at in his other works, are projected out into the Real during this film.[2]

The Structure of Psychosis

This need to represent Symbolic attributes in the Real can be, in part, explained by the central focus of the film, which is Norman Bates's psychosis. As Lacan has often pointed out, one of the major defining characteristics of psychosis is that certain Symbolic relations and concepts, that are "normally" abstract factors of structure and order, become perceived in the Real during psychotic states.[3] In the case of *Psycho*, the subject's Symbolic desire to identify with his mother will be acted out on the level of the Real, when he actually attempts to take on his mother's voice and clothing.

Another defining characteristic of psychosis is the rejection of the subject's super-ego and its externalization into the Real. Freud points out that all of us have a conscience, or what Lacan would call an "internalized Other," that listens to our thoughts and judges our desires. However, what happens in psychosis is that the subject actually perceives in the Real, the Other listening to his or her thoughts and desires.[4] Delusions of observation, as well as paranoia, can thus be explained by the externalization of the internalized Other.

If Norman Bates becomes his mother at the end of the film, it is, in part, because he has so identified with her law and desires after her death that he cannot separate his self from her conscience. Likewise, in the scenes where we believe that we hear his mother yelling at Norman, what is actually going on is that he has projected his own conscience outside of himself and he is now yelling at himself from the position of the (m)Other. We must read this film, therefore, on the level of a long extended psychotic delusion that forces all of Hitchcock's more subtle themes out into the open.

One way that the structure of this film has been read is by dividing it into three sections: the first section concerns the sexuality and criminality of the female subject, Marion Crane; the next section switches focus and is more concerned with the desire and fears of the masculine subject, Norman Bates; and the final section deals with the social search for the missing woman and the assumption by Norman Bates of his mother's voice and identity. According to Barbara Klinger, this three-part structure centers on a dialectical discussion of feminine sexuality, "The narrative of *Psycho* can be seen to function in its movement to present this problem [feminine sexuality], to repress it (the switch in narratives) and restate it (Norman-the mother), and finally to contain/solve it in the name of the family and the law."[5] In this structure, the problem of sexual difference is, in part, resolved through the psychotic resolution of the film. However, I would like to argue that what this film presents is a radically ambivalent representation of feminine sexuality that does not fit into any type of dialectical resolution, but rather serves to materialize a radical splitting of the female subject through the emergence of bi-textual desire.

From the opening credits of *Psycho*, this projection of the split subject is evident. When we first see the names and the titles of the film appear, each name is sliced into sections. Hitchcock will later reuse this method in *The Birds*, when he shows the titles being eaten away. Of course Hitchcock's own name is shown to be divided, reunited, and then split again, and I believe we can read this as an indication of his identification with the divided female subject.

One may initially respond to my stress on the female subject in this film by claiming that the central focus is on Norman Bates, who is a male figure that finally gets united with his Other half at the end of the movie. Thus, it would seem that *Psycho* is not about feminine sexuality and division, but rather concerns masculinity and the desire to reunite with the lost maternal love-object. In fact, I would not argue with this second interpretation, and I would add that these two different readings represent two sides of the same coin. In other words, the male subject's desire to reunite himself with his other half demands that the female object be split and divided.

In order to demonstrate this latter theory, I will read the film backwards, starting with the long psychiatric explanation for Norman's behavior. According to the court-appointed psychiatrist, Norman's mind was divided between himself and the voice of his mother. We can read the name "Norman" as a condensation of the "normal man." What is normal, then, is for the male subject to be divided in half between his identifications with his mother and her desire and his identification with his father. Freud's theory of the universal bisexuality points to this fundamental subjective division that remains repressed in the unconscious for most subjects. However, what happens in psychosis is this unconscious bi-textual split is experienced as a Real perception.

In Norman's case, every time he has a masculine desire his mother's voice reacts against it. We can suppose that for most subjects this battle between desire and the voice of conscience goes on internally, but with Norman we actually hear his debate with his conscience out loud. The psychiatrist explains that the origin of Norman's psychosis occurred after he killed his mother and her lover. As in the case of a psychotic process of mourning, Norman identified with his lost object and took on his mother's identity. The transitive nature of this relationship is expressed when the psychiatrist points out that because Norman was so jealous of his mother, he assumed that she was so jealous of him.

Thus, when Norman met Marion and he became attracted to her, his mother's jealousy, or rather the projection of his own jealousy, called for Marion's murder. He then had to erase all of the traces of the crime, just as he erased all of the traces of his mother's death, in order to keep up the illusion that she was still alive. Moreover, to hold onto the presence of his mother in the Real, he kept her body in her bedroom.

The male's need to keep the female subject in the Real, which is so evident in Hitchcock's other films, is taken here to its logical extreme. The female body is transformed into a corpse that is now truly outside of the Symbolic order of law and discourse; this body remains a gaze or a dead stare that cannot be effaced by the subject.

This presence of the dead staring gaze is manifested in one of the last lines of the film, when Norman states through his mother's voice, "As if I could do anything except sit and stare like one of his stuffed birds. They're probably watching me. I'm not even going to swat that fly." The protesting inactivity of this subject, who can only sit and stare, can be related to the effacement of the female subject by the Symbolic order that attempts to pose and manipulate her body.

The final image in the film of a rope pulling a car out of the water echoes this notion of the female subject that has been reduced to being a pure inert object of resistance. For it is Marion's body that is hidden inside the car that has been pushed into the swamp and is now being dredged up. According to Klinger, this last view of the car reflects a process that began with the opening scenes of Marion in a hotel room:

> Marion is transformed in this progression from an overt erotic spectacle (semiclad, in postcoital embrace) to a figure entirely shrouded from view (a body in the trunk of a car): a figure initially manifested strongly as spectacle becomes an almost complete visual nonentity. (334)

The female image, which I have shown is often at the center of Hitchcock's field of representation, has now been reduced to being an absent object. The Lady has once again vanished but this time she will not return.

If the female subject has now been murdered, it is clear that Hitchcock and the process of filmmaking have killed her off. This connection between murder and representation becomes clear in the famous shower scene where each stab at Marion's body is matched with a cut of the film and camera angle. In other terms, the film editor and director are the ones that are cutting up the female body by breaking down her image into separate angles and views. Through the analysis of the ethics of representation, we learn that film feeds on the feminine body, but it can only represent it by cutting and ultimately killing it. Once again, I would argue that Hitchcock has hinted at this before, but here he is presenting the ethical connection between murder and representation in the Real; the male-dominated cultural order works by effacing the female subject and pushing her body towards the limits of the representable.

If we now look at the beginning of this movie, we can see that Hitchcock himself returns to one of his earliest films. Just as in the opening of *The Lady Vanishes*, the camera slowly and silently enters through a window and into a room at a cheap hotel. We see Marion partially undressed and laying on a bed while she talks to her lover, Sam. She tells him that this will be their last time together and that she is tired of meeting secretively.

Sex as a secret is a common theme in Hitchcock's work; yet, in this film, the female body is presented in a more explicit way than in most of his other films. Rarely in a Hitchcock picture do we see a female character so undressed, and perhaps the most revealing scene in all of his work up to this point is the shower scene, which results in such a violent reaction. One could argue that Hitchcock's ability to create an atmosphere of suspense is dependent on his strong desire to repress his own sexual and violent urges. However, in this film, everything is pushed up a notch, and that which is usually concealed begins to be revealed. This movement of revelation is, in part, highlighted when Sam says to Marion: "You make respectability seem disrespectful."

Hitchcock's attempt to present sexuality in a respectful way has now crossed over to its crude opposite.

In the second scene of the film, this movement from concealed desire to overt representation occurs on the level of money. At the bank where Marion works, a wealthy client, Mr. Cassidy, can't help but to wave his $40,000 in front of everyone's faces as he flirts with Marion. She seems to ignore his passes; however, once she is entrusted with his money, she decides to take it for herself. We then see her return to a room where she changes clothing, and is now presented in black lingerie instead of white. This section of the film will be later repeated in *Marnie* where we find another female character who steals from her boss and whose name also starts off with the letters "Mar."[6]

In fact, the similarities do not stop here because Marnie also changes colors and names like Marion. While Marnie changes her name to Mary, Marion, and Martha; Marion changes her name to Marie Samuels. The stress on the "mar" in all of these names points to the marring effect that representation has on women. Although, in *Psycho* the female subject will not only be marred on a Symbolic level, but she will be effaced in the Real.

This marring effect of language on the feminine body is doubled in the film by the connection between money and sexuality. In the first scene at the hotel, Marion stresses to Sam that she also pays for their secret affair. Then in the next scene at the bank [the real estate office—ed.], the flirting man proposes to buy her love. After she steals his money, so that in part he cannot do this, she hears his voice in her head saying, "If anything is missing, I'll replace it with her fine smooth flesh." As Lacan has argued, the signifier attaches itself to the body by removing a pound of flesh.[7] Here, the process of signification is tied directly to the commodification of the female body. She has stolen money from him, so he feels that he is entitled to some of her flesh—it is not only the name that demands to become flesh, but it is also the almighty dollar.

Furthermore, the dollar as an object of exchange doubles the presence of the female object as an object of circulation in the masculine economy. Once Marion steals the money, she then upsets these two circuits of exchange. Hitchcock highlights the way that this object is the material residue of all Symbolic exchanges by having the letter full of money always sticking out of Marion's purse. Like the object (*a*), this part of the Real that has been submitted to the Symbolic order refuses to be completely negated. The protruding envelope points to the final image of the protruding car trunk that hides the remains of the negated female body.

When Marion finally does pull into the Bates Hotel, her approach to the large house in the rain recalls the second Mrs. de Winter's approach to Manderley in *Rebecca*. Both homes loom large and are filled with the presence of a murdered female/maternal figure. Like Norman, Max in *Rebecca* has killed a woman and has placed her in a vehicle that is now submerged under water. And like the reemergence of Rebecca's body from the sea, Marion's body will reemerge at the end of *Psycho*.

The Real(m) of the Birds

Once Marion is inside Norman's parlor, we see that he is quite obsessed by birds. In a room that is filled with stuffed birds, he says to Marion, whose real last name is Crane, that she eats like a bird. All of these references point to the association between his mother and the birds, which becomes explicit at the end of the film. Marion is thus placed in the same position as his mother; she must be contained by being stuffed and reduced to being a pure, dead stare.

Of course, these references to birds anticipate the movie that Hitchcock will later make, which has this animal as its central figure. If the bird represents the maternal super-ego as [Slavoj] Žižek has argued, then we must ask what does the stuffed bird represent and how does it relate to Norman's attempt to stuff his mother's voice into his own body?[8]

A partial response to this question is provided by Norman's

soliloquy on the human condition that he delivers to Marion in his back parlor:

> I think we're all in our private traps, clamped in them
> and none of us can ever get out. We scratch and we claw,
> but only at the air and at each other, and for all of it, we
> never budge an inch.

Here, Norman is no longer saying that Marion is like a bird, or that his mother is like one, but rather that all subjects are trapped in cages like birds that are going to be stuffed. But what is this human cage if not the solitude of our own bodies and consciousness? Isn't Hitchcock's point, in this very self-revealing moment, that all connections between people are fundamentally impossible because we are all trapped within our own cages or bodies?

On the other hand, if we are all stuck in our own private hells, that does not mean that other people don't try to place us in other forms and hellish places. When Marion suggests to Norman that he should place his mother "in" a mental institution, he becomes enraged and replies:

> Put her in some place! What do you know about caring?
> Have you ever seen the inside of one of those places? The
> laughing and the tears, the cruel eyes studying you, my
> mother there! She's as harmless as one of those stuffed
> birds.

This resistance of the subject who has identified with his mother is a resistance to being placed within the Symbolic structure of the Other and under the Other's observation. In order to prevent this, he would rather kill her and stuff her like a bird. If we now apply this argument to Hitchcock's own conflicted attempts at reducing and representing female bodies and fluids (*Notorious*) in fixed forms, we see that his desire to control his own horror of the feminine results in a transformation of feminine presence into being a fixed dead object.

Connected to this mortification of the female body, we find the unconscious insistence of letters and writing. After their extended exchange of views on birds and human nature, Marion goes back to her room, but she makes a mistake by using her real name instead of her false one. Norman then goes back and checks her signature in his guest book, and he realizes that she has been lying. This scene repeats in its essence the scene in *Spellbound* where Constance compares signatures and discovers that Dr. Edwards is not who he says he is. As in many of Hitchcock's other films, the first sign of guilt and material proof comes in the form of writing. Once again, it is an unconscious slip and the insistence of the letter that provides evidence for the resolution of the mystery.

After Norman makes this discovery, he then goes back into his room, and he removes a picture so that he can watch Marion undress in her room. Here we have a restating of the *Rear Window* theme of voyeurism, which is another film where a woman's body is cut into pieces. Of course, in the first film, we only hear about this murder—it is only reproduced in the Symbolic—but in this version, we actually get to witness it visually.

Before the cutting of the female body occurs in *Psycho*, there is a prefiguring of this event. Marion decides that she is going to return the money she has stolen, and she calculates on a piece of paper how much she owes. She then rips up the paper and flushes it down the toilet. The camera focuses on the water and the ripped paper being sucked down into the hole of the toilet. Later, after Marion herself is cut up in the shower, we will see her blood being sucked down into the hole of the bathtub. She is, thus, placed in the same position as the ripped-up letter. In fact, the first clue that her sister will find of her presence at the Bates Hotels [sic] will be a piece of this paper that has resisted being flushed.

Later on as we watch Marion's blood spin down the shower drain, we see superimposed an image of her open eye which begins to spin around. This eye recalls the female eye that we see at the beginning of *Vertigo*. This female subject has now been truly reduced to being a dead gaze, which stares, but can no longer see. She is the material residue of the negation of the Real by the Symbolic order. In this sense, she resists being completely ab-sorbed by the system of the Other. It is precisely this resistance of the Real and the feminine subject/object that I have placed at the center of Lacan's theory of ethics. Hitchcock not only shows us the murder of the feminine Thing, but he also forces us to acknowledge this act of Symbolic destruction by having the dead eye of the woman stare at us as her blood runs down the drain.

In order to further instill this image of the blood running into a hole, Hitchcock shows Marion's car, which now holds her dead body, slowly sink into the swamp. As we watch this car begin to submerge, we see a round white circle that slowly disappears into nothingness. This image then recalls the flushing toilet bowl and the shower drain, but now in a reversal of structure, a solid object is being surrounded by water, instead of a solid form sucking in water.

This reversal of the flow of water relates to the theme of feminine fluidity that I have traced in *Notorious*. While Norman might attempt to mop up all of Marion's feminine fluids, like Lady Macbeth, he will never be able to erase all of the blood from his memory. This horror of the ineffaceable blood becomes evident when we hear Norman yell, "Mother, oh God mother, blood!"[9]

Discourse around the Missing Object

The next section of the film is started by the private investigator, who says to Sam and Marion's sister, "Let's all talk about Marion." For a great deal of the rest of the film, no one will do anything else, but precisely this—talk about the missing feminine object and attempt to absorb this lack into the Symbolic order of discourse. The role of the investigator is to seek out clues to account for the disappearance of Marion and the money. At one point, he insists that she must be visible because "Someone always sees a girl with $40,000." The idea, here, is that money as a material form of Symbolic circulation makes the absent feminine body present. As in the case of *Rebecca* and *The Lady Vanishes*, the only proof of a woman's existence is the material traces of the Symbolic order. In *Psycho*, the first clue for the investigator is her signature in the guest book. Even though she has signed a different name, the investigator makes the connection by comparing her handwriting.

The second clue that this detective sees is what appears to be a person's face in a window at the big house. When he confronts Norman about this, Norman first denies it, and then he admits that it is his mother, but she is an invalid. This spotting of the invalid female in the window is another direct quote from *Rear Window*. And like this previous film, the attempt of the subject to investigate this gaze, by entering into the home of the other, will result in a scene of violent confrontation. However, in the case of *Rear Window*, Lisa survives this encounter, while in *Psycho*, the investigator is brutally murdered.

While Sam and the sister are waiting to hear from the detective, they become suspicious, and they go see the sheriff of the town. They tell him that the investigator said something about seeing Norman's mother at the window. The sheriff replies that this is impossible because Norman's mother has been dead for over ten years and is buried at a cemetery nearby. This situation of the buried female body, that is not really buried, is another reference to *Rebecca*, whose body everyone thought was already identified and buried a year before she is rediscovered.

When Marion's sister finally enters the Bates' home, she first becomes convinced that the mother is still alive because she sees a bodily indentation in her bed. While she is exploring the inside of Norman's house, Sam is questioning Norman outside in his office. He confronts Norman and states, "I've been talking about your mother, your motel." In a strange equation, the mother is, here, equated with the hotel; both are empty structures that are filled with vacancy.

Right after this exchange between Sam and Norman, we see Marion's sister discover Norman's mother in the basement. As she slowly turns a chair around, we begin to view the mother's dead skeleton and staring, empty eye sockets. This empty gaze, the look without vision, refers back to the relation between the mother and the empty, vacant hotel. The maternal body is only a shell, a place of enclosure that is filled with nothingness. When

Norman then attempts to identify with his mother in the Real by taking on her voice, he is, in part, trying to reoccupy and reanimate her body. This return to the maternal body and the attempt to give it a voice represents the movement of Hitchcock's work itself. In order to materialize the absent Real of the female body, he can only reenact its destruction and attempt to let it speak through him.

I have been calling this return of the repressed female subject an "ethical" relationship because it allows us to see the way that our systems of representation work by killing off the Real of human existence. At the end of the film, we have the situation where a murdered female voice is communicating through a possessed male body. This structure represents a reversal of the classical filmic relationship between the masculine voice and the female form. Instead of the male character telling the female body where to go and what to do, we have the invasion of a female voice within a masculine form. The result of this process is a highlighting of the bisexual and divided nature of every human subject.

Through the discourse of psychosis, Hitchcock is now able to bring out into the open his own cross-gendered identifications. The voice of this subject has become the bi-textual voice of the unconscious that calls out of the void and articulates the ethical demand for a return to the Real. Furthermore, Norman's bi-textual psychosis subverts the feminist en-gendering of the Real by highlighting the cultural horror of bisexual desire and unconscious discourse. From this perspective, we can read *Psycho* as the projection of Hitchcock's most profound cultural fears and desires.

This horror of the bi-textual Real that surfaces in *Psycho* points to one of the main mechanisms of control that the dominant heterosexist Symbolic order employs in order to contain and silence diverse forms of desire and identification. In order to work against this process of containment and repression, cultural workers need to explore the ways that the unconscious and the Real become equated with feminine and queer subjects. Linked to this process of exposing the en-gendering of the Real is an awareness of the ways that Symbolic castration is rejected and projected onto debased Others. Hitchcock's work has offered us the opportunity to view the ways that bi-textuality challenges and subverts the imposition of the death drive and the Symbolic order of law and sexual regulation.

Notes

1. Freud, *Three Essays on the Theory of Sexuality*, ed. James Strachey (New York: Basic Books, 1962), pp. 56–57, n.1.

2. My use of the Lacanian notion of the "Real," here, attempts to relate together the reality of perception with the limits of all forms of Symbolization.

3. For a detailed analysis of the relationship between the Real and psychosis, see Robert Samuels, *Between Philosophy and Psychoanalysis* (New York: Routledge, 1983), pp. 27–55.

4. Sigmund Freud, "On Narcissism: An Introduction," in *General Psychological Theory*, ed. Philip Rieff (New York: Collier Books, 1963), p. 75.

5. Barbara Klinger, "*Psycho*: The Institutionalization of Female Sexuality," in *A Hitchcock Reader*, ed. Marshall Deutelbaum and Leland Poague (Ames: Iowa State University Press, 1986), p. 334.

6. For an extended analysis of the meaning of these "mar" names, see my chapter in [*Hitchcock's Bi-Textuality: Lacan, Feminisms, and Queer Theory* (Albany: State University of New York Press, 1998)] on *Marnie*.

7. This same relation between money, language, and a pound of flesh is of course a central theme to Shakespeare's *Merchant of Venice*.

8. Slavoj Žižek, *Looking Awry* (Cambridge: MIT Press, 1992).

9. Norman's horror of blood connects him to Marnie and the general connection between femininity, abjection, and male anxiety.

9

Gender, Reception, and the Postmodern

◆　◆　◆

◆　◆　◆

Linda Williams has been writing on a variety of gender issues for many years. One of her essays, "When the Woman Looks," focuses on gender in horror film and points out quite convincingly the ways in which the genre equates the woman with the monster—as does *Psycho*. In the following essay, Williams thinks about gender in *Psycho* but encapsulates it in a larger context of the critical and popular reception of the film and places it in a still larger context of postmodernism. She attempts to take seriously Hitchcock's insistence that *Psycho* is a funny, or at least "fun" film and does this without denying its seriousness. In the course of her essay, she manages a survey of methodologies used throughout the history of film studies, as well as the history of post-*Psycho* films that have been deeply influenced by it.

Some terms need clarification: "postmodernism" is a contested concept, as Williams admits. It was developed as a response to modernism, which itself was the aesthetic response to modernity—the loss of simple, secure, knowable positions that an individual could take in a world of continual progress and change. Williams holds that postmodernism is a response to modernity as well, and she is correct; I think she is not correct in suggesting that high modernism was against pleasure. It was serious, and the art it produced demanded a great deal from its viewers, readers, or listeners. But it was also highly ironic and very playful. The early modernist writer, Franz Kafka, like Hitchcock, was surprised when people did not laugh at his strange and troubling narratives. In general, postmodernism is defined by a breaking down of traditional separations, a liquidation of boundaries between high and low, serious and comic, ironic and sarcastic. It is the art of the pastiche, of "sampling," bringing together disparate elements of art and culture. And unlike modernism, it is pointedly ahistorical and, if such a thing is possible (which it never is), apolitical.

Williams mentions "subject positions," which is an important concept in contemporary film theory, having to do with the ways a film and its audience collude to create a perfect viewer, a universal viewer who will respond the same way at the same time. Hitchcock claimed that this is what he wanted, when he speaks of playing the audience like a pipe organ, and almost all the writers in this collection have alluded to it. But Hitchcock, as Williams shows, disrupts this goal of classic Hollywood cinema by disrupting his narrative, tossing viewer expectations and identification back and forth. Finally, the term "Baudrillardian simulacra" refers to Jean Baudrillard, an influential French theorist whose concept of the simulacrum—an imitation of something that never existed, an imitation without an origin, as Williams states it—has had such wide influence that a copy of one of his books is prominent in the first *Matrix*, a film about simulacra.

LINDA WILLIAMS ◆ Discipline and Fun: *Psycho* and Postmodern Cinema

> If you've designed a picture correctly, in terms of its
> emotional impact, the Japanese audience would scream at
> the same time as the Indian audience.
> —ALFRED HITCHCOCK, quoted in Houston, 1980: 488

Talk to psychoanalytic critics about *Psycho* and they will tell you how perfectly the film illustrates the perverse mechanisms of the medium. Talk to horror aficionados and they will tell you how the film represents the moment horror moved inside the family and home. Talk to anyone old enough to have seen *Psycho* on first release in a movie theater, however, and they will tell you what it felt like to be scared out of their wits. Fear of showers in the aftermath of the film's famous shower-murder ran rampant throughout the 1960s. Yet if it is popularly remembered how *Psycho* altered the bathing habits of the nation, it is oddly less well remembered how it fundamentally altered viewing habits.

The following study of the place of Alfred Hitchcock's *Psycho* (1960) in film studies is interested in the critical and popular reception of a film that I believe has been crucial to the constitution of new ways of seeing, and new ways of feeling, films. As we shall see, these ways of seeing and feeling are simultaneously more distracted and more disciplined than previous cinema. Released in the summer of 1960—a date which has been seen by some to mark the end of the "classical" Hollywood style and mode of production and the beginning of a much more amorphously defined "post-classical," postmodern cinema—*Psycho* has nevertheless not previously been viewed as a quintessentially postmodern film.[1]

The term postmodern is enormously complicated in its application to cinema by the way the medium of cinema has, since its inception, automatically, but unreflectingly been equated with modernity. Fredric Jameson (1984) sees postmodernism in cinema as a relatively recent occurrence determined by the "cultural logic of late capitalism" manifested in a schizophrenic, decentered subjectivity that can be seen in popular cinema in the pervasive mode of nostalgia and pastiche that flattens all time, or, more recently, in the prevalence of paranoid conspiracy thrillers in which communication technologies are often central metaphors. Anne Friedberg (1993) and Miriam Hansen ([2000]) on the other hand, have both argued for the need first to sort out cinema's problematic relation to the modern, before leaping to embrace the "p" word. For Friedberg the very apparatus of the cinema makes the stylistic categories of modernism and postmodernism inappropriate since it constructs a "virtual, mobilized gaze" through a photographically represented "elsewhere and elsewhen" that is already postmodern. Thus for Friedberg there is no precise moment of temporal rupture between the modern and the postmodern, but only a subtle transformation produced by the increasing centrality of the image-producing and reproducing apparatuses (1993: 170). For Hansen, the difficulty is the relation of the modernity of cinema and its so-called "classical" Hollywood tendencies. Since cinema history has so often been presented as the juncture between the classical popular and the modernist avant-garde, it has been difficult to perceive the extent to which the quintessentially modern phenomenon of movies have also been popular.

I agree with Friedberg that the basic elements of the so-called postmodern condition consist in the "instrumentalized acceleration of spatial and temporal fluidities" that have always operated in cinema (1993: 179). In this sense, all cinema *is*, as Friedberg puts it, "proto-postmodern." A mere thematics of nostalgia—or in this case of schizophrenia—does not adequately define a postmodern film. I also agree with Hansen that from the contemporary perspective of postmodernity, it becomes possible to see the limitations of both a purely "high modernist" understanding of cinematic modernism and a seemingly ahistorical popular "classicism." However, the temptation to identify specific films or genres which emphatically perform the kind of acceleration of fluidities Friedberg mentions and the kind of challenge to the "classical" Hansen mentions remains. My own particular temptation is to locate within the history of cinematic reception a moment in which the audience response to postmodern gender and sexual fluidity, schizophrenia, and irony began to become not only central *attractions* of "going to the movies" but the very basis of new spectatorial *disciplines* capable of enhancing these attractions.

The Place of Psycho in Film Studies

In order to argue for the postmodern nature of *Psycho*'s discipline and distraction, let me briefly survey the film's changing status within the field of film studies. David Bordwell's (1989) survey of the rhetoric of *Psycho* criticism is a good place to begin to identify what might be called the modernist appropriation of the film— approaches that Bordwell wishes to disparage. Bordwell's account of the interpretations of *Psycho* traces a remarkable process of legitimization whereby a film initially seen as a minor, low-budget, black-and-white Hitchcock "thriller," not up to the "master's" usual standards, was five years later the subject of an extremely influential chapter of a major auteur study, ten years later a classic worthy of close analysis, and fifteen years later an example of a subversive work of modernism. All subsequent interpretations, including those by [William] Rothman (1982), [Fredric] Jameson (1990), and [Slavoj] Žižek (1992), assume the centrality of the film to cinema studies as constituted and legitimized by reigning psychoanalytic paradigms of film theory in the 1970s. Yet, as Bordwell shows, what is missing from such interpretations is a quality mentioned by Hitchcock himself and cited in an epigraph to Robin Wood's influential auteur study: this quality is "fun."

> You have to remember that *Psycho* is a film made with quite a sense of amusement on my part. To me it's a *fun* picture. The processes through which we take the audience, you see, its rather like taking them through the haunted house at the fairground. (Bordwell, 1989: 229; Wood, 1965: 106)

With *Psycho*'s entrance into the canon of the twenty or so most frequently taught and critically revered films, discussion of this fairground appeal to sensational fun fell by the wayside. The more exalted Hitchcock's critical reputation became, the less he, or anyone else, learned about the secrets of this fun. As he once noted, "My films went from being failures to masterpieces without ever being successes" (Spoto, 1983: 456–57). So interested was Hitchcock in understanding the powerful effect *Psycho* had on audiences that he proposed that the Stanford Research Institute devote a study to understand its popularity. But when he found out they wanted $75,000 to do the the research, he told them he was not that curious (Spoto, 1983: 457).

One reason so much academic film criticism has passed over the question of the film's fun has to do with psychoanalytic and feminist paradigms aligned with what David Rodowick has called the discourse of political modernism in which the notion of an endlessly deferred, insatiable *desire* was central and the notion of visual pleasure (let alone "fun") was anathema.[2] Within these paradigms *Psycho*'s modernism could only be understood as a rupture with "readerly," and "classical" forms of visual pleasure. This "classical" pleasure might be understood judgmentally as transparent realism's support of bourgeois ideology (as in most 1970s' film theory) or, somewhat more neutrally, as a dominant style and mode of production (as in Bordwell, Staiger, and Thompson's monumental work, *The Classical Hollywood Cinema: Film Style and Mode of Production, 1917–1960* (1985)). Of course it makes a difference which form of classicism a work like *Psycho* is seen to rupture.

For Kaja Silverman, it ruptures the classical "system of suture" whereby coherent forms of meaning and unified subject positions are upheld. Silverman asserts the exceptional and deviant status of a film that obliges its viewing subject "to make abrupt shifts in identification," at one juncture inscribed as victim, "at the next juncture as victimizer" (Silverman, 1983: 206). However, Silverman's psychoanalytic characterization of the viewer as "castrated" comes close to presenting the experience of viewing the film as a form of punishment. For her—and for most critics who wrote about the film in this mode—the film is about painful castration and perversely thwarted desires. Spectators who are first identified with the neurotic desires of Marion are abruptly cut off from her and subsequently unwittingly caught up in the perverse and psychotic desires of Norman and are then, presumably, punished for such errant identification by a narrative that does not follow the "classical" realist narrative trajectory of resolution and reassurance.[3] For Silverman, and many others, the transparency and unity of the suture system are "synonymous with the operations of classic narrative" and its ideological effects (1983: 214).

In contrast, in the Bordwell–Thompson paradigm of the "classical" cinema, classic stands not so much for realism and suture as for Aristotelian (and neo-Aristotelian) values of unity, harmony, and tradition that have endured in American cinema since the late teens. This classicism is seen as consisting in a strong narrative logic, coherence of cause and effect, space and time, psychological motivation, and character-driven events. To Bordwell and Thompson it is so stable and permanent a style that it is capable of absorbing whatever differences are introduced into the system. This is precisely what Bordwell argues with respect to *Psycho*. Noting that it is "certainly one of the most deviant films ever made in Hollywood" because of its attack on such fundamental classical assumptions as the psychological identity of characters and the role accorded to narration, he nevertheless argues that "*Psycho* remains closer to *His Girl Friday* than *Diary of a Country Priest*" (Bordwell, Staiger, and Thompson, 1985: 81).

For Bordwell, *Psycho*'s deviation from "classical" unity is transitory and fleeting: "in Hollywood cinema, there are no subversive films, only subversive moments"—moments ultimately absorbed by the relatively static hegemony of the group style (Bordwell, Staiger, and Thompson, 1985: 81). For Silverman, *Psycho*'s deviation from classical style is subversive, but it is a subversion that partakes of the unpleasure—even the quasi-punishment—of high modernism. Thus, although the answer to the questions of what *Psycho* ruptures, and how it does so, differs slightly depending on whether it is the 1970s version of "classical realist narrative"—often equated with the novel—or the "classical Hollywood style"—often traced back to the well-made play, and to neoclassical values—the common wisdom of both approaches is that the classical can be opposed to the innovation and rupture of the modern. Classicism thus seems to acquire something akin to a universal static appeal in tension with, but ultimately overpowering any deviation posed by, the modern.[4]

What is missing from both Bordwell's and Silverman's account of *Psycho*'s deviance from "classical" norms is any sense of the popular, sensory pleasures of either the mainstream cinema from which it supposedly deviates or the specific nature of the different and "deviant" pleasures of *Psycho* itself. The deeper problem may be, as Miriam Hansen has suggested, that the very category of the classical verges on anachronism when we are using the term to refer to "a cultural formation that was, after all, perceived as the incarnation of *the modern*" in its methods of industrial production and mass consumption (2000: 337, emphasis in original). In other words, the category of the classical to which Bordwell wants to assimilate *Psycho*, and from which Silverman and others want to differentiate it, might better be reconceived as a form of what Hansen calls "popular modernism." From this perspective, the Bordwell–Thompson–Staiger model of the tendency of the classical cinema to devour and assimilate the modern, and the 1970s' film theory model of classical realism's neutralization of the modern, are both inadequate to the task of understanding what was new, and fun, in popular, mainstream cinema.

My project with *Psycho* is therefore to account for some of its more sensational and "fun" appeals. However, this fun does not represent a completely radical rupture with a popularly conceived, mainstream, Hollywood cinema in the business of providing sensually based thrills and pleasures. It represents, rather, a new intensification and destabilization of the gendered components of that pleasure. Following both Anne Friedberg and Miriam Hansen, then, I would like to argue that *Psycho* offers an intensification of certain forms of visuality, and certain appeals to the senses through the image-producing and reproducing apparatuses that were already evident in what is more properly called the popular modernism of mainstream Hollywood cinema, but which changed under the incipient pressures of postmodernity.[5]

Psycho's Story of an Eye

Alfred Hitchcock's *Psycho* opens on a famous "bird's eye" view of the Phoenix skyline; after surveying the city laterally the camera moves forward towards a half-open window blind, then through the window to allow us to become voyeurs of the aftermath of illicit sex in a sleazy hotel. Marion Crane and her lover Sam are half naked after a lunch-hour tryst. Never before in the history of mainstream American film had an erotic scene been played horizontally on a bed (Rebello, 1990: 86). Never before had a film so blatantly enlisted voyeuristic pleasures. Marion begins the scene supine, in bra and slip; Sam, with his shirt off, stands over her. Soon he joins her on the bed; they kiss and express frustration at having to meet like this.

Marion later steals $40,000 in order not to have to meet in cheap hotels. When she gets lost en route to Sam, she meets Norman Bates who seems, like herself, caught in a "private trap." After a cathartic conversation with Norman in the parlor of the motel, Marion decides to return the money. Norman peers through a peephole as she prepares for her shower. In extreme close-up we see a gigantic (male) eye gazing at a partly disrobed (female) body. Yet the twist of *Psycho* will turn out to be that this "male gaze" unleashes not a conventional, masculine heterosexual desire (or assault) but a new being: the schizo-psychotic Norman–Mother who will act to foil Norman's heterosexual desire.

The sudden, unexplained violence of the attack in the shower came as a great shock to audiences who had been set up by the first third of the film to expect the slightly tawdry love story of Marion and Sam. The shower-murder's destabilizing effect on audiences was perfectly enacted by the shots that followed this attack. The same roving, voyeuristic camera eye that began the film appears to want to pick up the pieces of a narrative trajectory. But where should it go? What should it now see? The inquisitive, forward-propelled movement that inaugurated the story is now impossible; the camera can only look at the bloody water washing down the drain. Tracking "down the drain" graphically enacts what has just happened to all narrative expectation with the murder of the film's main character and star. From the darkness of the drain, and echoing the counterclockwise spiral of the swirling water, vision re-emerges in a reverse pull-back out of the dead, staring eye of Marion.

This baroque camera movement "down the drain" and back out of a dead, unseeing eye enacts a spectatorial disorientation that was one of the most striking features of watching *Psycho*. In a moment this abyss will be filled by a new focus on Norman who will enter to clean up the mess and protect "Mother." But from this point on, the audience cannot comfortably settle into a conventional narrative trajectory. What it will do instead is begin to anticipate "Mother's" next attack and to register the rhythms of its anticipation, shock, and release.

The above are familiar observations about *Psycho*'s abrupt rupture with supposedly "classical" narrative expectation. Yet anyone who has gone to the movies in the past twenty years—a period in which the influence of Hitchcock in general and *Psycho* in particular has become increasingly apparent—cannot help but notice how elements of this "roller-coaster" sensibility—a sensibility that is grounded in the pleasurable anticipation of the next gut-spilling, gut-wrenching moment—has gained ascendance in popular moving-image culture.[6] Although *Psycho* is certainly not the direct antecedent of all these films, it does mark the important beginning of an era in which viewers began going to the movies to be thrilled and moved in quite visceral ways, and without much concern for coherent characters or motives.

The New "Cinema of Attractions"

Scholars of early cinema have recently shown the importance of visual sensation in this period (see Gunning, [2000: 316–331]). As these scholars have learned to appreciate the sensational pleasures of this pre-narrative, pre-"classical" cinema, they have often noted affinities between this cinema and the contemporary return to sensation in special effects, extreme violence, and sexual display. While narrative is not abandoned in ever more sensationalized cinema, it often takes second seat to a succession of visual and auditory "attractions." Tom Gunning's work on the early "cinema of attractions" is based on this cinema's dual ability visually to "show" something new or sensational and to "attract" viewers to this show. Gunning shows how most early cinema before [D. W.] Griffith placed a premium on calling attention to the ability of the apparatus to offer attractions over its ability to absorb spectators into a diegetic world (Gunning, 1986). The term *attraction* is borrowed from Sergei Eisenstein whose theory of the "montage of attractions" laid stress on the "sensual or psychological

impact" of images on spectators in their ability to disrupt spectatorial absorption into "illusory depictions" (Eisenstein, 1988: 35).
It was, in fact, the destabilizing, shock effect of the fairground
roller coaster that Eisenstein had most in mind when he coined
the term.[7] And it is very much a quality like a roller-coaster ride
that is the primary attraction of the new cinema described above.

The point of invoking the term "attractions" (and the further
association of the actual roller-coaster ride) is not to argue that
contemporary postmodern American cinema has reverted to the
same attractions of early cinema. While there is certainly an affinity
between the two, this new regime entails entirely different spectatorial disciplines and engages viewers in entirely different social
experiences.[8] We might distinguish between these experiences by
considering the attractions of the fair which beckon to viewers,
surrounding them with sights and shows from which they might
choose, to the experience of being caught up in the literal sensations of falling, flying, careening in the roller coaster. Film his-
torian Thomas Schatz has attempted to specify the institutional,
economic, technological, and generic changes that have constituted the new attractions of what he prefers to call "the New
Hollywood" (Schatz, 1993). Schatz isolates a common feature of
"high-cost, high-tech, high-speed thrillers" which, in his predom-
inantly negative account, were most dramatically ushered in by
the 1973 blockbuster *Jaws* and followed by the *Star Wars*, *Close Encounters*, *Raiders of the Lost Ark*, *E. T.*, *Exorcist*, and *Godfather* mega hits.[9]
He characterizes these "calculated blockbusters" as genre pastiches
which are "visceral, kinetic, and fast-paced, increasingly reliant on
special effects, increasingly 'fantastic' . . . and increasingly targeted
at younger audiences" (Schatz, 1993: 23).

What is especially interesting in Schatz's description is the attention to the new packaging of thrills and the connection of
these thrills not simply to the fairground of Eisenstein's attractions, but to the postmodern theme park of Baudrillardian simulacra. For the crucial point about all the films Schatz mentions
is not simply that some of them actually *are* theme-park rides
(for example, Universal's "E.T." and Disneyland's "Star Tours"),
but that many films now set out, as a first order of business, to

simulate the bodily thrills and visceral pleasures of attractions that not only beckon to us but take us on a continuous ride punctuated by shocks and moments of speed-up and slow-down. Since Schatz wrote his essay, one of the highest grossing movies ever is a film about a dinosaur theme-park ride run amok (*Jurassic Park*, 1993). The fact that this film has now itself become a theme-park ride only confirms the observation that the destabilized ride, the ride that seems to career most wildly out of control, is the one we increasingly want to take.

We might consider as well a telling moment in *Titanic* (James Cameron, 1997), the film that has now passed *Jurassic Park* to become the biggest box-office hit of all time. Just before the stern end of the Titanic—the only part of the ship still afloat—sinks, it rides high up into the air and poises perpendicular to the water. With desperate passengers clinging to the railings, the towering upended stern pauses a breathless moment before plunging straight down into the deep. During this moment, behaving for all the world like a kid on a roller coaster preparing to ride the downhill plunge after the dramatic pause at the top, the film's hero Jack Dawson (Leonardo DiCaprio) cries out with more excitement than fear: "This is it!" Dawson's exclamation, pinpointing the exact moment of the ride's greatest anticipation and fear speaks for the roller-coaster thrill of yet another film ride that has careened wildly out of control. Can the theme-park simulation be far behind?

Perhaps the best way to understand this specific appeal to the roller-coaster sensibilities of contemporary life is to compare a traditional roller-coaster ride—say the rickety wood and steel affair on [the] Santa Cruz, California, boardwalk, part of the fun of which is riding high above the boardwalk, beach, and ocean—with the roller-coaster-style rides at Disneyland. These latter rides borrow from cinema in one of two ways. Either they simulate a diegetic world through cinematic *mise-en-scène*—but still literally move the body through actual space—such as the "Matterhorn," or they are elaborate updates of early cinema's Hales Tours, "moving" the audience through virtual, electronically generated, space, such as Tomorrowland's motion-simulation "Star Tours." This ride, which literally goes nowhere, feels just as harrowing as an actual roller coaster, even more so when the added narrative informs us that the robot pilot has malfunctioned causing us nearly to collide with a number of objects. The narrative information that we are out of control enhances the virtual sensation of wild careening.

In both forms of ride, traditional roller coasters have become more like the movies; and movies, in turn, have become more like roller coasters. In this convergence of pleasures the contemporary, postmodern cinema has reconnected in important ways with the "attractions" of amusement parks. But these attractions have themselves been thematized and narrativized through their connection with the entire history of movies. (Even the Matterhorn is based on a now forgotten 1959 movie, *Third Man on the Mountain*.) It would be a mistake, therefore, to think of these new forms of attractions as simply reverting (or regressing) to the spectatorial sensations of early cinema. Rather, we need to see them as scopic regimes demanding specific kinds of spectatorial discipline.

One aspect of that discipline was already being cultivated in the long lines beginning to form in the late 1950s at the newly built Disneyland. Just as the newly thematized roller coasters such as the Matterhorn and the later motion-simulation roller coasters such as Star Tours base their thrills on destabilizing movement through real, or simulated, narrativized space, so a film such as *Psycho* introduced, long before the blockbusters Schatz describes as defining the New Hollywood, what might be called a roller-coaster concept to the phenomenon of film viewing. For *Psycho* the ride began, like the rides at Disneyland, with the line and its anticipation of terror. It continued in the film proper with an unprecedented experience of disorientation, destabilization, and terror. When the forward-moving, purposeful voyeuristic camera eye "washes" down the drain after the murder of Marion and emerges in reverse twisting out of her dead eye, audiences could, for the first time in mainstream motion picture history, take pleasure in losing the kind of control, mastery, and forward momentum familiar to what I will now resist calling the "classical" narrative and will instead call popular modern cinema.

Billy Crystal's joke at the 1993 Academy Awards ceremony that *The Crying Game* proved that "white men *can* jump" offers a good example of the kind of pleasurable destabilization that I am trying to identify. The shocking attraction of this film is the appearance of a masculine mark of gender where none was expected. This gender shock would not have been possible without the remarkable ability of audiences and critics to keep the secret of a key protagonist's gender. Gender shock is, of course, what *Psycho* also gave to its audience. The "shock" of the surprise depends on the discipline of the kept secret. *Psycho* is the film that first linked an erotic display of sexual attractions to a shocking display of sexualized violence. But its attractions were no longer deployed within a stable heterosexual framework or within the hegemony of an exclusive masculine subjectivity. This new twist on some very "basic instincts" is at the heart of postmodern gender and sexuality in popular cinema.

Psycho and Genre Study

If today it is becoming possible to recognize *Psycho* as fun, it is partly because the popular contemporary slasher film has taught us this lesson through generic repetitions of what was once so strikingly original in *Psycho*. But it is also because genre study has sometimes been the one place in film studies where repeatable audience pleasures, as opposed to thwarted or punitive desires, have been scrutinized. Genre study is also the place where some of the major truisms of contemporary film theory have been most thoroughly re-examined in the face of the social experiences of spectators. It is thus not surprising that it is in the study of the horror genre that we have received, however indirectly, an implicit appreciation of *Psycho*'s pivotal place in the transition to a postmodern visual culture.

Approached as a horror film, *Psycho* is often regarded as a turning point in the history of the genre: the moment when horror moved, in Andrew Tudor's words, "from collective fears about threatening forces somewhere 'out there'" to a "sexuality, repression and psychosis" that is frighteningly close to home and potential in us all (1989: 46–47). Carol J. Clover's study of contemporary horror film, *Men, Women, and Chain Saws*, has also commented on the enormous influence of a tale "of sex and parents" (1992: 49) inaugurated by *Psycho*. In her chapter on the contemporary "slasher film" that forms the nucleus of her book, Clover notices how powerfully a masculine viewer casts his emotional lot with a "female-victim-hero."[10] This "final girl," survivor of gruesome slice and dice mayhem, is, in her knife-wielding or chain-saw-wielding triumph at the end, anything but passive and not very feminine. Where traditional views of the horror genre have too simply polarized gender to active male monster and passive female victim, Clover's analysis of the low exploitative subgenre of the slasher film discovers that a vicarious "abject terror, gendered feminine" is crucial to the genre, and that this terror is merely the starting point of a roller-coaster ride that careens wildly, between the gendered poles of feminine abjection and masculine mastery.

Clover develops Kaja Silverman's insight that identification in *Psycho* shifts between victim and victimizer, though she develops this mostly in relation to the contemporary horror tradition spawned by this film and she develops it as masochistic *pleasure*, not punishment. In order to understand sadomasochistic pleasures that are perhaps more basic to contemporary film viewing than any modernist rupture, Clover argues that all forms of contemporary horror involve the thrill of being assaulted—of "opening up" to penetrating images. Using horror's own metacommentary on itself to fill in what she calls the "blind spots" of theories of spectatorship by [Christian] Metz and [Laura] Mulvey, Clover asserts the importance of "gazes" that do not master their objects of vision but are reactive and introjective (Clover, 1992: 225–26).

Today, *Psycho*'s relation to the slasher genre and its peculiar gendered pleasure seems obvious. Yet, it is only in retrospect that we can place it "in" the slasher subgenre, or perhaps only if we wish to include its sequels of the 1980s—*Psycho II, III*, and *IV*—as part of its text.[11] What, then, is *Psycho*? Or, more precisely, what was *Psycho* on first viewing and what has it become since? Through subsequent viewings it has become the familiar antecedent for familial "slice and dice" horror. But audiences who first went to see it did not go to see a slasher horror film; they went to see a *Hitchcock* thriller with a twist—about which there was a great deal of excitement and quite a bit of mystery. The crucial significance of *Psycho*, measurable today in terms of its influence on the slasher film, but measurable then in its new "attractions" challenging certain production code taboos against depictions of both sex and violence, is not that it actually showed more sex or more violence than other films—which it, literally speaking, did not—but rather, as Clover notes, that it sexualized the motive, and the action, of violence (Clover, 1992: 24).

Just how we understand this sexualization of violence seems to be the key issue in assessing the impact, the influence, and the postmodernity of *Psycho*'s particular roller-coaster ride of attractions. The shower sequence is one of the most analyzed sequences in all American film. Certainly, part of its fame derives from the technical brilliance of the way it is cut. Many a film teacher, myself included, has taught the importance of editing by punning on its powerful effects of cutting—of both flesh and film.

It was almost a reflex of post-structuralist psychoanalytic criticism to "read" the shower sequence as an act of symbolic castration carried out on the presumably already "castrated" body of a woman with whom spectators have identified. Marion's body—insisted on by some form of undress in two scenes prior to the shower-murder—unleashes Norman's desire for her which in turn unleashes "Mrs. Bates," the mother who kills to protect her son from the sexual aggressions of "loose" women. As I once put it: "the woman is both victim and monster. . . . Norman, the matricide and killer of several other women, is judged the victim of the very mother he has killed" (Williams, 1984: 93–94). The female monster unleashed by the female victim seemed to permit the simultaneous vilification and victimization of women. Yet as

Carol Clover has correctly pointed out, such a feminist critique does not do justice to the obvious bisexuality of the slasher killers spawned by Norman, nor to the new-found strength and resourcefulness of the female victims spawned by Marion and her sister (Clover, 1992: 21–64).

Barbara Creed has tried to argue that what has been missing from psychoanalytically based studies of horror film has been an appreciation of the disturbing power of the "monstrous feminine."[12] Creed has a point about the Kristevan [the critic, Julia Kristeva's notion of the] powers of (abject, female) horror. However, because she points to the monstrous feminine as an archetype, she fails to account for the remarkable emergence of this monstrosity in the wake of the influence of *Psycho*, or for the historical importance of *Psycho* itself. For the really striking fact about this film is not its illustration of a previously unacknowledged archetype, but its archetype's influential emergence in 1960. This is not to say that there had not been female monsters before *Psycho* or that conventional male monsters of classic horror were not often sexually indeterminate.[13] It is to say, however, that *Psycho*'s array of dislocations—between normal and psychotic; between masculine and feminine; between Eros and fear; even between the familiar Hitchcockian suspense and a new, frankly gender-based horror—are what make it an important precursor of the thrill-producing visual attractions Schatz discusses as crucial to the New Hollywood and which I would like to identify as postmodern. Thus Hitchcock's decision to make the traditional monster of horror cinema a son who dresses up as his own mummified mother was a decision not so much to give violent power to "the monstrous feminine," but, much more dramatically, to destabilize masculine and feminine altogether.

"He's a transvestite!" says the district attorney in a famously inadequate attempt to explain the root cause of Norman's disturbance. The line has been criticized, along with the psychiatrist's lengthy speech about how Norman became his mother, as Hitchcock's jab at the inadequacies of clinical explanation. Certainly Norman is not a mere transvestite—that is, a person whose sexual pleasure involves dressing up as the opposite sex—but rather a much more deeply disturbed individual whose whole personality had at times, as the psychiatrist puts it, "become the mother." Yet in the scene that supposedly shows us that Norman has finally "become the mother," what we really see is Norman, now without wig and dress, sitting alone in a holding area reflecting, in the most feminine of the many voices given Mrs. Bates, on the evil of "her" son.

In other words, while ostensibly illustrating that Norman now "is" the mother, the film provides a visual and auditory variation on Norman's earlier sexual indeterminacy. The shock of this scene is the combination of young male body and older female voice: visual evidence of male, aural evidence of female. It is thus not the recognition of one identity overcome by another that fascinates so much as the slippage between masculine and feminine poles of an identity. The film's penultimate image drives this home. Briefly emerging as if from under Norman's face is the grinning mouth of Mrs. Bates's corpse. Again, the shock is that of indeterminacy: both Norman *and* mother. Thus the psychiatrist's point that Norman is entirely mother is not visually or aurally proven. Instead, these variations of drag become overtly thematized as ironic, and almost camp, forms of play with audience expectations regarding the fixity of gender.[14] Norman is not a transvestite, but transvestitism is a major "attraction" of these scenes for audiences.

A similar point can be made for the earlier climax of *Psycho* during Norman–Mrs. Bates's thwarted attack on Lila in the fruit cellar. Here again the "attraction" is neither the appearance of Mrs. Bates as woman, nor the revelation, when "her" wig falls off in the struggle, that "she" is her son. At the precise moment that Norman's wig begins to slip off in his struggle with Sam— when we see a masculine head emerging from under the old-lady wig—we witnessed what was at the time a truly shocking absence of gender stability. Gender of the monster is revealed in this film in very much the terms Judith Butler offers: as an imitation without an origin, a corporeal style of performance, a construction (1990: 138–39).

There can be no doubt, however, that one primary "attraction" of the film's horror is its spectacular mutilation of a woman's naked body. Abject terror, as Clover puts it, is "gendered feminine" (1992: 51). There is also no doubt that the introduction of certain psychoanalytic conventions on screen conspire to vilify the mother and her sexuality as cause of Norman's derangement. These are certain misogynist features of a film that, for a variety of reasons, struck a responsive chord with American audiences in a way that Michael Powell's similar, but more truly modernist, "laying bare" of the device of voyeurism in *Peeping Tom* (also 1960) did not.[15] Over the next twenty years the horror genre would begin to establish a formula for reproducing, and refining, the various sexual and gendered elements of this experience in ways that would not lessen the attraction of the violence against women but which would empower the "final girl" to fight back and invite spectators to identify alternately with her powerless victimization and the subsequently empowered struggle against it.

Psycho thus needs to be seen not as an exceptional and transgressive experience working against the classical norms of visual pleasure but rather as an important turning point in the pleasurable destabilizing of sexual identity within what would become the genre of slasher horror: it is the moment when the experience of going to the movies began to be constituted as providing a certain generally transgressive sexualized thrill of promiscuous abandonment to indeterminate, "other" identities. To undergo this abandonment, however, audiences had to be *disciplined*, not in Silverman's sense of being punished, but in [Michel] Foucault's sense of voluntarily submitting to a regime.

Disciplining Fear: "The Care and Handling of *Psycho*"

From the very first screenings of the film, audience reaction, in the form of gasps, screams, yells, and even running up and down the aisles, was unprecedented. Although Hitchcock later claimed to have calculated all this, saying he could hear the screams when planning the shower montage, screenwriter Joseph Stefano claims, "He was lying. . . . We had no idea. We thought people would gasp or be silent, but screaming? Never" (Rebello, 1990: 117).

No contemporary review of the film ignored the fact that audiences were screaming as never before. Here are some typical reviews:

> Scream! Its a good way to let off steam in this Alfred Hitchcock shockeroo, . . . so scream, shiver and shake and have yourself a ball. (*Los Angeles Examiner*, 8 November 1960)

> So well is the picture made . . . that it can lead audiences to do something they hardly ever do any more—cry out to the characters, in hopes of dissuading them from going to the doom that has been cleverly established as awaiting them. (Callenbach, 1960: 48)

And on the negative side:

> Director Hitchcock bears down too heavily in this one, and the delicate illusion of reality necessary for a creak-and-shriek movie becomes, instead, a spectacle of stomach-churning horror. (*Time*, 27 June 1960: 51)

> *Psycho* is being advertised as more a shocker than a thriller, and that is right—I am shocked, in the sense that I am offended and disgusted. . . . The clinical details of psychopathology are not material for trivial entertainment; when they are used so they are an offense against taste and an assault upon the sensibilities of the audience . . . it makes you feel unclean. (Robert Hatch, *The Nation*, 2 July 1960)

Having unleashed such powerful reactions, the problem now was how to handle them. According to Anthony Perkins, the entire scene in the hardware store following the shower-murder, the mopping up and disposal of Marion's body in the swamp, were inaudible due to leftover howls from the previous scene. Hitchcock even asked [Universal] Studio[s] head Lew Wasserman to allow him to remix the sound to allow for the audience's vocal reaction. Permission was denied (Rebello, 1990: 163).

Hitchcock's unprecedented "special policy" of admitting no

one to the theater after the film had begun was certainly a successful publicity stunt, but it had lasting repercussions in its transformation of the previously casual act of going to the movies into a much more *disciplined* activity of arriving on time and waiting in an orderly line. As Peter Bogdanovich (1963) has noted, it is because of *Psycho* that audiences now go to movies at the beginning. One popular critic wrote in a Sunday arts-and-leisure section about the new policy:

> At any other entertainment from ice show to baseball games, the bulk of the patrons arrive before the performance begins. Not so at the movies which have followed the policy of grabbing customers in any time they arrive, no matter how it may impair the story for those who come in midway. (*View*: 1)

This reviewer then takes it upon himself to advocate the exhibition policy so important to *Psycho*'s success and impact on audiences: that no one be admitted late to the film. Hitchcock defended this policy in an article published in the *Motion Picture Herald* saying that the idea came to him one afternoon in the cutting room.

> I suddenly startled my fellow-workers with a noisy vow that my frontwards-backwards-sidewards-and-inside-out labors on *Psycho* would not be in vain—that everyone else in the world would have to enjoy the fruits of my labor to the full by seeing the picture from beginning to end. This was the way the picture was conceived—and this was how it had to be seen. (6 August, 1960: 17–18)

This "policy," unheard of in the United States at the time, necessitated important changes in the public's movie-going habits: audiences had to be trained to learn the times of each show; if they were late they had to wait for the next screening; and, once they bought their tickets, they had to be induced to stand patiently in ticketholder lines. The theater managers' new buzzwords were to "fill and spill" theaters efficiently at precise intervals, thus affording more screenings. The unprecedented discipline required to "fill and spill" the theater was in paradoxical contrast to the equally unprecedented thrills of the show itself.[16]

Here is how another columnist described the discipline and thrill of seeing the film over a month after its release:

> There was a long line of people at the show—they will only seat you at the beginning and I don't think they let you out while it's going on. . . . A loudspeaker was carry-ing a sound track made by Mr. Hitchcock. He said it was absolutely necessary—he gave it the British pronunciation like "nessary." He said you absolutely could not go in at the beginning. The loudspeaker then let out a couple of female shrieks that would turn your blood to ice. And the ticket taker began letting us all in. A few months ago, I was reading the London review of this picture. The Brit-ish critics rapped it. "Contrived," they said. "Not up to the Hitchcock standards." I do not know what standards they were talking about. But I must say that Hitchcock . . . did not seem to be that kind of person at all. Hitch-cock turned us all on. Of all the shrieking and screaming! We were all limp. And, after drying my palms on the mink coat next to me, we went out to have hamburgers. And let the next line of people go in and die. Well, if you are reading the trade papers, you must know that *Psycho* is making a mint of money. This means we are in for a whole series of such pictures. (Delaplane, 1960)

How shall we construe this new disciplining of audiences to wait in line? Michel Foucault writes that "discipline produces subjected and practiced bodies, 'docile' bodies" (1978: 138). He means that what we experience as autonomy is actually a subtle form of power. Obviously the bodies of the *Psycho* audience were docile. Indeed, the fun of the film was dependent upon the ability of these bodies to wait patiently in line in order to catch the thrills described above. No one coerced them to arrive on time and wait in line. This discipline is for fun. And the fun derives partly from the exhilaration of a group submitting itself, as a group, to a thrilling sensation of fear and release from fear. In this highly ritualized masochistic submission to a familiar "master," blood turns to ice, shrieking and screaming are understood frankly as a "turn on," followed by climax, detumescence, and the final the recovery and renewal of (literal and metaphorical) appetite.

The passage also offers a rich mix of allusions to gender, class, and nationality: the mink coat next to the columnist is clear indication that these pleasures were not for men only, as well as evidence that a wide variety of the public participated. Hamburger counters mink; snooty English "standards" are foils to America's favorite fantasy of the leveling democratic entertainment of "the movies." What we see here is a conception of the audience as a group with a common solidarity—that of submitting to an experience of mixed arousal and fear and of recognizing those reactions in one another and perhaps even performing them for one another.[17]

This audience, surveilled and policed with unprecedented rigor outside the theater, responding with unprecedented vocalized terror inside the theater, is certainly disciplined in the sense of Foucault's term. But it is also an audience with a newfound sense of itself as bonded around the revelation of certain terrifying visual secrets. The shock of learning these secrets produces a camaraderie, a pleasure of the group, that was, I think, quite new to motion pictures. A certain community was created around *Psycho*'s secret that gender is often not what it seems. The shock of learning this secret helped produce an ironic sadomasochistic discipline of master and slave with Hitchcock hamming up his role as sadistic master and with audiences enjoying their role as submissive victims.

An important tool in disciplining the *Psycho* audience were three promotional trailers, two quite short and one six-minute affair that has become a classic. All hinted at but, unlike most "coming attractions," refrained from showing too much of the film's secret. In the most famous of these Hitchcock acts as a kind of house-of-horrors tour guide at the Universal International Studio set of the Bates Motel and adjacent house (now the Universal Studios Theme Park featuring the *Psycho* house and motel). Each trailer stressed the importance of special discipline: either "please don't tell the ending, it's the only one we have"—or the importance of arriving on time. But there was also another trailer, not seen by the general public but even more crucial in inculcating audience discipline. Called "The care and handling of *Psycho*" this was not a preview of the film but a filmed "press book" teaching theater exhibitors how properly to exhibit the film and police the audience.[18]

The black-and-white trailer begins with a scene outside the DeMille Theater in New York where *Psycho* began a limited engagement before being released nationwide. To the accompaniment of Bernard Herrmann's driving violin score we see crowds in line for the film. A man in a tuxedo is a theater manager, the narrator urgently informs us, in charge of implementing the new policy, which the trailer then explains. The sly voice of Alfred Hitchcock is heard over a loudspeaker explaining to the waiting audience that "This queuing up is good for you, it will make you appreciate the seats inside. It will also make you appreciate *Psycho*." The mixture of polite inducement backed up by the presence of Pinkerton guards, and a life-size lobby card cut-out of Hitchcock pointing to his watch, add up to a rather theatrical, sadomasochistic display of coercion. We hear Hitchcock induce the audience to keep the "tiny, little horrifying secrets" of the story while insisting on the democracy of a policy that will not even make exceptions for the Queen of England or the manager's brother.

Perhaps the most striking thing about this trailer is that it worked; not only did audiences learn to arrive on time but they eagerly joined the visible crowds on the sidewalks waiting to see the film. When shaken spectators left the theater they were grilled by those waiting in line but never gave away the secret (Rebello, 1990: 161). By exploiting his popular television persona as the man who loves to scare you, and the man audiences love to be scared by, Hitchcock achieved the kind of rapt audience attention, prompt arrival, and departure that would have been the envy of a symphony orchestra. Yet, he achieved this attention with the casual, general audience more used to the distractions of amusement parks than the discipline of high culture.

On 17 July 1955, Disneyland had already opened its doors to

large numbers of visitors taking in the total visual attraction of a variety of film-orientated "fantasy lands." In August 1964, Universal Studios began offering tram ride tours of its movie sets and would eventually expand to a more movie-related and thrill-inducing competitor to Disneyland, including the *Psycho* set and a presentation of how certain scenes from the film were shot.[19] Clearly, the sort of discipline that Hitchcock was teaching was more like that of the crowds at these theme parks than any kind of simple audience taming. Lawrence Levine has written compellingly about the taming of American audiences during the latter part of the nineteenth century. He argues that while American theater audiences had in the first half of the nineteenth century been a highly participatory and unruly lot, spitting tobacco, talking back to actors, arriving late, leaving early, stamping feet, applauding promiscuously, they were gradually tamed by the arbiters of culture to "submit to creators and become mere instruments of their will, mere auditors of the productions of the artist" (1988: 183).

Levine tells, for example, of an orchestra conductor in Cincinnati in 1873 who ordered the doors to be closed when he began to play, admitting no one until the first part was finished. When he was resisted his argument was "When you play Offenbach or Yankee Doodle, you can keep your doors open. When I play Handel . . . they must be shut. Those who appreciate music will be here on time" (1988: 188). Levine argues that this late-nineteenth-century American audience lost a sense of itself as an active force, a "public," and became instead a passive "mute receptor" of the will of the artist through this discipline. New divisions between high and low meant that it was more and more difficult to find audiences who could serve as microcosms of society, who felt like participants in a general culture, and who could articulate their opinions and feelings vocally (Levine, 1988: 195).

With Hitchcock's policy trailer we certainly see some elements of Levine's tamed audience: Pinkerton guards, loudspeakers, "docile bodies" waiting patiently in line, not to mention Hitchcock's disembodied voice insisting that seeing the film from the beginning is "required." Certainly, Hitchcock asserts "the will of the artist" over the audience. However, this will is in the service of producing visceral thrills and ear-splitting screams that are a far cry from the politely suppressed coughs of the concert hall. It seems that the efficiency and discipline demonstrated outside the theater need to be viewed in tandem with the unprecedented patterns of fear and release unleashed inside.

Hitchcock's discipline, like that of the emerging theme parks, was not based on the stratification of audiences into high and low, nor, as would later occur in the ratings system, was it based on the stratification of different age-groups. Nor was it based on the acquisition of the same kind of passivity and silence that Levine traces in late-nineteenth-century America. In Hitchcock's assumption of the persona of the sadist who expects his submissive audience to trust him to provide a devious form of pleasure, we see a new bargain struck between filmmaker and audience: if you want me to make you scream in a new way and about these new sexually destabilized secrets, the impresario seems to say, then you must line up patiently to receive this thrill.

Hitchcock is, of course, only doing what he often did in his trailers: teasing the audience with their paradoxical love of fear, shock, surprise, and suspense—all emotions which he can rely upon audiences to know that he will manipulate for maximum pleasure. His famous cameos in the early parts of most of his films are another way of teasing the audience, though also of disciplining them to pay close attention. Like the patient crowds standing in line at Disneyland, or the crowds that would eventually stand in line to see the *Psycho* house and motel at Universal Studios,[20] these disciplined audiences were a far cry either from 1970s' film theory's notion of distanced, voyeuristic mastery or Levine's passive, mute receptors.

Psycho is popularly remembered as the film that violated spectatorial identification with a main character by an unprecedented killing off of that character in the first third of the film. But in order for audiences to experience the full force of that violation, Hitchcock required the kind of rapt entrance into the spell of a unified space and time that the so-called "classical" theories of spectatorship assume but which the popular Hollywood cinema, with its distracted viewers wandering into theaters at any old time, had perhaps only rarely delivered. *Psycho* thus needs to be viewed as a film in which disciplined audiences arrived on time in order to be attentively absorbed into the filmic world and narrative, and in which distracted "attractions" of the amusement-park variety are equally important. The more rapt viewers' initial attention, the more acute the shock when the rug was pulled out from under them.

Lawrence Levine's analysis of the nineteenth-century taming of the audience argues a singular process of repressing unruly body functions. Theaters, opera houses, large movie houses were, for him, agents in teaching audiences to adjust to new social imperatives, training them to keep strict control of emotional and physical processes. Levine may be right that bodily repression was necessary to concert- and theatergoers. But the (mostly unwritten) history of cinema reception[21] will require more than a concept of bodily repression to understand the various disciplines of film-going that have taken place in this century. It will certainly require a more Foucauldian concept of discipline as productive of certain precise bodily regimes of pleasure rather than the mere repression of the physical. For, as we have seen, *Psycho* simultaneously elicits more bodily reaction along with greater bodily discipline.[22]

The lesson of the "care and handling" of *Psycho* is thus how first Hitchcock, and then Hollywood, learned how greater spectatorial discipline could pay off in the distracted attractions of a postmodern cinema. *Psycho* needs to be seen as a historical marker of a moment when popular American movies, facing the threat of television, in competition and cooperation with new kinds of amusement parks, began to invent new scopic regimes of visual and visceral "attraction." In this moment visual culture can be seen getting a tighter grip on the visual pleasures of film spectators through the reinstitution of a postmodern cinema of attractions.

One way of picturing the variety of these regimes and this perhaps unique moment of discipline and distraction that was

Psycho is to consider an entire series of publicity photos of audiences watching *Psycho* published in the same trade publication. These photos were taken at the Plaza Theatre, London, during the film's first run in Britain. Figures 9.1 and 9.2 show fragments of a very intense-looking audience, jaws set, looking hard except for a few people with averted eyes. We can note here the some-

FIGURES 9.1 and 9.2. Fragments of the audience at the Plaza Theatre, London: bracing itself to view *Psycho*. Reproduced courtesy of the Academy of Motion Picture Arts and Sciences.

what defensive postures indicating moments of anticipation—arms crossed; one person holding ears, suggesting the importance sound has in cueing the anticipation of terror.

Figure 9.3 shows closer detail of what may be the same audience. Here we begin to note significant gender differences. Whereas the men look intently, most women cringe, refusing to look at the screen as I had once suggested women do at horror films (Williams, 1984), or they cover their ears. On the other hand, figure 9.4 shows just how dramatically male viewers seem to assert their masculinity by looking (note the "cool" man with clenched jaw who both looks and clutches his tie).

Let us suppose, for the sake of argument, that these scared women in the audience are looking at one of the following: the "scary woman" (Mrs. Bates) or a terrified woman being attacked (Marion, figure 9.5). What is the best way to describe the specifically gendered reactions of these women spectators? Consider the experience of watching the first attack on Marion in the shower. At this point in the film all viewers can be assumed to be somewhat identified with Marion and to be relatively, though not completely, unprepared for the attack—after all the film is called *Psycho*. They are taken by surprise by this first irrational irruption

FIGURE 9.3. Fragment of the audience at the Plaza Theatre, London: gendered responses to *Psycho*. Reproduced courtesy of the Academy of Motion Picture Arts and Sciences.

FIGURE 9.4.

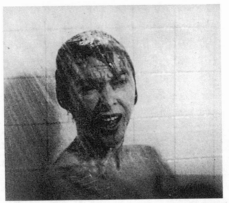

FIGURE 9.5. Marion in the shower, *Psycho* (1960).
Reproduced courtesy of the Academy of Motion
Picture Arts and Sciences.

of violence, mystified by the lack of a distinct view of the attacker,
shocked by the eerie sound and rhythms of screaming violins
blending with screaming victim, and energized by the rapid cutting of the scene. This much is true for all spectators. Why then
do women appear so much more moved, often to the point of
grabbing ears, averting and covering eyes? The question, it seems,

is whether female viewers can be said to be more closely identified with Marion, especially at the height of her fear and pain, than the males. Do we identify more, and thus find ourselves more terrorized, because we are insufficiently distanced from the image in general and from this tortured image of our like in particular? Men, in contrast, may identify with Marion, but they forcefully limit their correspondence to her. Since terror is itself, as Carol Clover aptly notes, "gendered feminine," the more controlled masculine reaction immediately distances itself from the scared woman on the screen. It more quickly gets a grip on itself (as does the man with his tie) and checks its expression. Yet at the same time that it exercises this control, this masculine reaction fully *opens up* to the image to, as Clover puts it, "take it in the eye" (1992: 202). If, as Clover argues, all forms of contemporary horror involve the masochistic and feminine thrill of "opening up" to, of being "assaulted" by, penetrating images, we might say that the men can be seen to open up more because they feel they "correspond" less to the gender of the primary victims (and to the femininity of fear itself).

For the woman viewer, however, this "taking it in the eye" pleasures her less, initially, than it does the man. Because women already perceive themselves as more vulnerable to penetration, as corresponding more to the assaulted, wide-eyed, and opened-up female victim all too readily penetrated by knife or penis, women's response is more likely to *close down*, at least initially, to such images. This is to say that the mix of pleasure and pain common to all horror viewing, and aligned with a feminine subject position, is negotiated differently by men than by women. Thus all viewers experience a second degree of vicarious pain that is felt as feminizing. But in their greater vulnerability, some women viewers react by acting to filter out some of the painful images. I once took the woman's refusal to look at the screen as a sensible resistance to pain (Williams, 1984). Now I am more inclined to think that, like the general audiences who were disciplined to arrive on time, a much more complex and disciplined negotiation of pleasure and pain is taking place, and that this negotiation takes place over time, as we watch first this film and then its host of imitators—something these instantaneous photos cannot register.

In involuntarily averting their eyes, for example, women viewers partially rupture their connection with the female victim. In the process, we may also establish a new connection with the other women in the audience whose screams we hear. This new connection then itself becomes a source of highly ritualized feminine pleasure. We enjoy being scared *with one another*—a camaraderie that also allows us to measure our difference from Marion. Notice, for example, the smile on the half-hidden mouth of the woman in figure 9.6.

Thus, while our first reactive, introjective experience of fear may elicit almost involuntary screams and the "closing down" response of not looking, we do not stop feeling the film because we stop looking. In fact, our reliance on musical cues may even induce us to feel more at this juncture. What are the violins saying about the danger of looking again? What is my girlfriend's posture as she leans into me telling me about how I might respond? Eventually, however, through the familiarity afforded by the film's repeated attacks, we begin to discipline ourselves to the experience of this reactive, introjective gaze. At this point some women may discipline themselves to keep their eyes more open.

Of course, these pictures do not really tell what audiences felt, and like all still images these are frozen moments, a few hundredths of seconds out of a 109-minute film. They could also have been faked. Nevertheless they dramatize, in acute body language, some general points about the changing distractions and disciplines of film spectatorship inaugurated by *Psycho*.

The first point is that however much we speak about the disembodied and virtual nature of cinematic, and all postmodern, forms of spectatorship, these are still real bodies in the theater, bodies which acutely feel what they see and which, even when visually "assaulted," experience various mixes of vulnerability and pleasure. These people are on a kind of roller coaster which they have been disciplined to ride, and discipline is an enormously important part of the social experience of going to the movies.

A second point is that this discipline may involve the audience

FIGURE 9.6. Fragment of the audience at the Plaza Theatre, London: the gendered pleasure of fear. Reproduced courtesy of the Academy of Motion Picture Arts and Sciences.

in a new level of performativity. While learning to enjoy the roller-coaster ride of a new kind of thrill, the audience may begin to perceive its own performances of fear as part of the show. As we also saw in the extended description of seeing *Psycho* by the columnist, these performances—screaming, hiding eyes, clutching the self as well as neighbors—may be important to the pleasures audiences take, as a group, in the film. Such spectatorial performances are certainly not new with *Psycho*. However, the self-consciously ironic manipulations of "the master" eliciting these performances from audiences in a film that is itself about the performance of masculinity and femininity represents a new level of gender play and destabilization that I take to be a founding moment of the greater awareness of the performativity of gender roles increasingly ushered in by a postmodern, "post-classical" reception of cinema.

A final point is that the discipline involved here—both inside and outside the theater—takes place over time. Spectators who clutched themselves, covered eyes, ears, and recoiled in fear at the shower-murder may have been responding involuntarily, the first time, to an unexpected assault. But by the film's second assault this audience was already beginning to play the game of anticipation and to repeat its response in increasingly performed and gender-based gestures and cries. By the time the game of slasher-assault became an actual genre in the mid-1970s, this disciplined and distracted, this attentive, performing audience will give way to the equivalent of the kids who raise their hands in roller-coaster rides and call out "look Ma, no hands!"

To find the experience of the popular, fun *Psycho* beneath the layers of high modernist critique or an all-embracing classicism is neither to denigrate the film's intelligence, nor the intelligence of the audiences who have enjoyed it. It is to recognize, rather, how important the visual and visceral experience of narrativized roller coasters have become and how assiduously audiences have applied themselves to the discipline of this fun.

Notes

This is a revised and altered version of an essay from *Culture and the Problem of the Disciplines*, edited by John Rowe. Copyright © 1998 by Columbia University Press. Reprinted with permission of the publisher.

Thanks to Agnieszka Soltysik for much of the research concerning the reception of *Psycho*, to Nita Rollins and Christine Gledhill for the significance of roller coasters, to Michael Friend of the Margaret Herrick Library for all sorts of advice and information, including access to "The Care and Handling of *Psycho*." Thanks also to members of the University of California Irvine Critics Theory Institute and to many other University of California Irvine colleagues, and to the Bay Area Film Consortium for helpful suggestions.

1. Slavoj Žižek, for example, claims that it is "still a 'modernist' film because it has maintained a dialectical tension between history and the present," which he sees embodied in the contrast between the old family house and the modern hotel (Žižek, 1992: 232). Psychoanalytic critics seem to agree with this assessment. David Bordwell, as we shall see below, goes to some trouble to argue for the film's "classical" status despite the fact that the release date of the film corresponds with the endpoint of his and his colleagues' study of the classical Hollywood era of cinema. This date would be quite convenient for the argument I propose about the postmodernity of *Psycho* if Bordwell, Staiger, and

Thompson actually argued that 1960 represented a real change in the Hollywood style of filmmaking. In fact, however, they argue that while the mode of production has changed, moving from studio system to a package-unit system relying on the enormous profits of occasional blockbusters to drive economic expansion into related acquisitions in the leisure field, the Hollywood style has not changed that much (1985: 360–77). I think it has and that *Psycho* is a good example of the nature of this change.

2. One measure of the high seriousness of this tradition could be seen in Robin Wood's straight-faced interpretation of Mrs. Bates's famous line about the fruit cellar—"Do you think I'm fruity?"—as offering the "hidden sexual springs of his behavior" yet then simply explicating the line as "the source of fruition and fertility become rotten"—with not a word about the gay implications of Norman's fruitiness.

3. In this passage, Silverman introduces the seeds of a sadomasochistic dynamic that she and others have fruitfully developed in later work. But she cannot develop it here, in relation to *Psycho*'s viewing pleasure, because her analysis is still wedded to a Mulveyan formula that sees all viewers seeking to escape an unpleasurable threat of castration. Since such escape is presumably thwarted by *Psycho*, the film seems to Silverman to disrupt classical narrative. However, this disruption was, in effect, saved from popular and suspect pleasures by its supposed enactment of castration: "When the stabbing begins, there is a cinematic cut with almost every thrust of the knife. The implied equation is too striking to ignore: the cinematic machine is lethal; it too murders and dissects" (1983: 211).

4. For an excellent critique of limitations of this way of formulating cinema history, see Miriam Hansen (2000). For a critique of the glaring omission of the mode or genre of melodrama from this history, see Altman (1992), Gledhill (1987), and Williams (1998).

5. This unfortunately leaves open the vexed problem of what to call this cinema, given the general acceptance of the term *classical* by so many scholars. I have become convinced that very often the old-fashioned, industry term melodrama—along with additional descriptive terms (western melodrama, gangster melodrama, racial melodrama)—offers a more precise description of both the narrative form and the spectatorial pleasures of a certain mainstream Hollywood product than does the term classical. But that is a matter for another essay (see Williams, 1998).

6. Consider, for example, the collections of films that have often (rather loosely) been called thrillers: erotic thrillers as different as *Blue*

Velvet (1986), *Fatal Attraction* (1987), and *Basic Instinct* (1992); older-style paranoid political thrillers such as *The Parallax View* (1974) or *All the President's Men* (1976); or the more recent political thrillers *JFK* (1991) and *The Pelican Brief* (1993); action thrillers, whether of the slightly more realistic Harrison Ford variety or the more stylized Hong Kong-influenced variety; older-style gross-out horror such as *The Texas Chain Saw Massacre* (1974) or *Halloween* (1978) and the hundreds of sequels of these and many other titles, or the newer-style mainstream horror thrillers (with similar "psycho-killer" monsters) such as *The Silence of the Lambs* (1991); or, finally, the paranoid political thriller turned gender-destabilized romance of *The Crying Game* (1992).

7. Gunning writes, for example, "the relations between films and the emergence of the great amusement parks, such as Coney Island, at the turn of the century provides rich ground for rethinking the roots of early cinema" (1990 reprint: 58). A similarly rich ground for rethinking postmodern cinema might be to consider the relation between cinema and the theme parks of the second half of the twentieth century.

8. Miriam Hansen, for example, has (sibilantly) argued that American films have in some way returned to attractions which "assault the viewer with sensational, supernatural, scientific, sentimental or otherwise stimulating sights" (Hansen, 1995: 137). Yet, as Hansen certainly is aware, it is also important to see how these sensational and stimulating sights have changed.

9. Though Schatz himself would have no truck with such theoretical grand narratives as the rupture of the modern by the postmodern, his description of the appeal of these films nevertheless exemplifies both Jameson's "cultural logic of late capitalism" as well Friedberg's more modest description of the gradually increasing centrality of the image-producing and reproducing apparatuses.

10. Clover does not consider the female viewer as a significant component of the audience of slasher films.

11. Although the basic conventions of gender-confused *Psycho* "killer," "terrible place," "phallic weapon," and "multiple victims" are already in place with *Psycho*, the convention of the powerful and triumphant "final girl" is only incipient with the survival (though not yet the self-rescue) of Marion's sister Lila. Since this "girl's'" reversal from abject victim to triumphant victor is crucial to the energy of the genre, it is possible to say that *Psycho* does not fully "fit" the psycho-killer genre.

12. This power challenges the prevalent view—especially in discus-

sions of horror cinema—that femininity constitutes passivity. Creed goes on to argue in a chapter on *Psycho* that the really important story of this film is precisely the story of the castrating mother. While it has become conventional to interpret the phallic mother as endowed with a fantasy phallus whose function is to disavow the male fear of castration—and thus the "actual" "lack" in the mother's body—Creed insists that *Psycho* does not offer an image of a phallic mother disavowing lack, but of a castrating mother whose power is located, presumably, in her difference from the male. Creed does not make this point about difference specifically in relation to *Psycho*, but she does make it generally with respect to the monstrous feminine.

13. Rhona Berenstein's study of classic horror film (1995), for example, extends Clover's insights into an earlier realm of horror often considered the province of the sadistic "male gaze" to argue that viewing pleasures were a more complicated form of role play than even Clover's masochistic pleasure of being assaulted can account for. In a genre in which monsters are masked and unmasked, heroes are feminized and doubled with monsters, heroines are both victimized and aligned with the monster's potency, viewer pleasure cannot be accounted for by simple binaries of masculine/feminine, Oedipal/preOedipal, homo/hetero. Berenstein thus argues not for a subversion of a monolithic male gaze through a challenge to pleasure, but for an account of viewing pleasures that entails a play of shifting gender and sexual identifications. Audiences themselves, Berenstein argues, become performers of gender roles in the game of attraction–repulsion played out in the genre.

14. See, for example, Butler (1990), Garber (1992), and Berenstein (1995).

15. Both films are about knife-wielding psycho killers. Both begin with illicit sex—sex in a hotel room in *Psycho*; the initial filmed assignation-murder of a prostitute in *Peeping Tom*—both then travel down a circuitous garden path to sexually motivated murder. Both films were more "graphic" in their displays of sex and violence than previous narratives. In both we are led to identify with the impulses of murdering Peeping Toms who are presented as sympathetic and with young men beleaguered by oppressive parents—Norman by his dead mother, Mark by his dead filmmaker father. The films differ, however, in one very important respect: Hitchcock initially fools us, in effect, about the perversions in which we are enlisted. Powell "plays fair" and lets us know immediately that the nice boy who is so damaged by his private family

romance is in fact a psycho killer who murders women while filming them and then projects what amounts to a snuff film for his private pleasure. Hitchcock, on the other hand, plays devious and does not let on that the nice young man who seems to be protecting his mother is really a sexually confused psychotic condemned to murder anyone who interferes with his totally psychotic relation to his mother–himself. Thus Powell's construction of the audience's relation to Mark, who is actually a moral being who destroys himself rather than destroy the "good" woman who breaks into his psychotic repetition compulsions, is ironically more threatening to moral and psychological certainty than Hitchcock's construction of the audience's relation to Norman. For Norman has no moral awareness of his deeds at all since they are done "by" Norman-as-mother. Thus *Peeping Tom* is the film that took the critical heat for being truly perverse while *Psycho* acquired the reputation of the self-reflexive critique of perversion. Powell claims that the strong negative reaction to this film, coupled with its poor box office, virtually ended his career. In contrast, the initially negative critical reaction to *Psycho* did Hitchcock no harm at all.

16. This is not to say that absolute mayhem in inside the theater contrasted to absolute discipline in the lines formed outside. Hitchcock's project was, after all, to control the audience reaction inside the theater as well: "If you've designed a picture correctly, in terms of its emotional impact, the Japanese audience would scream at the same time as the Indian audience" (Houston, 1980: 487–502). To the extent that he could not remix his film, Hitchcock did not, finally, obtain optimum control over audience reaction.

17. In 1971, film critic William Pechter pinpoints this camaraderie of the audience in his own description of how it felt to watch *Psycho*:

The atmosphere . . . was deeply charged with apprehension. Something awful is always about to happen. One could sense that the audience was constantly aware of this; indeed it had the solidarity of a convention assembled on the common understanding of some unspoken *entente terrible*; it was, in the fullest sense, an audience; not merely the random gathering of discrete individuals attendant at most plays and movies. (1971: 181)

18. The recent Universal Studios "rides"—with the possible exception of the fanciful flight on E. T.'s bicycle, or the in more jolting experiences of catastrophic earthquake (*Earthquake*) and fire (*Backdraft*) seem to operate in the more sensationalizing, blockbuster, Hitchcock tradition of catas-

trophe and terror, to move audiences quite seriously. In April 1992 the guide on the tram ride portion of the tour showed how thoroughly the Hitchcockian model of assault on the body had been absorbed: "At Universal Studios we not only like to show you the movies, we like you to feel them too." For an excellent discussion of the "hypercinematic" nature of the Disney experience see Bukatman (1991).

19. It is worth noting that Hitchcock's next project was to have been a film set against the background of Disneyland with Jimmy Stewart as a blind pianist whose sight is restored in operation and who goes to Disneyland in celebration. While there he discovers that the eyes he has been given are those of a murdered man. He thus begins to hunt down "his" killer. After the manifest perversions of *Psycho*, the then child-centered and family-centered Disney claimed that not only would he not permit Hitchcock to shoot in his park, he would not permit his own children to see *Psycho* (Spoto, 1983: 471).

20. Hitchcock was greatly disappointed. Yet he may have had at least partial revenge. In a filmed address made sometime later to a British film society, we can see Hitchcock inventing the rudiments of what would one day become the Universal Studio's Tour. Called the Westcliffe Address—basically a filmed speech overlaid with documentary shots of the Universal Studio backlots featuring, of course, as the movie-centered amusement park now does, the *Psycho* house as one of its main attractions—the speech is fascinating for its anticipation of the Hollywood rival to Disneyland which would include a most catastrophic, Hitchcockian, assaultive approach to its attractions. As we have already seen, what Hitchcock anticipated, not only in this address but in *Psycho* itself, was the process whereby amusement parks would become more like movies and movies would become more like the new amusement parks. The Westcliffe Address is in the archives of the Margaret Herrick Library [the Academy of Motion Picture Arts and Sciences Library in Los Angeles].

21. One important exploration in the theory and practice of cinematic reception study is Janet Staiger's *Interpreting Films* (1992).

22. Berenstein (1996) argues that such performances were a common feature of "classic" horror cinema. She cites the publicity stunt of a woman planted in the audience of each screening of *Mark of the Vampire* as an extreme example. Her task was to scream and faint at predetermined moments so that ushers would whisk her away in a waiting ambulance.

References

Altman, Rick. 1992. "Dickens, Griffith and Film Theory Today." In Jane Gaines, ed., *Classical Hollywood Narrative*. Durham, NC: Duke University Press, pp. 9–47.

Berenstein, Rhona. 1995. "Spectatorship as Drag: The Act of Viewing and Classic Horror Cinema." In Linda Williams, ed., *Viewing Positions: Ways of Seeing Film*. New Brunswick, NJ: Rutgers University Press, pp. 231–69.

————. 1996. *Attack of the Leading Ladies: Gender and Performance in Classic Horror Cinema*. New York: Columbia University Press.

Bogdanovich, Peter. 1963. *The Cinema of Alfred Hitchcock*. New York: Doubleday.

Bordwell, David. 1989. *Making Meaning: Inference and Rhetoric in the Interpretation of Cinema*. Cambridge, MA: Harvard University Press.

Bordwell, David, Janet Staiger, and Kristin Thompson. 1985. *The Classical Hollywood Cinema: Film Style and Mode of Production, 1917–1960*. New York: Columbia University Press.

Bukatman, Scott. 1991. "There's Always Tomorrow Land: Disney and the Hypercinematic Experience." *October* 57: 55–78.

Butler, Judith. 1990. *Gender Trouble: Feminism and the Subversion of Identity*. New York: Routledge.

Callenbach, Ernest. 1960. *Film Quarterly* 14(1): 47–49.

Clover, Carol. 1992. *Men, Women and Chain Saws: Gender in the Modern Horror Film*. Princeton, NJ: Princeton University Press.

Creed, Barbara. 1993. *The Monstruous Feminine: Film, Feminism, Psychoanalysis*. London: Routledge.

Delaplane, Stan. 1960. *Los Angeles Examiner*, 12 August.

Eisenstein, Sergei. 1988. "The Montage of Attractions." In *Eisenstein, Writings, Vol. 1, 1922–1934*, Richard Taylor, ed. and trans. Bloomington: University of Indiana Press.

Foucault, Michel. 1978. *Discipline and Punish: The Birth of the Prison*, Alan Sheridan trans. New York: Vintage Books.

Friedberg, Anne. 1993. *Window Shopping: Cinema and the Postmodern*. Berkeley: University of California Press.

Garber, Marjorie. 1992. *Vested Interests: Cross-Dressing and Cultural Anxiety*. New York: Routledge.

Gledhill, Christine. 1987. "The Melodramatic Field: An Investigation." In

Christine Gledhill, ed., *Home Is Where the Heart Is: Studies in Melodrama and the Woman's Film*. London: British Film Institute, pp. 5–39.

Gunning, Tom. 1986. "The Cinema of Attractions: Early Film, Its Spectator and the Avant-Garde." *Wide Angle* 8(3–4): 63–70; reprinted in Thomas Elsaesser and Adam Barker, eds., *Early Cinema: Space, Frame, Narrative*. London: British Film Institute, 1990, 56–62.

————. 2000. " 'Animated Pictures': Tales of Cinema's Forgotten Future, after 100 Years of Films." In Cristine Gledhill and Linda Willams, eds., *Reinventing Film Studies*. London: Arnold, 316–31.

Hansen, Miriam. 1995. "Early Cinema, Late Cinema: Transformations of the Public Sphere." In Linda Williams, ed., *Viewing Positions: Ways of Seeing Film*. New Brunswick, NJ: Rutgers University Press.

————. 2000. "The Mass Production of the Senses: Classical Cinema as Vernacular Modernism." In Cristine Gledhill and Linda Willams, eds., *Reinventing Film Studies*. London: Arnold, 332–50.

Hatch, Robert. 1960. *The Nation*, 2 July.

Hitchcock, Alfred. 1960. *Motion Picture Herald*, 8 August, pp. 17–18.

Houston, Penelope. 1980. "Alfred Hitchcock: I." In Richard Roud, ed., *Cinema: A Critical Dictionary*, vol. 1. Norwich, England: Martin Secker and Warburg, pp. 487–502.

Jameson, Fredric. 1984. "The Cultural Logic of Late Capitalism." In *Postmodernism, or, the Cultural Logic of Late Capitalism*. Durham, NC: Duke University Press.

————. 1990. *Signatures of the Visible*. New York: Routledge.

————. 1992. *The Geopolitical Aesthetic: Cinema and Space in the World System*. Bloomington: Indiana University Press.

Levine, Lawrence. 1988. *Highbrow/Lowbrow: The Emergence of Cultural Hierarchy in America*. Cambridge, MA: Harvard University Press.

Pechter, William S. 1971. *Twenty-Four Times a Second*. New York: Harper and Row.

Rebello, Stephen. 1990. *Alfred Hitchcock and the Making of Psycho*. New York: HarperCollins.

Rothman, William. 1982. *The Murderous Gaze*. Cambridge, MA: Harvard University Press.

Schatz, Thomas. 1993. "The New Hollywood." In Jim Collins, Hilary Radner, and Ava Preacher Collins, eds., *Film Theory Goes to the Movies*. New York: Routledge, pp. 8–36.

Silverman, Kaja. 1983. *The Subject of Semiotics*. New York: Oxford University Press.

————. 1992. *Male Subjectivity at the Margins*. New York: Routledge.

Spoto, Donald. 1983. *The Dark Side of Genius: The Life of Alfred Hitchcock*. New York: Ballantine.

Staiger, Janet. 1992. *Interpreting Films: Studies in the Historical Reception of American Cinema*. Princeton, NJ: Princeton University Press.

Tudor, Andrew. 1989. *Monsters and Mad Scientists: A Cultural History of the Horror Movie*. Oxford: Basil Blackwell.

Williams, Linda. 1984. "When the Woman Looks." In Mary Ann Doane, Patricia Mellencamp, and Linda Williams, eds., *Re-Vision: Essays in Feminst Film Criticism*. The American Film Institute Monograph Series, vol. 3. Frederick, MD: University Publications of America, pp. 83–99.

Williams, Linda. 1998. "Melodrama Revised." In Nick Browne, ed., *Refiguring American Film Genre*. Berkeley: University of California Press, pp. 42–58.

Wood, Robin. 1965. *Hitchcock's Films*. New York: Paperback Library.

Žižek, Slavoj, ed. 1992. *Everything You Always Wanted to Know about Lacan but Were Afraid to Ask Hitchcock*. London: Verso.

10

The Man Who Knew More
Than Too Much

◆   ◆   ◆

◆   ◆   ◆

Hitchcock, as all the ...iters in this book have pointed out, was a master
of cinematic form. In his best work, films such as *Shadow of a Doubt*
(1942), *Notorious* (1946), *The Wrong Man* (1956), *Vertigo* (1958), *North by
Northwest* (1959), and, of course, *Psycho*, he created a fictional realm out of
the composition and the editing of images. Directors ever since have been
trying to discover and reproduce the Hitchcockian vision, but only a very,
very few have succeeded. In the following, I have attempted to pick up a
number of the ideas developed by other authors in this book and re-see them
by means of a close visual analysis of *Psycho* that may indicate why the
intricacy and thoughtfulness of his image and narrative making creates the
Hitchcockian universe, and at the same time is so personal a style that
others have a difficult time imitating it. More than that, I want to examine a
film that is in fact a kind of cinematic machine, engineered so tightly that
every part refers and is tightly linked to every other part. I want to look at
the engine of the fun-house ride Linda Williams discusses.

ROBERT KOLKER ◆ The Form, Structure, and
Influence of *Psycho*

There is a lingering question about *Psycho*. Here is a film so grim
and dark, a film that, as George Toles puts it in the title of his
essay, is the art of infection, showing its audience that the more
they look, the more they will see death, madness, and, finally,
the abyss, the unknowable; a film that takes them down the drain
and out from the swamp. It would seem to be the kind of film
people would flee from, and yet we all keep coming back. Why?
Even after the thrills, frights, and surprises are revealed, it is a
film we want to see yet again. Perhaps, in psychological terms,
we want to go through a kind of "mastery" proceess in which
we keep returning to an anxiety-provoking memory in order to
try and get the better of it; to feel better about it; to overcome
the fears it provokes. At the opposite pole, it may be that we find
Psycho so fascinating in both what it says and the way it articulates
it, we keep wanting to look again to experience the pleasure of
it, the pleasure of fear, and the ways in which that pleasure is
created.

It is possible to look at or listen to works in other media—
painting, photography, music—over and over again, no matter
what their content, and continue to receive pleasure. The reason
is because a great work is formally complete and contextually
open. A well-made painting, for example, whether it is an abstract
work or representational image, manifests a design, a way of dealing with line, color, shape, that is completely realized, "closed"
in the sense that the design, the composition, the way the various
pictorial elements have been put together, express completely
what the artist had in mind—the work could not be imagined
differently without being something else. But, at the same time,
that closed form opens up the picture (or the piece of music)
and allows it to keep communicating with us at emotional and
intellectual levels often so profound that we either experience
more at each viewing or hearing or we take pleasure in having

the original experience over and over again. The "closed" work of art is open to us continuously.

Narrative art is no different. When you examine the details of a great novel, you will probably find no word that could be changed, no combination of paragraphs, chapters, characters, dialogue—of the narrative flow itself—that could be made different without destroying the book. Admittedly such examples of narrative perfection are rare, although not as rare as in film where the emphasis is on story told quickly and cheaply. But the response is the same. There are some complex films that one can look at over and over and some not-so-complex films that also bring us back many times—some for their pleasure and complexity, others simply for their pleasure, a few for both.

Psycho brings us back for all the reasons we have outlined: to attempt to come finally to grips with its bleak vision; to revel again in the intricacy of its form, and the dark power of its images; to take even more pleasure from its shocks and surprises—even when we know the springboards of all of these.

Previous essays in this volume present questions about whether *Psycho* is or is not a modernist work. *Modernism* is a slippery term and not easily applied to most conventional, commercial film, which depends on an invisible style in which all loose narrative, moral, and emotional ends are tied up at the end. *Psycho* does none of this. As in a modernist work, an abstract painting, for example, Hitchcock foregrounds form, and was always happy to talk about it. He insisted that film tell its story cinematically, creating a narrative that is open and closed simultaneously. *Psycho* ties up no ends: it is as stark as the madness it portrays; its world is closed off from any humane impulses; it represents its characters as small, fearsome, or monstrously mad. As Linda Williams suggests, the film also touches on the postmodern as well, in the fluidity of its genre and, most important, in its treatment of gender, especially that of its central monster, Norman Bates—part man, part woman. Like almost all of Hitchcock's major works, it dissallows comforting stability, and it makes the viewer both observer and moral or immoral accomplice of its characters. Mod-

ernist or postmodernist, the film closes itself, opens us: it is per-
meable to our desires and anxieties.

The Pattern

What are the structural plans for the well-made machine of *Psycho*? To begin with, we must understand that every artist contends,
even does battle, with the form of his or her art. Every imaginative work—film, painting, the novel, poetry, music, architec-
ture—is a formal structure with conventions to be followed or
broken, with structures and a history that the individual imagination must accept or work against. Content or meaning is created through this struggle with or against form. The right word,
the perfectly framed image, the exact place to break a line in a
poem, or make a composition or a cut in a film, determines how
the reader or viewer will respond and comprehend—or be left
in a state of incomprehension. Form is everything, a realization
that made modernism possible.

Think for a moment of the paintings of Jackson Pollock, the
great American abstract "action" painter, who appeared merely
to be dripping and splashing paint on a canvas lying flat on the
floor. The fact is that Pollock was not splashing and dripping, but
forcing that apparently free form of paint application into a
rhythmic arrangement of line and color that allows the viewer
to "read" his paintings, to visually trace its patterns and texture.
Look at a Pollock closely and at length, and you will detect patterns of color and a rhythm of line and volume, making up an
intricate visual pattern. Hitchcock was not Pollock and might be
appalled at his working methods, but not necessarily at their
results—in fact, as we can see in figure 10.1, from *North by Northwest*, and as we will see in many aspects of *Psycho*, he does create
visually abstract patterns. But essentially, Hitchcock was an artist
who insisted on tight, prearranged control of his work from beginning to end—a control that expressed an explosion of disorder. He did not splash and drip, but drew his images, constructed
his movies on paper, making them, in fact, before actually making

FIGURE 10.1. A high-angle, abstract pattern looking down from the United Nations building in Hitchcock's *North by Northwest* (1959).

them. With *Psycho*, he made a very conscious effort to control the form and structure of the film by deliberately setting boundaries, even obstacles.

First, he chose the production methods and some of the crew of his television show to make the movie. He would make a feature film under the tight production restrictions of a television program, yet one that would transcend anything that might ever appear on television. He chose less than well-known actors. Tony Perkins was almost unknown. Janet Leigh's name had some panache, but Hitchcock killed her off one-third of the way into the film. No one in the film was of the class of Hitchcock's former players: Cary Grant, James Stewart, Grace Kelly. And none of the characters was physically or morally attractive in the Hollywood mode. He chose a gruesome story of a serial killer to recreate into a film that would be compact, demanding, even unfriendly, and at the same time a great joke. With all of this, he created an airtight box; nothing could be changed, and nothing makes this clearer than taking a very brief look at the 1998 "remake" of *Psycho*, by an interesting, although hardly Hitchcockian, director, Gus van Sant.

Van Sant decided, by and large, to recreate the original, shot for shot—but in color, which Hitchcock explicitly rejected in order to create a bleakly gray world. (There is a legend that in a vault there are some test reels that Hitchcock made in color.) The copying aspect of Van Sant's *Psycho* is merely boring. Hitchcock's shots were perfect; there was no reason to redo them. Ocassionally, van Sant tried a slightly different angle, and whenever he did, it was the wrong one. He did not understand the design or the orginal's sense of mise-en-scène (see figures 10.2 and 10.3). He finally attempted to "open out" the film's ending. The closure of Hitchcock's film (which is no closure at all, in the sense of a satisfactory conclusion that ties up all the loose ends) is grim and airless. We are left with the image of a car, containing a body, being winched out of a stinking swamp, with Herrmann's great chords that have supported the film throughout, upping, rather than resolving, our anxiety. Van Sant, on the other hand, zooms back from the scene; we see the surroundings. Cars go by. He places us safely back into the world, exactly what Hitchcock did not want to happen.

FIGURE 10.2. Gus van Sant's imitation of the parlor scene in *Psycho*. Here, he changes the camera angles and puts the background in soft focus, destroying the effect of the dark, swooping bird on top of Norman's head in the original.

FIGURE 10.3.

There is no reason to further criticize the remake, which was essentially Universal Pictures' attempt to wring some further profit from their property. The point, to repeat, is that *Psycho's* tight, abstract, visual design is unique to the film, and something that few other filmmakers are able or willing to create for their own. To understand this design, we need to recall Hitchcock's statement to François Truffaut in their interview: "Definitely, that's our composition: a vertical block and a horizontal block." In other words, *Psycho* begins with an abstract design concept of verticals and horizontals that assists Hitchcock in maintaining the compactness, the compression even, of his mise-en-scène—the spacial coherence of his film. Hitchcock depended on articulate spatial configurations in most of his films. Composition, lighting, camera movement, the relationship of the character to the camera—all were calculated for maximum effect. In *Psycho*, the mise-en-scène is calculated and compressed even more. The film itself is tight and closed. And the way Hitchcock achieves this compression and tightness is through the horizontal/vertical design. This patterning of the film can be seen to begin in *North by Northwest*, the titles for which were designed by Saul Bass, who did the credits and acted as visual consultant on *Psycho* as well. Like *Psycho*, *North by Northwest's* credit sequence begins with animated abstract lines, which dissolve into the United Nations building in New York (see figures 10.4 and 10.5). The pattern is not followed throughout the rest of the film, as it will be in *Psycho*, although it is suggested in the modernist house where the spies live, above the Mount Rushmore monument (see figure 10.6).

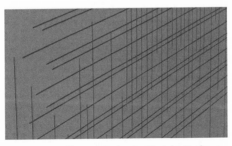

FIGURE 10.4. Abstract design in *North by Northwest*.

The controlling horizontal and vertical pattern in *Psycho* appears immediately in the Paramount logo that precedes the film. The logo is scored with horizontal lines from top to bottom (figure 10.7). This could be a Hitchcockian joke. Since he was making a film under the constraints of television production, why not play with the Paramount logo to make it look like a television screen? More likely is that Hitchcock and Bass wanted to start

FIGURE 10.5.

FIGURE 10.6.

FIGURE 10.7.

the graphic pattern of the film immediately, and the vertical peak
of the Paramount mountain with the addition of the horizontal
lines sets the visual tone, which is immediately picked up by the
first two credit shots, animated as they all are, here with vertical
lines streaming across the screen, culminating first with the appearance of the film's title and finally the director's name, fitting
itself together like a jigsaw puzzle (see figures 10.8, 10.9, and 10.10).
The film's title is pushed away with a flow of lines from top to

FIGURE 10.8.

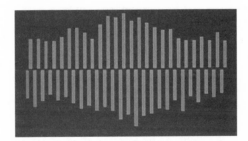

FIGURE 10.9.

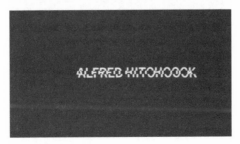

FIGURE 10.10.

bottom, emanating from a horizontal black line in the middle. Variations on these patterns continue through the credits, until after the director's name, which, when the vertical lines disappear, zigzags into place, suggesting, as other contributors to this volume have, a premonition of dismemberment and bifurcation. The name itself is pushed out of sight by an uneven set of vertical lines, under which a bird's-eye view of Phoenix, Arizona, is dissolved, and, for a moment, the lines and the cityscape are superimposed over each other (figure 10.11).

The superimposition sets the film's compositional pattern, and almost every shot in the film is impressed with it, based on it, or laid over it. The uneven vertical lines that end the title sequence point to some important breaks in the pattern, which I will discuss further on. But it is important to notice this repeated composition, which appears over and over, from the hotel sequence that opens the film (figure 10.12) to an almost abstract composition that occurs when Norman cleans up after Mother's killing spree (figure 10.13).

Most famously and importantly, the vertical and horizontal lines occur in the contrast between the motel and Norman's old dark house (figures 10.14 and 10.15). These are the core images of the film, actually seen only a few times. The first occurs early in the film, when Norman comes running down after the murder he/she committed. The second is very late in the film, when Sam and Lila pull up to begin the film's climax. The latter suggests the

FIGURE 10.11. The vertical lines alternate with the horizontals throughout the credit sequence. In this dissolve into the narrative itself, the grid is firmly established.

FIGURE 10.12. Sam towers over Marion, his position echoed in the verticals of the bedstand.

FIGURE 10.13. This almost abstract composition occurs for only a moment as Norman cleans up. The diagonal spray of the shower is an important break in the vertical/horizontal blocks.

FIGURE 10.14.

FIGURE 10.15.

normality of a roadside motel whereas the former indicates the unknown terrors in the old dark house, their juxtaposition the
breakdown of boundaries between order and chaos the two structures represent.

The grid focuses our gaze and, beyond providing a control
structure for the film, also implies a sense of order for a narrative
that is precisely about the breakdown of order, about madness
appearing from nowhere, and our helplessness in its face. That is
why this strong grid is broken from time to time by either a
diagonal or arc-shaped line. It can be seen in the image of the
bathroom shown in figure 10.13. The diagonal stream of water
from the shower breaks the hard horizontals and verticals of the
bathroom and the door. It can be seen more clearly in the motion
of the windshield wipers of Marion's car during her escape from
Phoenix. The windshield becomes a kind of screen on which she
projects her imaginary conversations. The slashing of the blades
create an arc-like motion that foreshadows Marion's horrible
death in the shower (figures 10.16 and 10.17). That movement is
itself foreshadowed in the animated lines during the credit graph-
ics of the film (see figures 10.8–10.11).

The breaking of the horizontal and vertical stability—and of
life itself—sends Marion's blood down the shower drain in a
counter-clockwise swirl that is an extension of the arc-like motion. It echoes the circle of the shower head that, Marion
thought, would produce a cleansing of body and soul and, even
more ironically, the circle that Marion wanted to follow, returning to Phoenix and renewing her life. Instead, life goes down the

FIGURE 10.16.

FIGURE 10.17.

drain: the end of seeing, of order, of morality, and redemption, surrounded by symmetrical images of drainage and sewage—the toilet bowl down which Marion flushes a piece of paper and Norman's sinking of her car in the swamp. (The images appear later in this chapter in the discussion of the shower sequence [figures 10.62–10.66].) These movements, set against the grid and its destruction, all represent the breaking down of the banal order of Marion's life, partly due to her naïveté, partly due to contingency—the chance meeting with Norman.

Her affair in a cheap hotel with Sam, which we gaze at early in the film like Peeping Toms, is a meeting of two lower-middle-class people who cannot break out of their own private islands. Marion's escape with her boss's money, which briefly turns *Psycho* into a road movie, moves her in a straight line to an abyss she could not see. Her life ends when she steps into Norman's parlor (an extraordinary sequence I will analyze later) and winds up, in the darkest metaphor in the film, in the sewer. The metaphor is made literal in *Psycho*'s last shot, with a compositional line that has not yet been seen. In a complex dissolve from Norman's insane, grinning face, with Mother's skull beneath it, Hitchcock presents us with a heavy chain, pulling the car with Marion's body out of the swamp. The chain moves, pulling the car out of the detritus, in a sharp diagonal, almost pushing through the screen surface. In the dissolve of Norman-Mother-chain, the latter seems attached to Norman's neck (figure 10.18).

It is a hard, monolithic, and chaotic image, contrary to the surprisingly elegant, carefully composed images of the rest of the film. *Psycho* is a delicately composed and edited film, and the sudden, heavy last image is the final surprise, a rough, enigmatic reminder of the violence that lay under, and often over, the film as a whole. It is also a visual assault, one of many, such as the shower murder, the killing of Arbogast, and the discovery of Mrs. Bates's corpse, that pushes the viewer back, that reminds us of Hitchcock's control, that discomforts us and, like the characters in the film, reminds us that our world is not as comfortable as we would like it to seem. The chain pulling the car from the swamp does not supply closure; it supplies further discomfort; it imposes, confuses, and frightens. It leaves us powerless. The hauling of the car from the sewer restores or redeems nothing—and this lack is what *Psycho* is about.

FIGURE 10.18.

The Anxiety of the Frame

Part of the elegance of *Psycho*'s structure is demonstrated not only in the geometrical patterns that bolster the composition of the images, and tell part of its story, but in the way those images themselves are composed on or in reaction to the pattern. Composition, in most films, rarely rests on a prearranged, abstract pattern, but rather on the way the director frames each shot, using his camera, lighting, and position of characters to transmit their experiences or comment on them, communicating to us, in Hitchcock's case, the danger, the unknown, the violence that awaits. Hitchcock does this in a number of ways, through pre-arranging every shot for maximum effect. One subtle example of his framing is to move his camera off center when gazing at a character in the middle of trouble, putting the viewer off balance by breaking the rules of a centered, eye-level composition of the shot. We can observe this in almost all of his films. Look at the frames from *North by Northwest* (1959), the simultaneously light-hearted and terrifying film of mistaken identity and the performance of the self that preceded *Psycho* (figures 10.19 and 10.20). Here the Cary Grant character, Roger O. Thornhill, who the spies believes is a CIA agent named Kaplan, is in a hotel room, where "Kaplan" (who doesn't exist) receives a call from the spy's hench-

FIGURE 10.19. In *North by Northwest*, Thornhill re-ceives the phone call, and the camera remains at eye level and at a comfortable distance.

men. The camera begins at a conventional position, eye level with Thornhill sitting on the bed, but slowly moves upward and left, tilting down somewhat so that the loss of an eye-level, symmetrical gaze causes unease and foreshadows the further disorientation that will occur in Thornhill's world.

We can see this compositional approach in *Psycho* in many sequences, for example, in the opening scene in the hotel room where Marion and Sam have their lunchtime rendezvous—one of the grimmest sequences in the film. Hitchcock keeps pushing us to intuit the portentousness of what is going on, hinting that disaster will follow (see figure 10.21). Some of this is done in the dialogue, with references to Mother, especially when Marion talks about having a respectful dinner at home, with Mother's picture on the mantle. Sam responds, "And after the steak, send sister

FIGURE 10.20. As the call continues, the camera tracks around and up, knocking the composition off center and communicating Thornhill's own anxiety.

FIGURE 10.21.

to the movies, turn Mama's picture to the wall . . . ?" But we really only get the joke in the dialogue after a second viewing of the film, realizing that all references to "Mother" throughout *Psycho* reverberate back to the film's core joke, that "Mother" is Norman, and vice versa. What we see immediately, however, provokes us. The camera is too high, and it strains the grid. There is nothing authorizing its gaze, except of course the director of the film, who, as its ultimate narrator, is telling us to look at this scene askew, to detect that something is wrong, and will become more wrong. We see this also in the shower sequence, which I will examine in detail later. After the parlor sequence at the motel, Marion, having made the decision to return to Phoenix with the money, unaware that she has already been "infected" by Norman's gaze, looks to the shower as a cleansing agent on all

FIGURE 10.22. When Marion enters the shower, the camera is at eye level. There is no expectation or anxiety emanating from the composition. In fact, the shower begins with a kind of ecstasy.

FIGURE 10.23. When Mother is about to enter the room, the shot changes abruptly, becoming high, distant, and close simultaneously; threateningly.

counts. She washes herself clean of her sins (figure 10.22). When Mother enters the bathroom—a vaguely seen figure through the curtains, the camera suddenly looks at the scene at a high, canted angle, similar to the off-center compositions I discussed earlier. And the shot seems to be taken through a telephoto lens, which distances the scene while compressing space, withdrawing it from our immediate gaze, and, along with the figure emerging from the door, begins to disturb us deeply (figure 10.23).

If Hitchcock puts the frame off-kilter to provoke an anxiety equal to or foreshadowing that of the characters in his films, he will take a much more radical stance when his characters are either in very deep trouble or in a hazardous moral state. He will cut or move his camera to a ninety-degree position looking directly down at the character, isolating him or her, taking a god's- or bird's-eye view (literally, as in the image from *The Birds* [1963] shown in figure 10.24). This visual strategy occurs in almost every Hitchcock film and leads to some speculation. Why remove our gaze from the characters at their moment of impending doom or extreme moral crisis? Is it Hitchcock's response of noninvolvement, as some have suggested, or of leaving the character in a state of isolation and helplessness, or, more pointedly, of placing the viewer in as helpless position as that of the character? It is an assertion of the director's power to manipulate what we see and to leave his character to fate (a fate, of course, Hitchcock fashions), therefore becoming a stylistic signature, repeated in one way or another in almost every Hitchcock film. But it is also an ambiguous and ironic moral position: in conventional film, when

FIGURE 10.24. The birds attack.

a character is in profound danger, the director usually moves to a tight close-up of his or her face. Hitchcock may do this before the character is in danger, but at the moment either of recognition of trouble or its imminent occurance, he will place his camera far above.

Two astounding ninety-degree shots, fully in the Hitchcockian style, occur outside of Mother's room. The first is when Arbogast

FIGURE 10.25.

FIGURE 10.26.

FIGURE 10.27.

slips into the house and mounts the stairs (figure 10.25). We first see him climbing the stairs in midshot, the camera in front, moving before him. The background is actually a process shot—a moving image projected behind Arbogast, creating a disconcerting, spatially disharmonious effect. Hitchcock happily explains this trickery in his interview with Truffaut. He then cuts to the door opening slightly, a shot that is probably not Arbogast's point of view, but rather Hitchcock's (figure 10.26). The camera returns to Arbogast and then cuts to a full ninety-degree shot, Herrmann's music screeching, as Mother comes tearing out, knife held high (figure 10.27). The surprise and the ensuing gruesomeness of the stabbing, as Arbogast falls backward down the stairs, again against a rear-screen projection, are created by and for viewer expectation as to what he will find when he enters the house (recall that the sequence occurs after the shower murder); fear when the door opens; near hysteria as the camera leaps to its high position, leaving Arbogast completely vulnerable and removed; and the breaking of this ordered arrangement of shocks as he tumbles downstairs, face bloodied, and finally stabbed to death.

I said that *Psycho* is an experiment in the compactness of form, an experiment that requires much problem solving to get narrative things done quickly. The next instance of the ninety-degree shot solves the problem of how to continue the joke about Norman and Mother and continue audience anxiety as well. It also shows Hitchcock's and his cameraman, John Russell's, skill with a moving camera. Concerned that there will be more visitors, Norman has to hide "Mother." Hitchcock's problem, as he states in the Truffaut interview, is how to do this without revealing that there is no mother. The solution is breathtaking. Norman ascends the stairs to Mother's room. The audience is already primed to expect danger from this action, even to Norman, who is still looked upon as innocent. No danger occurs, except for a growing anxiety on the viewers' part. After Norman goes up the stairs, the camera follows, assuming, again, a life of its own—or the eye the director—created not only to ratchet up our anxiety even more, but to see his virtuosity, and then, perhaps, discover the joke. The camera cranes up the stairs and literally creeps up the side of the doorjamb, doing a seemingly impossible twist into the ninety-degree position (perhaps too impossible—there may be a hidden edit in the camera's movement. (Figures 10.28–10.35.)

When the camera reaches its apex, at the same ninety-degree angle it assumed when Arbogast was stabbed, out comes Norman, carrying Mother to the fruit cellar, she all the while complaining and even making a pun. "You think I'm fruity?" she asks. One

FIGURE 10.28.

FIGURE 10.29.

FIGURE 10.30.

FIGURE 10.31.

FIGURE 10.32.

FIGURE 10.33.

FIGURE 10.34.

FIGURE 10.35.

FIGURE 10.36.

small item gives the joke away: one of Mother's dangling legs hits the side of the staircase, with no reaction from "her": hardly noticed, we are again offered an explanation of the "mystery" of Norman and mom (figure 10.36).

The Parlor

I want to examine in some detail the most famous sequence in *Psycho*, the shower murder, and the sequence in Norman's parlor that precedes it. Each demonstrates different formal properties aimed at different effects. The parlor sequence is a perfect example of mise-en-scène, the way space is organized through all the various elements that make up a shot: framing, lighting, movement, distances between characters and objects. Hitchcock's mastery of this is evident here, where it serves a number of purposes: it advances what is, we finally discover, the fraudulent plotline of Marion and the stolen money. Fraudulent because it has little to do with the film other than to get Marion to the motel. It's what Hitchcock calls the McGuffin, that plot object of interest to the characters in film, and perhaps the audience, but that has nothing to do with events in the film that are really important. *Psycho* has two McGuffins. The stolen money, for example, is a literal dead end. The most important McGuffin is Mother herself, the end of the dead.

The parlor is a setup sequence, leading us up and down many paths, establishing a false character for Norman, a false redemptive surge for Marion, and through its visual and verbal construction, not only foreshadowing the shower sequence, but giving away the film's essential joke, that Norman and Mother are one and the same. It is the also the counterpart of Mother's house where, later, in the fruit cellar, Lila Crane will finally reveal the film's secret. The parlor is a double of the heart—or heartlessness—of the old dark house, that staple place of horror films, the archetype of home, where all should be secure and safe but in horror films is saturated with foreboding, danger, and monsters.

Doubling is basic to Hitchcock's work. It not only supplies a creepy symmetry to things, but indicates that malevolence is not centered in a single character, a single action, or a single place. Hitchcock brings individuality and uniqueness into question, and shows that the ubiquity and banality of evil is shared across the board. Perhaps the most infamous doubling in *Psycho* occurs in the film's penultimate shot, as the camera tracks in on Norman in his cell, as Mother's voice boasts that she would not even hurt a fly; Norman looks up and breaks into a smile of absolute madness, and the two are briefly superimposed over one another (see figure 10.18). This image harks back to Lila's discovery of Mother in the fruit cellar and is also tripled (or quadrupled) if we recall a look on Marion's face on the road, where she is imagining conversations that might be going on in her office when the money is found stolen. She breaks into a grin that is all but a foreshadowing of Norman-Mother's own lunatic smiles. (George

Toles points this out in his essay.) Figure 10.37 shows a composite image of the three grinning figures: Marion, Mother, Norman are bizarre and perverse distorted reflections of each other; all are not what they appear, all "go a little mad sometimes," and one isn't there at all—he's his own double for his dead mother.

Other doublings in the film often appear as literal reflections in mirrors. One such image appears earlier in the film, when Marion begins her conversation with Norman in the motel office, preceding the parlor scene (figure 10.38). Another mirror image, much commented upon, occurs later, in the same place, when Sam and Norman confront each other (figure 10.39). The joke contained in the sequence from which the first image is taken is that Marion believes she has found a pitiable kindred spirit in Norman. She decides to change her thieving ways and return home. But the fact that both characters are seriously deluded, one about her future, the other about who he actually is, is brought home by Marion's reflection in the mirror and the sym-

FIGURE 10.37.

FIGURE 10.38.

FIGURE 10.39.

metrical composition with Norman. In the second image, Norman has finally met his match. Or has he? Sam may briefly over-power Norman and allow Lila to make her discovery. Sam may even be relatively sane. But "relatively" is exactly what Hitchcock is talking about. Sam's life, like Marion's, is as bleak and dead-ended as Norman's, and Norman, finally, is a reflection of the nascent madness in everyone. "We all go a little mad sometimes."

Things become complicated in the parlor and shower sequences. The doubles split off: Marion and Norman are, of course, nothing like each other, except for a kind of cunning innocence. Norman does have an actual double—his mother, who is himself, as he is she. All the doubling in the film points to this. Marion becomes, for a moment, at the end of the parlor sequence, a new and upstanding woman. Norman turns back into Mother and kills Marion. The doubles merge in death.

The parlor sequence proper begins just before the two enter the room. Norman goes to the house to get the milk and sand-wiches, and from her room, after wrapping the stolen money in a newspaper with the ironic headline, "OKAY," clearly visible, she hears the taunting, foul voice of "Mother" warning her son about his carnal desires. Marion had already seen "Mother" in the win-dow, when she first pulled up to the motel and was about to leave when Norman appeared to give her and us a taste of his naïve, adolescent persona. Now, when she looks at the old dark house, with the clouds looming above it, she sees nothing, only hears the voice of a madman/woman (figure 10.40).

Norman returns with the food, excusing Mother's outburst

("she isn't quite herself today"), and before going inside, we see both Marion and Norman as if in mirror image (figure 10.41). The office, Norman says, is too "officious," and they proceed to the parlor. As Norman turns the light on, Marion catches sight of something (figure 10.42). The reverse shot of her gaze reveals

FIGURE 10.40. The Old Dark House, from Marion's point of view, as Norman returns after being scolded by "Mother." The composition of the image foreshadows what is to come.

FIGURE 10.41.

FIGURE 10.42.

a stuffed owl in a predatory position and a stuffed crow, like the raven out of Edgar Allan Poe's poem (figures 10.43 and 10.44). The images immediately start the ironic foreshadowing that is at the heart of the sequence. Throughout, reference is made to stuffed things. It is Norman's hobby, stuffing things; although he does not admit here that Mother was one of his subjects, and the brazenness of the discussion only becomes clear when we see the sequence again. What Norman does admit, while petting a stuffed crow, is that it is more than a hobby. "A hobby," he says "is supposed to pass the time, not fill it." And fill things he does, surrounding himself—and the audience itself—with surrogates for his masterwork of taxidermy.

Images of the stuffed birds come to a visual climax when the conversation proceeds to talk of Mother and putting her "someplace," a madhouse. Norman is photographed in a tilted composition, against painting of a classical nude and a rape—surrogates for his repressed sexuality—his stuffed owl seeming to

FIGURE 10.43.

FIGURE 10.44.

swoop at his head (figure 10.45). The paintings hint at Norman's deeply repressed sexuality and, although we have no idea at this point of the power his stuffed mother holds over him, there is a hint of the aggressiveness and violence to come in this composition, as the dead bird seems ready to pounce on Norman, as Mother pounces *through* Norman. When Marion begins to talk about putting Mother away, the framing of Norman changes. In tighter close-up now, one of the ravens is turned toward him, its sharp beak pointed at his head (figure 10.46).

This change of space between the characters delivers more information. Most of the parlor sequence is edited into one shots. That is, we see Marion and Norman together only when they first enter the parlor and briefly when they leave (see figure 10.47). Otherwise, throughout the scene, until they leave, they are isolated from one another, each in their own frame, despite the fact they are inhabiting the same space. They are each cut off, literally and emotionally, trapped in their own "private islands." For the

FIGURE 10.45.

FIGURE 10.46.

first part of the sequence they are held in midshot, the camera at a comfortable distance from each; the only threat coming from the birds aimed at Norman and the slightly-below-eye-level framing of both (see figures 10.48 and 10.49). However, when the conversation turns to the way Marion heard Mother "talk" to Nor-

FIGURE 10.47. When they first enter the parlor, Norman and Marion are seen in a two shot.

FIGURE 10.48.

FIGURE 10.49.

man, and then to putting her "someplace," the composition changes dramatically. Both Marion and Norman are reframed so that the camera, and our gaze, are closer to them, tighter, below eye level on Norman, more anxiety provoking—or, more accurately, creating in us the anxiety being experienced by the characters (figures 10.50 and 10.51). The close shot of Norman, taken a bit earlier than the image we saw earlier (figure 10.45), begins this turn in the conversation and is terrifying. This shot almost appears to be taken in another place. Even though we have seen Norman earlier with the owl over his head, the closeness of this shot and the lighting are different. The pools of half light and dark are different from what we have so far seen in the parlor. This is, indeed, another place. Hitchcock, at his expressionist best, reflects a state of mind, a state of being, a half boy, half mother under assault, who will immediately assault Marion.

Further, as Norman becomes upset over the talk of putting

FIGURE 10.50.

FIGURE 10.51.

Mother "someplace," he leans forward, literally invading the screen space, our space, and Marion's (figure 10.52). It is the first time in the film that we get a sense of Norman being a threat, and the shot is doubled later in the film, with an even more extreme close-up of Norman during his interrogation by Sam (figure 10.53). But in the parlor, the threat is only suggested. Hitchcock is giving away a great deal in this sequence, but he does not yet want his audience to know anything, barely to suspect anything, only feel a growing anxiety. Shortly after his outburst, Norman sits back in his chair again, the raven pointing at his head, and resumes his boyish ways.

I have been talking about mise-en-scène, about the way Hitchcock organizes the space we are allowed to see in the parlor in order achieve a foreshadowing of things to come. Dialogue, as I have suggested, also plays an important part here. In fact, in the context of *Psycho* being a "twice-told tale," it is the funniest dialogue in the film because once we know what will go on, we

FIGURE 10.52.

FIGURE 10.53.

realize that much of what is said is not merely small talk, but cloaked exposition of who and what Norman and Mother are. As soon as Norman talks about his hobby, the secret is out. "A man should have a hobby," Marion politely affirms. Norman's response, as noted above, is strange. He pets his raven and says, "A hobby is supposed to pass the time, not fill it." When Marion solicitously asks if his time is so empty, up comes Mother directly: Norman says he looks after the motel, "and do . . . ah . . . little errands for my mother—the ones she allows I might be capable of doing." Norman, of course *is* Mother's little errand boy, a person emptied of personality and filled instead with a murderous dead woman. "Do you go out with friends?" Marion asks. "Well, a boy's best friend is his mother." The most chilling words in the film. Or anywhere. Marion's response is silent, but her look is more than a little suspicious and disturbed (figure 10.54).

Matters come to a head with the discussion of putting Mother in an asylum. I have noted how the visual style changes drastically, but there is also a marked change in Norman's responses. Marion has already shown her prickly side when Norman, in all innocence, asked what she is running away from. He even leans forward in his chair, though not into the frame, and speculates that "we're all in our private traps. . . . We scratch and claw, but only at the air, only at each other." The metaphor clings to the stuffed birds and suggests—with its scratching and clawing—what is about to happen to Marion. The real intrusion comes next. When Marion tells him that no one should talk to him the way she heard Mother talk, the cut is back to Norman in that

FIGURE 10.54.

extreme composition in which he is thoroughly trapped. And when they talk about putting Mother "someplace," his angry response, his seeming familiarity with th~ horrors of an asylum strongly suggest that it might have been he who was locked up. Though whether it was he or Mother makes little difference.

The parlor sequence is prelude and, in a way, climax. It sets the tone and generates the anxiety for what, on first viewing, we do not know is coming. At the same time, because it depends on visual and verbal interplay, it is, no matter how obliquely, a more complete explanation of Norman than the psychiatrist offers near the film's end. All of Norman's secrets that can be known are revealed here without our knowing it. The parlor is at the center of the tightly made box Hitchcock has created. Now the time has come for the violence that is implicit in all that has preceded to burst out.

The Shower

Psycho's shower sequence was—and no matter how many times it has been imitated, or even made banal, as when Bernard Herrmann's music is used in television commercials or promos— continues to be an assault on the viewer as well as an experiment in ways to depict the violence that causes that assault. There had been nothing like it in film before. Even Linda Williams's sugges- tion that *Psycho* is like a theme park ride does not detract from the fact that this sequence unnerves because it reaches into deep fears—of privacy, security, even, in Marion's case, happiness— and slashes it to pieces. Hitchcock, as if taking the metaphor literally, constructs the sequence as a series of slashes. And this needs some background explanation.

While the mise-en-scène of the parlor sequence is rich and unnerving, its cutting is fairly conventional, except in the ways Hitchcock plays with our proximity to the characters. Mostly, the sequence depends on composition for effect, which is an aspect of mise-en-scène rather than editing. Hitchcock can cut uncon- ventionally, as in one of his favorite patterns, which, like the high-angle shot, can be found in almost any of his films. To borrow Andrew Sarris's name for it, the pattern is called "cross-tracking."[1] Hitchcock will intercut a character in motion with the object toward which he or she is moving, also shown in motion. The effect is a point-of-view shot (a staple of the classical Hollywood style) taken to an extreme in which the kinetics of movement and approach—often with a sense of impending dread and danger—put us either within a character's state of mind, or beyond it, since we may know more than she does. The best example in *Psycho*, commented upon by many of the authors in the book, is Lila Crane's approach to the Old Dark House, where she will discover Mother's corpse. Through the cross-tracking, the house becomes a kind of presence. Once in the house, Hitchcock continues the intercutting, although mostly with a nonmoving camera. He does this with such rhythmic regularity that, not only are we surprised by the things Lila does (and does not) see, but are situated so that he can create a trick that makes both Lila and the viewer jump (see figures 10.55–10.61).

We have already examined Hitchcock's use of the moving camera and the long take. Hitchcock went through a period in which he experimented rather boldly with the long take, and his film

FIGURE 10.55. The first four images represent, as best as still images can, the cross-cutting that occurs as Lila approaches the house. Helpless not to play another joke on us, Hitchcock creates a fright when Lila, inside the house, believes she sees someone in the mirror. The images are rapidly cut, but when we isolate them, we see the trick—we see also that what might have frightened Lila is . . . us!

FIGURE 10.56.

FIGURE 10.57.

FIGURE 10.58.

FIGURE 10.59.

FIGURE 10.60.

FIGURE 10.61.

Rope (1948) was made with no visible cuts at all. Whenever a camera reel was about to run out, Hitchcock had the camera retreat behind a couch or a curtain. *Rope* was not a very successful film, and Hitchcock himself told the French critic, Andé Bazin, that he wished he had material to create some montage during the editing process.[2] But long after *Rope*, Hitchcock showed his fondness for a moving camera. In *Psycho*, the crane up the door-jamb when Norman removes Mother to the fruit cellar; the track from Marion's dead eye that ends the shower murder (a track that is actually two shots, the cut hidden when the camera moves by the wall); the track back from the rear of Sam's hardware store immediately following Norman's cleanup after the murder; and the track toward Norman in his jail cell—all indicate how acutely he was aware when such a shot could be used to draw the audience into a state of anxiety, or to fool them, or to play a joke. As opposed to crosscutting, which communicates to us a character's perceptions, the moving camera allows Hitchcock to guide the viewer directly into intriguing places, or show what a dead eye cannot see.

But the shower murder itself is different. There is no moving camera, no cross-tracking. It employs the most rapid montage Hitchcock had created, made up of some forty shots (depending on where one decides the sequence begins and ends), most lasting only a few frames, with the entire scene taking approximately forty-five seconds. Its construction has roots in the work and writing of the Russian filmmaker, Sergei Eisenstein, who wrote about and practiced a dynamic editing in which the juxtaposition of each shot created an emotional and intellectual response from the viewer. For Eisenstein, montage was a dynamic, political form that allowed the director to construct effects that would energize the viewer.[3]

Like Eisenstein's, although not as apparently political, Hitchcock's method in *Psycho* is about stunning the audience, if not (as Eisenstein would have liked) to enlighten them. The montage of the shower murder does have the shock effect that Eisenstein often sought out, and its rapid cutting of images, going by so fast that we can barely make out any one of them, has the effect of an assault, on Marion, of course, but more important, on the audience itself. It speaks to the assaultive power that makes up the politics of rape, and it has no equal in this until, perhaps, Kathryn Bigalow's *Strange Days* (1998), where a woman is forced to wear a camera that will not merely photograph her rape, but allow others to experience it.

In the early thirties, about the time that Eisenstein was writing and practicing montage in the Russia, the French theater director Antonin Artaud was developing what has been called a "Theater of Cruelty," in which the drama onstage would overflow into the audience, shocking it, making it vibrate, in effect, to the events it was watching. There is something of Artaud in *Psycho*, and the shower murder made audiences (as Linda Williams points out) almost literally vibrate in terror. But their terror is based—as Hitchcock was always happy to point out—on illusion, or, more appropriately, allusion. The shower scene alludes to a stabbing, without showing one. This is not a snuff film, but a narrative fiction. No one is hurt, save for the audience's sensibility. Yet Hitchcock made the cuts, the edits, seem like actual cuts; he made murder and death as palpable as had ever been seen. In his eye and hands, the attack becomes a tactile representation, almost being there emotionally, coming very close to feeling it.

The parlor prepares us, and there are a number of further steps that bring us to the point of Marion's destruction. We glimpsed Norman's madness, however briefly, when talking to Marion about putting Mother "someplace," subtly suggesting that Norman himself had once been an inhabitant of "someplace." Oppositely, Marion achieves a state of calm, deciding to return to the scene of her crime, make amends, and achieve redemption. She fails. Leaving the parlor, Marion goes to her room in the motel, where Norman proceeds to stare at her through a hole that has obviously been there for some time and for similar purposes.

That hole, and Norman's eye, set up an unusual series of visual rhymes that echo throughout the sequence and tie its parts together. Many of the authors in the book have commented on this. Consider the seven images presented in figures 10.62–10.68. The vertical-horizontal pattern that structures the film is broken with these circular forms, signaling that the rigid order of things is now, like Marion's life, swirling down the drain. As many of the essays in this book note, Hitchcock structures most of his films on this dialectic of order and chaos, though in none other, even *The Birds* (1963, made right after *Psycho*), where the whole natural order of things is turned upside down, is this breakdown

FIGURE 10.62.

FIGURE 10.63.

FIGURE 10.64.

FIGURE 10.65.

FIGURE 10.66.

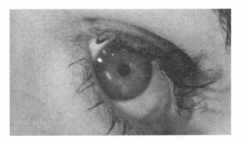

FIGURE 10.67.

FIGURE 10.68.

as fierce and stark. The circle cut in the wall to allow Norman to peer at and become aroused by his female guests (thus releasing his murderous activities, carried out by "Mother") becomes the drain down which Marion's blood flows, as his peering eye leads to the events that become the stare of Marion's dead eye and the foul waters of the swamp.

Until the stabbing itself, Hitchcock retards the events leading up to it. Norman peeps and then leaves for the house, where we see him sitting at the kitchen table. Marion, now relieved of her guilt, figures the amount of money she spent on the car and what she has left to return to its owner, flushes her notes down the toilet, and steps into the shower. The spray head, which we see from Marion's point of view, becomes, for a moment, the fount for the cleansing of body and soul, and she shows an almost sexual delight in the rejuvenating spray (see figure 10.22). But the diagonal of the spray prepares us for another set of diagonals, the blade that will begin slashing down (and, at the end, the chain pulling the car from the swamp). The murder sequence proper begins when Hitchcock moves to his favorite high angle—although not ninety degrees—this time above Marion in the shower, signalling danger and a brief momentary visual retreat. Along with the high angle, the lens Hitchcock uses seems to change as well. This angle, along with the lens that seems both to widen and compress the close quarters, appears to push figure and background away from proximity with the viewer. The fact that Hitchcock gets to this shot by means of a 180-degree reverse from the previous shot, first at eye level, then from high up (see figures 10.22, 10.23, 10.69 and 10.70), which places the camera in a physically impossible place—through the back wall of the shower and drawing closer to Marion and the backgrond—brings up our anxiety slowly to the point when we detect Mother's figure coming through the bathroom door (figure 10.71).

FIGURE 10.69. Hitchcock first cuts 180 degrees and then cuts again to a high shot, taken with a different focal length lens.

FIGURE 10.70.

FIGURE 10.71.

The stabbing is an act of visual frenzy, of vicious, unmotivated, destruction that attains its effect by using form to imitate the act. In its brief but unrelenting collision of images, the rapid cinematic cuts come to represent the rapid cuts to the body and to the sensibility of the viewer. I said earlier that the construction of the sequence is, in actuallity, an allusion. On the level of pro-filmic reality—that is, what goes on in front of the camera—no one, obviously, is getting hurt; Janet Leigh's body double takes her place in a number of shots, a dummy torso in others. But on the level of the diegesis (the world of the fiction), a woman is being sliced to death. The impact of the representation transcends the reality of the film. Between the individual shots and the "reality" we see on screen, the illusion is created. Hitchcock was so pleased with this particular illusion, and its impact, that he sounds in his interviews almost giddy when he explains it was all done with tricks and unfailingly states that we never actually see the knife enter the body.

However, if you look at one montage unit from the whole shower murder sequence (figure 10.72), you will see that the knife does indeed enter the flesh in this shot—the torso used here was most likely artificial. That doesn't matter. What does is Hitchcock's insistence on the lie, as if he took such great pleasure in the joke of the shower murder, he would not admit (perhaps for purposes of avoiding censorship he *could not* admit) that he did show an "actual" stabbing. That might bring *Psycho* perilously to the edge of being a snuff film. Hitchcock wanted to scare the

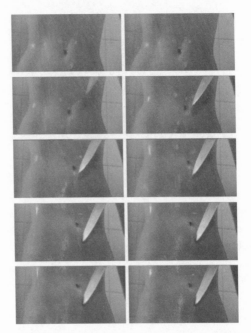

FIGURE 10.72.

audience with the stabbing, was delighted in its trickery, and was always aware of the pleasure of being scared. Again, we are caught in Linda Williams's fun house and the paradox of the deadly serious and the frightfully funny. We are also brought face-to-face with what Hitchcock liked to call "pure cinema," an event that could be effectively brought forth only by calling on the inherent forms of the medium.

Under the Influence

As some of the writers in this collection have noted, *Psycho*, with its dependence on cinematic form and its narrative that creates a bleak, hopeless world at the mercy of terrifying forces of violence, is an important American modernist film. Its dark vision of human individuality, its formal presence and compactness, place it within the tradition of modern painting, the novel, and poetry. It was made at the time that modernist filmmaking was beginning in Europe, in the work of Jean-Luc Godard in France and Michelangelo Antonioni in Italy, among others. And of course, even before they made their films, before *Psycho* itself was made, the French modernists recognized in Hitchcock a film-maker who transcended the Hollywood system with a willingness to foreground cinema's formal properties that were usually made invisible by average directors.

The commercial, critical, and, later, scholarly success of *Psycho*, the fact that it was a catalyst for a whole series of "slasher" films that have now gone on for so long that they are consciously made as parodies, and its formal methods and its darkness, have made it tempting to imitate. Curiously, *Psycho* is itself influenced by Orson Welles's *Touch of Evil* (1958). Janet Leigh and Mort Mills are in both films (Mills plays the district attorney in *Touch of Evil* and the policeman in dark glasses in *Psycho*). Hitchcock used Robert Clatworthy, who was art director on *Touch of Evil*, to be the same on his film. There is a motel with a loony night man in *Touch of Evil*, and in both films Leigh is badly mistreated in a motel, although she survives under Welles's hands. Welles and Hitchcock were extremely different filmmakers, yet both depended on the camera to achieve their effects. In this instance, it was not only the camera, but the seeds of an idea in *Touch of Evil* that was part of the inspiration for Hitchcock's film.

I briefly want to separate out three kinds of influence that *Psycho* and Hitchcock in general had on other filmmakers and concentrate on one particular variety. The first is the slasher film itself—the *Halloween, Friday the 13th, Nightmare on Elm Street* variations and sequels, where adolescent sexuality leads to death, and the monster always rises to kill again. More important, the heroic figure in these films is a young woman, "the final girl," to use Carol Clover's felicitous phrase from her book *Men, Women, and Chain Saws*, to describe the heroine who, at film's end, faces the monster.[4] The Final Girl is a direct descendent of Lila Crane, who confronts the man/woman monster of *Psycho*. The second group of *Psycho* imitations are the direct ones, some of which started immediately, such as J. Lee Thompson's *Cape Fear* (1962), itself remade by Martin Scorsese in 1991. Martin Balsam (who plays Arbogast in *Psycho*) appears in the first (and the second) *Cape Fear*, Bernard Herrmann wrote the score, and Hitchcock's editor, George Tomasini, cut it. Robert Mitchum played the psychopath, and there are some direct imitations of actions and camera movements from *Psycho* (see figures 10.73 and 10.74).

Then, there are the films of Brian De Palma, who spent a career in a vain attempt to imitate and remake Hitchcock. He tried a disastrous remake of Hitchcock's most intricate and complex film, *Vertigo*, in his 1976 *Obsession*, as well as borrowing obvious Hitchcockian techniques (without understanding their narrative use) in other of his films. De Palma's work is a perfect example of skimming the superficialities of a technique without the depth

FIGURE 10.73. A Hitchcockian high angle in the 1962 *Cape Fear*.

FIGURE 10.74. Climbing the staircase in *Cape Fear*, similar to the staircase in *Psycho* (perhaps even the same one—studios often recycle sets).

of thinking that made the technique eloquent and inseparable from the narrative the technique creates.

The third is constituted by a very, very small group, filmmakers who understood Hitchcock, who didn't imitate him but absorbed the way he understood and expressed the world in cinematic terms. There are really only two—although Jonathan Demme's *Silence of the Lambs* (1991) and David Fincher's *Seven* (1996) and *The Game* (1997) might be included as films that recognize Hitchcock's irony and image-making strength. One is an original member of the French New Wave, whose work is not well known in the United States, Claude Chabrol. He coauthored the first full-length study of Hitchcock's films, and many of his own contain a subtle morality of violence that recognizes the Hitchcockian state of mind. The other is Martin Scorsese himself.

The difference between these filmmakers and the imitators is that they were able to understand the essential darkness, pessimism, and misanthropy of Hitchcock's vision. They grasp the complex moral structure of his films that insisted good and evil were reflections of one another and that the seemingly ordered world was always vulnerable to an unforeseen eruption of chaos. They comprehend the delicate balance between order and chaos, which, Hitchcock saw, almost always tipped vertiginously toward the latter. They know, as well, that filmic expression can be used to create a fictive world that reflects realities unfathomable, unable to be perceived, in daily life.

I will concentrate on Scorsese, who, in two films, caught the Hitchcockian spirit. The first, *Cape Fear*, has little to do with *Psycho*, even though its 1962 original did. Scorsese's remake largely drops most, but not all, direct *Psycho* references (although he uses Herrmann's score and Saul Bass's wife, Elaine, for the credits) and concentrates on larger Hitchcockian concerns of doubling—in this case of the not-so-moral lawyer, Sam Bowden, and his monstrous, psychotic other, Max Cady.

Just as Hitchcock used an abstract pattern to underpin the structure of *Psycho*, Scorsese uses the images of at least two other Hitchcock films to underpin his own: *Stage Fright* (1950) and *Strangers on a Train* (1951). The latter in particular is a film about doubles, an upstanding, unhappily married tennis player and a sociopath. Bruno, a psychopath, who asks Guy, the tennis player, if he would be willing to exchange murders, the result being a descent into chaos that ends only with a huge carousel careening out of control, destroying Bruno, who carried out Guy's murder of his wife. Guy kills no one, except through Bruno. Scorsese eschews the carousel for an over-the-top storm at sea to climax the film, but more important, he lays images and scenes from the Hitchcock films under his own, almost as if one image turned into a tracing of itself is placed under another image to suggest its Hitchcockian origins. Scorsese uses Hitchcock as an extended allusion in *Cape Fear*, understanding his motives and means, absorbing them into his work (see figures 10.75–10.78). Earlier, in *Taxi Driver* (1976), Scorsese does a more complex act of absorption, an act not so much of imitation, but of rethinking *Psycho*, remaking a narrative of the lunatic among us, enclosed in a world of his own perception. Scorsese ratchets up the Hitchcockian cross-tracking technique so that everything that Travis Bickle (Robert De Niro) sees is not merely a moving point-of-view shot, but a creation of Travis's bizarre notion of the world. The only things he sees are acts of violence and the most violent aspects of New York City. His, like Norman's, is a solipsistic world, his own distortions and terrors mapped over everything he sees. And many times what he sees is from a high shot down at what he is looking at, climaxing with a ninety-degree tracking shot of Travis and his vic-

FIGURE 10.75. In Scorsese's remake of *Cape Fear*, the roiling clouds over the prison that Cady leaves echo the clouds over the Bates house.

FIGURE 10.76. In Scorsese's film, Cady does Norman, dressing up as a woman to commit a murder in the Hitchcockian high angle shot.

FIGURE 10.77. Cady at a parade, staring at Sam Bowden, whom he wants to destroy.

FIGURE 10.78. One of the most famous Hitchcock images. From *Strangers on a Train*, Bruno watches his tennis-playing double, staring straight ahead as everyone in crowd follows the tennis ball.

tims at the end of the film. Scorsese also uses Hitchcockian off-center compositions, looking at Travis in ways that again suggest his disorientation and ensuing madness (see figures 10.79 and 10.80).

Bernard Herrmann wrote the score for *Taxi Driver* (the last before he died), and he refers to the dark, low chords of the *Psycho* score. And near the very end of the film, there is a strange and troubling reference to the eyes and to seeing, central metaphors in *Psycho*. When Travis talks to the young prostitute, Iris (Jodie Foster), he tells her that her pimp is a killer. She responds by asking if he's ever looked at his own eyeballs in the mirror. At the end of the film, as Travis drives through the dark streets of the city, he suddenly does catch sight of his eyes in the rearview mirror. With a loud squeak on the soundtrack, he reaches for the mirror and pushes it out of his view (figure 10.81).

The murderer refuses to recognize his own inner world, as Norman was unable to recognize his. But we are permitted to

FIGURE 10.79.

FIGURE 10.80.

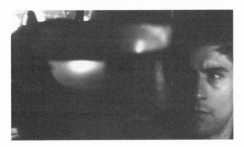

FIGURE 10.81.

see both. Each film ends with the face of madness, unknown and unknowing, with the world outside oblivious to its presence. Like Hitchcock, Scorsese understands the power of the image, especially images that allow the viewer to comprehend more than the characters do. Both filmmakers are masters at creating visual patterns and pushing them through their films. Both are poets of violence and anxiety.

Notes

William Rothman, in *Hitchcock: The Murderous Gaze* (Cambridge, Mass.: Harvard University Press, 1982), pp. 246–341, does a minute formal analysis of the *Psycho* that serves as a model for my own. There are inevitable overlaps, for we think similarly about the film, and I owe Rothman the debt of someone who has learned from his work.

1. Andrew Sarris talks about Hitchcock's cross-tracking in *The American Cinema* (New York: E.P. Dutton, 1968), p. 57.

2. Hitchcock told Bazin, "These continuous scenes were boring enough later during the montage; there was nothing to cut!" (André Bazin, "Hitchcock versus Hitchcock" in *Focus on Hitchcock*, ed. Albert J. LaValley [Englewood Cliffs, N.J.: Prentice Hall, 1972], p. 68).

3. Eisenstein's essays on montage can be found in Sergei Eisenstein, *The Film Form*, ed. and trans. Jay Leyda (New York: Harcourt, Brace, and World, 1949).

4. "The final girl" in horror movies is defined by Carol Clover in *Men, Women, and Chain Saws* (Princeton, N.J.: Princeton University Press, 1992).

Bibliography

◆ ◆ ◆

Jay Telotte and Steven Schneider contributed greatly to this bibliography. There are a few overlaps with the bibliography accompanying Linda Williams's essay in this volume.

Baer, William. "*Psycho*: An Interview with Joseph Stefano." *Creative Screenwriting* 5.5 (1998): 67–72.

Bellour, Raymond. "Psychosis, Neurosis, Perversion." In *A Hitchcock Reader*, ed. M. Deutelbaum and L. Poague. Ames: University of Iowa Press, 1986: 311–31.

Braudy, Leo. "Hitchcock, Truffaut, and the Irresponsible Audience." In *Focus on Hitchcock*, ed. Albert LeValley. Englewood, N.J.: Prentice Hall, 1972: 116–27.

Brottman, David. "Mrs. Bates in Plato's Cave: Reflections on the Self-Reflexive Signifying Chain Linking the Cellar to Cinema Cells within *Psycho*-tic Experience." In *Ethics and the Subject*, ed. Karl Simms (*Critical Studies* 8). Amsterdam: Rodopi, 1997: 173–88.

Cohen, Keith. "*Psycho*: The Suppression of Female Desire (and Its Return)." In *Reading Narrative: Form, Ethics, Ideology*, ed. James Phelan. Columbus: Ohio State University Press, 1989: 147–61.

Cohen, Paula Marantz. "The Emergence of Mother: *Psycho*." In *Alfred*

Hitchcock: The Legacy of Victorianism. Lexington: University of Kentucky Press, 1995: 142–50.

Corber, Robert J. *In the Name of National Security: Hitchcock, Homophobia, and the Political Construction of Gender in Postwar America.* Durham, N.C.: Duke University Press, 1993.

Crawford, Larry. "Looking, Film, Painting: The Trickster's In Site / In Sight / Insight / Incite." *Wide Angle* 5.3 (1983): 64–69.

———. "Subsegmenting the Filmic Text: The Bakersfield Car Lot Scene in *Psycho.*" *enclitic* 5.2/6.1 (1982): 35–43.

Durgnat, Raymond. "Inside Norman Bates." *Films and Feelings.* Cambridge: MIT Press, 1967: 209–20.

———. *A Long, Hard Look at* Psycho. London: BFI Publishing, 2002.

Eby, Douglas. "*Psycho*: Desecrating a Masterpiece?: Director Gus van Sant on Stepping into Alfred Hitchcock's Shadow." *Cinefantastique* 30.11 (1998): 3.

Garcia, Frank. "*Psycho*: Screenwriter Joseph Stefano on the Controversial Remake." *Cinefantastique* 30.12 (Jan. 1999): 40–41.

Garrett, Greg. "Hitchcock's Women on Hitchcock: A Panel Discussion with Janet Leigh, Tippi Hedren, Karen Black, Suzanne Pleshette, and Eva Marie Saint." *Literature/Film Quarterly* 27.2 (1999): 78–89.

Greenberg, Harvey Roy. "*Psycho*: The Apes at the Windows." In *The Movies on Your Mind.* New York: Saturday Review Press, 1975: 106–37.

Griffith, James. "*Psycho*: Not Guilty as Charged." *Film Comment*, July 1996.

Hendershot, Cyndy. "The Cold War Horror Film: Taboo and Transgression in *The Bad Seed, The Fly,* and *Psycho.*" *Journal of Popular Film and Television* 29.1 (2001): 20–31.

Jones, Alan. "Ed Gein, the Wisconsin Ghoul: Going Back to the Source for *Psycho* and *Texas Chainsaw Massacre.*" *Cinefantastique* 33.½ (2001): 10–12.

Kapsis, Robert E. *Hitchcock: The Making of a Reputation.* Chicago: University of Chicago Press, 1992.

Kolker, Robert. *A Cinema of Loneliness: Penn, Stone, Kubrick, Scorsese, Altman.* 3d ed. New York: Oxford University Press, 2000.

Klinger, Barbara. "*Psycho*: The Institutionalization of Female Sexuality." In *A Hitchcock Reader*, ed. Marshal Deutelbaum and Leland Poague. Ames: University of Iowa Press, 1986: 332–39.

Leitch, Thomas M. "101 Ways to Tell Hitchcock's *Psycho* from Gus van Sant's." *Literature/Film Quarterly* 28.4 (2000): 269–73.

Meola, Frank M. "Hitchcock's Emersonian Edges." *Hitchcock Annual* (2000–2001): 23–46.

Modleski, Tania. *The Women Who Knew Too Much.* New York: Methuen, 1988.

Morris, Christopher. "Psycho's Allegory of Seeing." *Literature/Film Quarterly* 24.1 (1996): 47–51.

Naremore, James. *Filmguide to Psycho*. Bloomington: Indiana University Press, 1973.

————. "Remaking *Psycho*." *Hitchcock Annual* (1999–2000): 3–12.

Perkins, V. F. "The World and Its Image." In *Film as Film* (1972): 71–115.

Pogue, Leland. "Links in a Chain: *Psycho* and Film Classicism." In *A Hitchcock Reader*, ed. Marshall Deutelbaum and Leland Pogue. Ames: Iowa State University Press, 1986: 340–49.

Rothman, William. "*Psycho*." *Hitchcock—The Murderous Gaze*. Cambridge, Mass.: Harvard University Press, 1982: 246–341.

Schneider, Steven Jay. "Manufacturing Horror in Hitchcock's *Psycho*." *CineAction!* 50 (1999): 70–75.

————. "Van Sant the Provoca(u)teur." *Hitchcock Annual* (2001–2002): 140–48.

Spoto, Donald. *The Art of Alfred Hitchcock*. New York: Hopkinson and Blake, 1976.

————. *The Dark Side of Genius: The Life of Alfred Hitchcock*. Boston: Little, Brown, 1983.

Taylor, John Russell. *Hitch: The Life and Times of Alfred Hitchcock*. New York: Pantheon, 1978.

Telotte, J. P. "Faith and Idolatry in the Horror Film." *Literature/Film Quarterly* 8.3 (1980): 143–55.

Thomas, Deborah. "On Being Norman: Performance and Inner Life in Hitchcock's *Psycho*." *CineAction!* 44 (1997): 66–72.

Thomson, David. "*Psycho* and the Roller Coaster." In *Overexposures: The Crisis in American Filmmaking*. New York: Morrow, 1981: 70–75.

————. "Salieri. *Psycho*." *Film Comment* 21.1 (1985): 70–75.

Williams, Linda. "When the Woman Looks." In Mary Ann Doane, Patricia Mellencamp, and Linda Williams, eds., *Re-Vision: Essays in Feminist Film Criticism*. American Film Institute Monograph Series, vol. 3. Frederick, Md.: University Publications of America, 1984: 83–99.

Wollen, Peter. "Hybrid Plots in *Psycho*." In *Readings and Writings: Semiotic Counter Strategies*. London: NLB, 1982: 34–39.

Zita, Jacquelyn. "Dark Passages: A Feminist Analysis of *Psycho*." In *The Paradigm Exchange*, ed. Rene Jara, et al. Minneapolis: University of Minnesota, 1981: 85–90.

Žižek, Slavoj. "In His Bold Gaze My Ruin Is Writ Large." In *Everything You Always Wanted to Know about Lacan (but Were Afraid to Ask Hitchcock)*. London and New York: Verso, 1992: 211–72.

Film Credits

◆ ◆ ◆

DIRECTION: Alfred Hitchcock

ASSISTANT DIRECTOR: Hilton A. Green

SCRIPT: Joseph Stefano, from a novel by Robert Bloch

PHOTOGRAPHY: John L. Russell

PRODUCTION DESIGN: Robert Clatworthy and Joseph Hurley

SET DECORATION: George Milo

TITLE DESIGN AND PICTORIAL CONSULTANT: Saul Bass

SPECIAL EFFECTS: Clarence Champagne

EDITING: George Tomasini

MUSIC: Bernard Herrmann

CAST: Anthony Perkins (Norman Bates), Janet Leigh (Marion Crane), Vera Miles (Lila Crane), John Gavin (Sam Loomis), Martin Balsam (Milton Arbogast), John McIntire (Sheriff Al Chambers), Simon Oakland (Dr. Richmond), Vaughn Taylor (George Lowery), Frank Albertson (Tom Cassidy), Lurene Tuttle (Eliza Chambers), Patricia Hitchcock (Caroline), John Anderson (Charlie), Mort Mills (Highway Patrol officer), Ted Knight (Cell Guard), "Mother" (Paul Jasmin, Jeanette Nolan, Anne Dore, Margo Epper, Virginia Gregg, Mitzi).

Produced by Alfred Hitchcock for Shamley Productions. Paramount Pictures. Universal Pictures. 1960. 109 min.